D0112109

The information provided within this book is for general
informational purposes only. While the author has made every
effort to provide up-to-date and accurate information, there are
no representations or warranties, express or implied, about the
completeness, accuracy, reliability, suitability or availability
with respect to the information, products, services, or related
graphics contained in this book. Any use of the information
contained within this text should be considered at your own risk.

i

Are You RV Ready?

Jeffrey E. Boyer
Albuquerque NM

To Joan,

Without whom, I'd be nothing.

To Nick and Liz,

Who fill me with pride.

To Ava, Zoe, and Lily,

Without whom, I'd be sad.

Table of Contents

Introduction

Are you recreational vehicle (RV) ready? The purpose of this book is to ensure that you are! The Recreational Vehicle Industry Association (RVIA) defines a RV as:[1]

> "A motorized or towable vehicle that combines transportation and temporary living quarters for travel, recreation and camping. RVs do not include mobile homes, off-road vehicles, snowmobiles, or conversion vehicles. RVs are sold by recreation vehicle dealers."

This is one of the better definitions I've found and it should be, based on the source. For our purposes, we'll stick pretty close to this. One exception in my opinion (which carries weight—I wrote the book) are the bus-style conversions, whether school bus or the larger diesel variants. I believe these fit squarely into the RV realm; they're just not sold by dealerships.

For clarity in this writing, I'm creating the following:

RV = recreational vehicle from this point forward
RVs = more than one RV
RVer = an individual RV user
RVers = a collective group of RV users—all of us!
RVing = the act of using an RV for its intended purpose
Rig or Coach = used interchangeably (referring to your RV)

As I am always learning new, interesting, and important things about RVing, I decided this book was an opportunity to share some of my experiences. This written effort is not an attempt at a "how-to guide" or "RVing, A to Z" (those exist already, with many wonderful examples), but is intended more as a primer for those, like me, who need a reminder once and again about the general systems in our RVs and their functions; what we need to look for and pay attention to; and topics we wished we knew a little more about. This book is not intended to make you an expert in anything.

The target audience for this book are those folks who may not yet own a RV, but are seriously contemplating getting one, and those folks who have a RV, but may need a reminder now and again about how the general systems function.

So, what makes this book different from others currently available? When I was researching our first RV, I found a tremendous amount of information available, both in book form and on forums, blogs, or other digitally delivered means. None of the individual reference sources I consulted ended up providing all of the material for which I was thirsting. Worse, I became worried about the contradictory information I encountered from the various reference sources I consulted, which made me wonder about the actual sources of information for some of the materials. It was often a struggle to differentiate fact from opinion. Contrary to the beliefs of some, just because it's on the internet, does not mean it's true.

Before purchasing our first RV—a 2008 Forest River, Berkshire— I spent a couple of years doing lots of research. This 38-foot diesel pusher was our first foray into the RV lifestyle (talk about jumping right in!). We went from never having camped to "_First Class Glamping_". Regardless, even after a of couple years reading and digesting every piece of reference material I could get my hands on about RVs and RVing, I was still struck by all that I didn't know, or by

13

what I thought I did, but really didn't. I was also confounded by the wide range of answers I found to what I believed were simple RVing questions.

As a result, I assembled this book to serve as a primer and source of information to help ensure that your RV experience is a positive one. Whether you're a well-seasoned RVer with many miles under your belt, or you're drawing closer to making your first (or maybe next) RV purchase, chapters of this book are intended to spark some thought, reflection, and discussion; and help you identify things you may have overlooked that indeed may be, ultimately, important to you. This book contains information varying from the most basic definitions, to detailed inspection criteria, all of which should be useful to even the most experienced of RVers.

My wife and I have met many wonderful, colorful, and truly helpful folks during our RVing journeys. The RVing community is full of people willing to help, share, and proffer advice.

Here is the first of many cautionary notes that this book contains. Folks who are into RVing have generally made a significant investment and as such, many are happy to tell you what to do and why. I've come to realize that every RVer is truly different, with varied needs and differing levels of expectations. If you want to see a couple of RVers get into a heated exchange, find owners of gas and diesel Class A motorhomes and ask them which engine choice is best! Then crack open a cool beverage and sit back. Significant investments marry people to decisions they have made—right, or almost right.

I attempted to assemble this book in chapters that flow together logically, make referencing information as simple as possible, and included a fairly detailed table of contents. The beginning chapters are geared toward readers who are contemplating getting into RVing, and include definitions, types of RVs, and discussions of pre-delivery inspections in some detail. The later chapters focus more on general systems in RVs, like electrical, plumbing, and weight management (i.e., weight distribution, axle weights, and combined weights) in great detail. Appendices to the text include several checklists, references, and some state-by-state information, including special licensing requirements. Also provided throughout the book are ideas, quick facts, and things that my wife and I have learned along the way.

Two specific chapters of the book comprise a significant portion of the overall text. The first is a very detailed chapter for Pre-Delivery Inspections (PDI) of the entire RV, regardless of type, and includes inspection items you should evaluate before buying a RV. The PDI reference material is more than a purchasing tool—it is also very useful as your annual inspection before hitting the road, to ensure that your RV is in sound, safe, operating condition.

The chapter covering weight and weight management, and the included checklists, are detailed and dry, but are critical to your safety. I've tried to keep them simple and concise while still capturing the information necessary for you to properly weight your RV. In each of these chapters, I was tempted to have written more on the subject, but a friend reminded me of the concept TL;DR – too long; didn't read.

My end goal for this book is that it's sufficiently detailed to allow you to understand RV general systems and technologies and potentially identify areas that you want (or, more importantly, need) to learn more about. If a chapter of this book leads you to the conclusion that you need to know more about a certain system, then that's my measure of success.

The text has many warnings to potential buyers. RVing is a wonderful lifestyle that I wouldn't trade, but it's not for everyone and I've tried to point that out, where it makes sense.

Lastly, a note on the couple of statements that I've made throughout this book: ***trust, but verify!*** I've tried to be very rigid with the information I've provided in this book and, where necessary, included references for you to research further should you warrant it helpful or necessary to do so.

Everyone has an opinion and, where I've stated mine, I've been careful to say so. ***Your mileage will vary.*** Nothing in the RV universe works exactly the same for any two users. Things with which you are inclined to like or prefer, others may find fault. You may feel that your RV is comfortable, others may complain that it rides like it has square wheels.

Do your own research. I've done a tremendous amount of reading and research, and thoroughly enjoyed writing this book over the past year. That said, the impact of how something affects you might be slightly (or radically) different. Read everything you can get your hands on about specific issues that you find interesting. Become your own expert. You'll be far better off in the long run.

Lastly, as you can see from reading just this introduction, a lot of jargon, slang, and acronyms are used when discussing RVing. To make the book a little easier to navigate, the next chapter is devoted to definitions. If you're just discovering RVing, the chapter will be handy for you; if you're a seasoned ole-timer, you may still discover something new.

Well, I hope that wasn't TL;DR! Now, let's see. *Are you RV Ready?*

 1910 is when the first auto-related camping vehicles were built for commercial sale. Known as "auto campers" or "camping trailers" a century ago, these vehicles were the forerunner of today's modern RVs. (Source: GoingRV.Com)

Chapter One

Definitions

12-Volt DC: 12-Volt direct current (DC), common in motor vehicles; power source is most often 12-Volt battery or 6-Volt batteries wired in series to create 12 Volts.

120-Volt AC: 120-Volt alternating current (AC), common in household wiring; 120-Volt AC is what the pedestal at a RV park/campground provides (referred to as shore power).

Adjustable ball mount: A typical ball hitch, which is mounted on a vertical bar with multiple adjustment options that allow the ball hitch to be raised or lowered incrementally to ensure the tow vehicle is level.

Airbag: Not the common safety airbag in passenger vehicles; RV airbag refers to a bag mounted to the RV suspension and/or chassis that allows the RV to ride on a cushion of air. Most often found on diesel pushers, these airbags are directly attributable to diesel pushers' exceptional ride quality. Airbags are also used in certain pickup models to help with ride quality and height adjustment.

Airbag (alternate): A know-it-all in the RV community who actually knows very little.

Anderson valve: A valve made by Anderson Brass Company, which allows you to select tank fill, city water, onboard water, or sanitize. Anderson Brass Company makes a wide variety of RV accessories, including the 4-function (or 4-way) RV fill valve.

18

Anode rod: A rod used only in steel (not in aluminum or glass-lined) water heater tank to attract corrosive contaminants found in supplied water. Corrosive contaminants attack the rod instead of tank's steel walls. The anode rod has limited life depending on quality of water run through water heater tank. At a minimum, the anode rod should be checked yearly and replaced when it is reduced to one quarter of its original size.

Auxiliary battery (or auxiliary battery bank): A battery (or series of batteries) specifically to run 12-Volt DC equipment, lights, and appliances.

Arctic pack: Specific packages offered by RV manufacturers that are used in cold-weather environments; extra insulation, heated water pipes, and ducted heat in basements are examples of some options.

Back-up camera and monitor: Rear-mounted camera that allows a vehicle's driver to view activity behind the vehicle; an electronic rearview mirror. Can be wired or wireless and transmit signals to the driver's area to be displayed either on a special dedicated monitor or often, a video screen of an embedded stereo head unit. Some backup camera units include side-mounted cameras for monitoring lane changes. Back-up cameras and monitors are commonly available on many larger RVs, vehicles, and trailers.

Ball mount: Portion of hitch to which hitch ball is affixed. Can be in the form of steel arm or bar, cross-member, or other hitch assembly; many different configurations of ball mounts and load ranges are available.

Basement: Storage area underneath your RV. Some larger RV models have very impressive, pass-thru basement storage.

Base plate: Assembly needed to tow your passenger vehicle behind your RV using a tow bar. The base plate mounts to the frame of the vehicle to be towed and allows tow bar to connect directly to vehicle so that it can be towed like a standard trailer.

Bat swing (also tail swing) effect: Effect created when that portion of RV that is physically behind the rear-most axle swings around like a bat when the RV is negotiating a corner. You must be cognizant of bat swing or you risk the potential of damaging the rear of your RV with a pole, street sign, or (worse yet) another vehicle.

Batwing antenna: Common name for the crank-up television antenna on an RV's roof. The Winegard antenna is shaped like a bat's wing.

Black water: Most commonly is wastewater from an RV's toilet. Black water tank is normally plumbed separately and must be emptied using a specific waste-dumping valve.

Blue-Boy: A container with wheels used to transport gray and black tank waste to a RV Park's dump station.

Boondocking: A wildly popular form of camping (also known as dry camping); camping without connecting to external utilities. Relies on RV's integrated systems for you to be self-sufficient.

Brake controller unit: A device, either mounted in or integrated into a tow vehicle that controls electric brakes of towed trailer. The tow vehicle operator calibrates the brake controller unit so that brake pressure is proportionate to the brake pressure applied by the driver. Most units also allow for manually braking the trailer, which can be useful in connecting and disconnecting from tow vehicle.

Breakaway switch/box: Connects from trailer to tow vehicle by means of cable or lanyard. If, during towing, there is a significant failure and the trailer becomes separated from the tow vehicle, cable or lanyard is pulled free from breakaway switch/box, which then applies full power to trailer brakes, hopefully bringing trailer to safe stop without further incident.

Bunkhouse: Popular with families and available in several RV models, the bunkhouse refers to an area where there are stacked "bunk-beds" or a specific children's' bedroom area.

Bypass valve: Most often associated with winterizing RV water system; allows a "bypass" of certain plumbing (e.g., water heater) so that water system can be winterized with RV-specific antifreeze.

Cabover area: Enclosed area directly over the driver and passenger front seats; area normally contains bed but, in some configurations, contains cabinets or RV entertainment system. Most common in Class C motorhomes.

Camper shell: Perhaps the most basic camper form, an enclosed cover that fits over bed area of pickup truck; no thrills, no frills.

Cargo weight: Weight of passengers, cargo, and any added equipment, including weight associated with hitch.

Cassette toilet: Portable toilets often found in very small RVs, like pop-ups, slide-ins, or conversion vans. Have small holding tank that can be removed to empty it.

CCC (cargo carrying capacity): This value is provided so that you are aware of how much cargo can be added to your RV. It is established by the manufacturer and is determined before adding any options and after-market items.

CDL (Commercial Driver's License): Required in many states to operate large RVs and many commercial-use vehicles.

Chassis: Frame and structure that supports an RV and running gear; truck and frame for motorhomes, or substructure for trailers.

Chassis battery: 12-Volt battery system used to control and manage 12-Volt requirements of the chassis ignition, engine controls, etc.

Chuck (or tire chuck): Tire air-pressure gauge; some include long stems to allow for RVs with dual tires to be checked with relative ease.

Chucking: Term used to refer to the rocking back and forth motion between a trailer and tow vehicle; most often caused by uneven roadways. Motion can be significant and create an uneasy feeling for the operator. If it is persistent, may indicate improper weight distribution or tire imbalance.

Class 1- 5 Receiver hitch: Very common, sturdy, reliable hitch assemblies for tow vehicles. Most often mounted to frame, making them very robust. Has an open box at the rear where hitch bar and ball mount are inserted. Classes of receiver hitch are ranked 1 thru 5. Class 1 are 1.25 in. square with 2,000-lb. capacity; Class 2 are 1.25 in. square with 3,500-lb. capacity; Class 3 are 2 in. square with 8,000-lb. capacity; Class 4 are 2 in. square 10,000-lb. capacity; and Class 5 are 2.25 in. square with 12,000-lb capacity.

Class A: RV Unit Class specifically built on manufacturer's chassis; largest offerings in motorized RVs. Class A RV box design offers excellent room, storage, and comfort. Class A RV units can be gas or diesel chassis and can come in lengths up to 45 ft.

Class B: RV Unit Class; smaller cousin of Class A RVs; most often built on larger van chassis, often with raised roofs. Recent additions of Mercedes and Dodge Sprinter Chassis and new offerings from Ford have created several new models in this class with more rigs to choose from than ever.

Class C (mini motorhome): RV Unit Class, incredibly popular, mostly built on van "cutaway" chassis. Class C RV has cab-over area above driver and passenger seating that incorporates bed or entertainment system. Class C RV units can be quite roomy with units up to 36 ft.

Coach: Term used synonymously with RV by many.

Cockpit: Area where driver sits and operates RV or motorhome.

Convenience panel: Single panel in many RVs where many of switches and controls used for slides, lights, and other RV systems are located in one place, for convenience.

Converter: Unit that converts 120-Volt AC (household [shore power]) to 12-Volt DC. Normally, RV lighting, slides, awnings, and some appliances are controlled by 12-Volt DC so that they can be used without hooking up to "shore power" (boondocking) and while on the road.

Coupler: "Cup," or ball socket, the point of a trailer frame that attaches to hitch ball. Available in different styles, all serve same function.

Curb-weight: Empty weight of RV or tow vehicle with full fuel tank and all required oils and operating fluids. Curb weight excludes passengers or accessories added to the RV after initial sale.

Curbside: Passenger side of RV that is adjacent to curb when parked.

Cut-off-switch: Mechanical switch found in many RVs; allows disconnection of RV batteries between use, thus avoiding parasitic drains that kill batteries.

Delamination: Term used to refer to deterioration and failure of laminated panels due to heat and freezing cycles or water infiltration of laminated, bonded products that are used to construct walls of many RVs. Many RV walls are constructed with a series of laminated products, sandwiched together using materials like luan plywood, insulation sheets, and core fiberglass panels. Once bonded together, these panels are smooth, strong, and offer manufacturers more construction options. Failure areas appear as swelled pockets or bubbles and can be quite large. Delamination should be taken very seriously; measures should be taken quickly to resolve root cause.

DH: Slang for Dear Husband—very common on forums and on-line posts.

Diesel puller: Diesel Class A motorhome with engine in front (also commonly referred to as FRED (Front-Engine Diesel).

Diesel pusher: Most common diesel Class A is the pusher; these units have rear-mounted motor.

Dinette: Eating area in an RV; many have fold-down tables and the booth seats that open to form full-size bed.

Dinghy: Term used for vehicle that is towed behind a motorhome on trailer or vehicle tow dolly. Tow dolly allows front two wheels to be strapped onto top of dolly so that vehicle can be towed. Commonly required for front-wheel drive/automatic vehicles where the front wheel cannot roll freely.

Donut: Rubber, or similar material, ring that helps create proper seal for RV dump hose where it mates to non-threaded RV campground or dump-station sewer inlet.

Dry camping (also known as boondocking): Wildly popular form of camping; relies on integrated systems within your RV for you to be self-sufficient; camping without connecting to external utilities.

Direct-spark ignition (DSI): Refers to electrical spark necessary to ignite propane appliances, such as furnaces, stove burners, and some refrigerators. Systems utilizing DSI do not require pilot lights.

DRW (dual rear wheels): Configuration available on larger, 1-ton pickups or RV Toters, mid-size specialty trucks used for larger trailer transportation.

DSS (digital satellite system): Portable or roof-mounted configurations available.

Dual electric: Capability to operate RV utilities using on-board batteries or by plugging into shore power.

Dually: Common term for 1-ton pickup truck with dual rear wheels (DRW) on each side; often required to pull heavy fifth-wheel trailers.

Ducted air conditioning: Much like a residential home's central air conditioning, ducted air conditioning provides air through a series of vents throughout an RV.

Ducted heat: Series of ducts and vents that provides and distributes warm air from a RV's furnace.

Dump station: Approved sewer inlet for dumping RV gray and black tank wastewater; often provided at campgrounds and some larger service stations along highways. Some dump stations are now automated or pay-as-you-need service facilities.

DW: Slang term meaning Dear Wife—very common on forums and on-line posts.

EMS (Electric Management System)**:** A system, often an aftermarket add-on, that can protect your RV against high and low voltages, lost or open neutral, ground faults, polarity problems, and more.

EPDM (Ethylene Propylene Diene Monomer): Term more commonly known as a rubber roof; very common on RVs.

EW (empty weight)**:** Weight of RV at the point it left the assembly line.

FHU (full hookup): Term used by many RV parks on their websites or flyers for site-specific details.

Fifth-wheel hitch: Term used to identify an entire class of trailers and the hitch necessary to pull them. Large hitch assembly that is solidly mounted in a pickup (or larger) truck bed to the vehicle's frame; allows for heavy trailers to be securely pulled. Hitch plate is commonly referred to as the fifth-wheel plate. Fifth-wheel trailers are the largest trailers in the category while being considered easier to pull because of their distributed weight across a tow vehicle's axles.

Fiver: Slang or abbreviated term for fifth wheel.

Fresh water: Water used for drinking, cooking, and bathing/showering; sourced from either a RV's fresh water tank or through a hose attached to a water tap.

Fresh water tank: One of three tanks common in RVs; can vary greatly in capacity, but intended to provide fresh water for drinking, cooking, and bathing/showering. Exert great care to properly maintain the cleanliness of the fresh water tank to prevent health concerns.

Full-timing/full timer: Terms used to refer to living year-round and/or permanently in an RV.

Galley: A RV's kitchen area.

Gas pusher: Less common variety of Class A RVs with a rear-mounted, gasoline engine. Most "pushers" are diesel, but some gasoline options appear from time to time.

Gasser: Slang term used to refer to gasoline engine-powered Class A motorhomes.

GAW (gross axle weight): Actual weight placed on axles from vehicle chassis and any added equipment and attached trailer. Actual weight on the axle; not the total axle rating (see GAWR).

GAWR (gross axle weight rating): Rating that applies to any axle on any platform; maximum allowable weight for specified axle.

GCW (gross combined weight): Actual combined weight of fully loaded tow vehicle and fully loaded trailer when weighed (not GCWR).

GCWR (gross combined weight rating): Absolute maximum weight that combined tow vehicle and towed vehicle can weigh. GCWR could be a motorhome and dinghy, a motorhome and enclosed trailer, a pickup and fifth-wheel trailer, or any combination of vehicles. In this case, the GCWR includes everything from the RV itself, fuel, water, luggage, propane, Cheetos and soda—everything. The GCWR weight rating is often overlooked, which can lead to dangerous vehicle conditions.

Generator: A portable or permanently installed power-generating device that runs on gasoline, diesel, or propane. A RV operator's requirements and RV type dictate what kind, if any, of generator is needed.

GENSET: A synonymous term used by some RV manufacturers' literature for the Generator.

Glamping: Slang term meaning Glamorous Camping. Many traditionalists believe that camping involves a tent and a sleeping bag and that those who use RVs are actually Glamping.

Gray water: "Used" water from an RV's sink(s) and tub/shower; captured into the gray tank, plumbed into the sewer drain, and dumped using a specific drain valve.

GTW (gross trailer weight): Actual weight of fully loaded trailer when weighed; not to be confused with GTWR, which represents the maximum allowable weight for a trailer.

GTWR (gross trailer weight rating): Maximum allowable weight for a trailer. GTWR includes everything you've loaded in or added to the RV (e.g., propane, food, water, cargo, etc.).

GVW (gross vehicle weight): Actual weight of a loaded vehicle when weighed; not to be confused with GVWR.

GVWR (gross vehicle weight rating): Maximum allowable weight for an RV based on manufacturer design specifications; rating includes everything you've loaded into the RV as well (e.g., propane, food, water, cargo, etc.).

High profile: Some RVs, most often fifth wheels, have an extremely tall roofline, which makes them spacious inside, but a little harder to maneuver in some circumstances. Towing a high-profile vehicle means you need to be paying attention to windy conditions, bridge heights, and any other potential obstructions, like tree limbs and building awnings.

Hitch bar: The removable bar that slides into the hitch receiver and has the hitch ball mounted at the end. The hitch bar is secured into the hitch receiver with a receiver lock or receiver pin and clip.

Hitch weight: The specific weight the trailer applies to the tow vehicle through the hitch. Hitch weights vary based on the trailer and hitch style. Hitch weight of a recessed box hitch is referred to as the tongue weight, which is somewhat lower than the pin weight you could expect to see when coupling a fifth wheel.

Holding tanks: Most traditional RVs have three holding tanks: fresh water, gray water, and black water. The gray and black water holding tanks are normally plumbed in line to be dumped into specific sewer drains using dump valves. A water inlet, using a fresh water hose, fills the fresh water tank. When using the fresh water tank, a 12-Volt water pump provides water throughout the RV as needed.

Honey wagon (also known as Blue boy): This term refers to the less-than-glamorous portable means used to empty RV gray and black holding tanks if a RV Park site does not include full hookups. The holding tank is emptied into the honey wagon, and hauled to the central dump station—a good workout, but not much fun.

Hookups: RV hookups (not the social variety) include water, electrical, sewer, and even cable television. Hookup types are determined by both what is available at the RV Park at which you're staying, and the type of site at the RV Park. Generally, the more hookups you opt for, the higher the fee at the RV Park.

House battery: A single battery, or group of batteries, in a RV that supply power to operate 12-Volt systems in a RV (e.g., lights, appliance controllers, awnings, slides, etc.).

Hula skirt: Skirting attached to the rear of a motorhome (or tow vehicle) to prevent debris from being kicked up onto the tow vehicle.

Inverter: The inverter in a RV takes 12-Volt DC from the house battery or sometimes from the chassis 12-Volt system, and creates 120-Volt AC. An inverter is necessary to run typical household appliances like televisions, computers, or audio-visual systems without being hooked up to shore power. Sometimes people confuse the inverter with the converter functionality; they are very different components.

Inverter generator: Type of portable generator that converts power from its internal engine to direct current (DC) power. The DC power is then fed into an inverter, producing clean and stable 120-Volt AC power.

Jackknife: A situation achieved usually as a result of backing or emergency braking, where the trailer becomes positioned at a 90% angle (or more) to the tow vehicle. While backing, jackknifing is very hard on the tow vehicle and trailer frame, often forcing the trailer wheels to skid (or slide) instead of rolling. In short-bed pickups (without specialized hitches), a jackknife situation can become costly as often there is not sufficient room between the rear of the pickup cab and the front nose of the fifth wheel to support a 90% turn, resulting in contact or physical damage to a vehicle and trailer.

Jackknife sofa: Very common in the RV industry, a jackknife sofa can be converted into a comfortable sleeping surface within seconds by applying a little force to the rear of the sofa, thereby allowing the sofa back to drop down and the bottom cushions to slide out.

King pin: The round steel shaft attached to the fifth-wheel pin box that mates with the fifth wheel plate on the tow vehicle and locks into place for towing.

Landing gear: The two most forward "legs" on a fifth-wheel trailer that are used to remove the trailer weight from the tow vehicle to allow the tow vehicle to disconnect; the landing gear then become part of the RV leveling process.

Leveling: The process of getting a RV as level as possible when setting up. Leveling can be accomplished by simply pushing a button (for auto leveling rigs), or be as complicated as driving up on leveling blocks or planks of wood one at a time until a bubble or level inside the RV ensures that the occupants' dinner will not slide off the table. Manual leveling can be very frustrating and time consuming.

LP (liquefied petroleum gas): Most RVs have some capacity to carry LP for cooking, water heating, and heat. Some refrigerators actually operate using LP.

MDT (medium-duty truck): Most often used as Toters or RV haulers, these custom medium-duty trucks are manufactured for use in towing or transporting RV trailers long distance or in ultimate comfort.

Motor coach/Motorcoach: Term used synonymously with motorhome.

MWL (manufacturer's weight label): Placard, plate or label applied to the vehicle by the manufacturer that details the specific weight capacities for the vehicle, including gross axel and vehicle weight ratings.

NCC (net carrying capacity): Term used by some manufacturers to reference the maximum weight of items you can add to your RV. The NCC is a calculation of a vehicle's dry weight subtracted from its gross vehicle weight rating.

Newbie: Someone new to the world of RVing.

Nonpotable water: Water that is not safe for human consumption and should never be put into your fresh water tank.

OPD (overfill protection device, or overfilling prevention device): Simple safety mechanism device used to ensure a cylinder is not accidentally overfilled; now required on all 4- to 40-lb. Department of Transportation cylinders.

Payload: Maximum cargo capacity a vehicle can carry; calculated by subtracting curb weight from GVWR.

PCS (power control system)/PMS (power management system): Systems that hook into a circuit panel and allow programming of the power requirement for each circuit in your coach. This allows the PCS to shed power loads when they exceed the power supply, eliminating tripped circuits. They also show power status to the RV.

PDI (pre-delivery inspection): Inspection that is conducted prior to accepting delivery of a RV unit that has been purchased. This inspection is also useful as an annual tool to ensure a RV is ready for the new camping year.

Pilot light: A small flame that is present at the burner of propane heating elements. When LP gas is introduced, the pilot light ignites gas as it enters the burner. More and more, newer gas appliances use mechanical or electrical ignition methods to replace the pilot light. Appliances that do use pilots most often have a thermocouple as a safety means to shut off the LP gas in the event the pilot is extinguished (see thermocouple).

Pin weight: Weight of the fifth-wheel applied to the tow vehicle through the fifth wheel hitch. Fifth-wheel pin weight is approximately 20% of trailer gross weight.

Pop-up: Common style of RV trailer that unfolds from a stored/towed position to create substantially larger living and sleeping area. Pop-up units have been around a long time and are produced in many different styles from several manufacturers.

Porpoising: Continual rocking-back-and-forth motion of a RV on uneven road surfaces.

Pressure valve: Often found on water heaters, is a safety valve that will open in the event the pressure inside a water heater exceeds a safe pressure, thereby preventing the tank from rupturing, or worse.

Propane: See LP

Pull through: A RV Park or campsite space that allows you to pull directly through the parking space instead of having to back into the space. RV Parks often have pull-through sites available for larger RVs (or for those of us who just can't back up!).

PUP: Slang term for pop-up camper.

Pusher: Diesel, or more rarely gasoline, Class A motorhome with engine mounted in rear of chassis.

Receiver hitch: Common form of hitch; usually mounted to frame of tow vehicle, thereby rendering the hitch very sturdy, reliable, and robust. Receiver hitch has an open box at the rear where the hitch bar and ball mount are inserted. Receiver hitches range in size from 1.25 in. to 2.5 in.. The most common sizes are 1.25 in. (Class I and II) and 2 in. (Class III and IV).

Refrigerator: The RV brand will dictate which of the several available types of refrigerator systems that will come stock in a RV. Some RVs use residential units, 120-Volt AC; other units can operate on either LP gas or 120-Volt AC; still other units have three-way refrigerators that can also operate on 12-Volt DC.

RVDA: Recreational Vehicle Dealers Association

RVIA: Recreational Vehicle Industry Association

Sani-Dump: Another term for dump station, either at a RV Park or a commercial facility that allows RVs to use (pay) for their dump services.

Safety chains: Used to connect a trailer A-frame to a tow vehicle frame. Many tow vehicle hitches have safety chain attachment points. The safety chains should crisscross each other from the front of the trailer to the tow vehicle attachment point. In the event of a hitch ball or coupler failure, the A frame would fall on to the crisscrossed safety chains and not impact the roadway.

SCWR (sleeping capacity weight rating): A RV manufacturers determined number of defined sleeping positions multiplied by 154 lbs.

Self-contained: A RV with the capability to sustain itself and its occupants for periods of time without any external support. This is important if you desire to boondock or periodically camp at sights with no accommodations.

Shore cord: Heavy-duty electrical cord that attaches from a RV to a camping ground electrical power pedestal.

Shore power: Electricity provided by a RV Park or campground, usually through a power pedestal. The power can range from 120-Volt 15 amp to 50 amp service.

Slide hitch: Common with owners of short-bed pickup trucks, allows the fifth wheel to slide to the rear of the pickup bed to allow for tight turns, thus avoiding vehicle body damage.

Slam-latch: Common type of compartment door latch on a RV.

Slide-in: A type of RV that slides into the bed of a pickup truck. These units are often self-contained and amazingly appointed for their compact size.

Slide out: Many RVs now can increase their living space by means of slide outs. These mechanical extensions literally slide out of a RV to increase available space. There are living room slides, bedroom slides, entire wall-slides—almost unlimited options.

Snowbird: Unrelated to the 1969 hit song for Canadian singer Anne Murray, the term Snowbirds refers to folks who take their RVs South during winter months.

Spring bars: Bars associated with weight distributing hitches that help distribute the hitch weight across all axles of the tow vehicle and attached trailer.

Stealership: Slang term for the dealership where a RV is purchased, particularly when the transaction involved a series of bad interactions and disappointment in having to pay to get things corrected—so as to provoke feelings of being stolen from or robbed.

Stinky-slinky: Slang name given to flexible sewer hose that connects from your RV to the dump station sewer inlet.

Street side: Side of a RV that, when parked, is adjacent to active traffic, or the driver's side.

Surge protector: Portable or permanently installed device that helps protect RV electrical components from unwanted electrical surges when attached to wayside power.

SURV (Sport Utility RV): A new entry into the toy hauler trailer market, a SURV resembles a flatbed trailer with a camper built on the back. This design allows for dirt bikes and ATVs to be carried with you and the luxury of not having the smell of fuel and oil in your living area.

Sway control: Device used in conjunction with the ball-mounted trailer hitch; designed to dampen and lessen the pivoting motion between the tow vehicle and trailer.

Tail swing (also referred to as bat swing): Effect created when the portion of a RV that is physically behind the rear-most axle swings around like a bat when the RV is negotiating a corner. Importance of being cognizant of bat swing is to avoid risking the potential of damaging the rear of a RV with a wall, tree, pole, street sign, or (worse yet), another vehicle.

Thermocouple: Used in LP gas appliances that use a pilot light to monitor the pilot. In the event the pilot becomes extinguished, a thermocouple turns off the gas supply.

TOAD (towed on all down): Term that refers to vehicles pulled behind motorhomes that do not use a tow dolly or require a trailer.

Tongue weight (synonymous with hitch weight): Weight a trailer imposes on a tow vehicle through a hitch. Tongue weights vary based on trailer and hitch style.

Toter (also known as RV hauler): Custom medium-duty truck manufactured for towing or transporting RV trailers long distance or in ultimate comfort.

Tow bar: Assuming your car can be pulled with all wheels on the ground, a tow bar is an excellent, reliable and safe way to pull your car behind your motorhome. The tow bar works in conjunction with the tow vehicle base plate.

Tow dolly: Used to tow a vehicle behind a RV if the vehicle cannot be pulled with all four wheels on the ground. Most automatic transmission cars cannot be pulled with all the wheels on the ground, as it would damage the drivetrain. In this case, either a trailer or tow dolly would be necessary.

Tow rating: Rating determined by the manufacturer of a tow vehicle based on numerous factors, including engine, drivetrain, cooling system, tires, and brakes.

Toy hauler: Refers to special floor models of RVs that include specific space to haul your toys. Some toy haulers, like specific fifth wheels, have a dedicated garage at the rear. Some toy haulers have a special slide to accommodate a motorcycle. There are numerous models in the industry now as this is one of the more popular offerings.

TPMS (tire pressure monitoring system): Safety system that is available in several varieties, including stem cap transmitters, valve stem units, and internal wheel bands. A TPMS monitors RV tires in real time, and notifies an operator about loss of pressure, over pressure, and temperature.

Travel trailer: A category of trailer that represents a major segment in the RV industry, travel trailers are conventional trailers that utilize an A-frame design with a hitch coupler to attach to a vehicle with a ball hitch. Travel trailers range in size from 10 ft to more than 40 ft, with every conceivable option in between.

Triple towing: More common in Western States, triple towing is a term used when two trailers are attached to a tow vehicle. An example might be a pickup truck pulling a fifth wheel that has a boat or motorcycle trailer in tow. As you might imagine, in the event of an incident where you might need to back up, triple towing presents several significant challenges.

TT: Term commonly used to refer to travel trailers.

TV: Term commonly used to refer to tow vehicle.

UDC (universal docking center): Many RVs have a specific bay or panel where plumbing inlets, coax connections and other RV utilities are managed. This specific panel, or bay, is referred to as the UDC.

Umbilical cord: Wiring harness that attaches between a tow vehicle and a trailer. Supplies 12-Volt DC power, running lights, brake lights, turn indicators, and signals to control the brakes.

Underbelly: Material used to cover and protect a RV's underside.

UVW (unloaded vehicle weight rating): Weight of a RV without any options or accessories of any kind.

Wally-Dock: Term used for those who use WalMart parking lots for an over-night stop.

Wallyworld: Slang for a local WalMart store.

Water heater bypass valve: Valve that allows winterizing of a RV water system by bypassing certain plumbing, most often the water heater.

Wayside power: A term often used in the railroad industry for equipment to power parked locomotives from the trackside, the term is also used synonymously with shore power.

WDH (Weight Distributing Hitch): A hitch assembly enhancement for receiver hitches used to attach to conventional trailers. By design, weight-distributing hitches use spring bars, rods, and chains to distribute the trailer's tongue weight across both the tow vehicle and trailer chassis.

Weights:

> Diesel fuel – 6.6 lbs/gal.
> Gasoline – 6.3 lbs/gal.
> LP Gas – 4.4 lbs/gal.
> Water – 8.3 lbs/gal.

W.E.S. (water, electric and sewer): Abbreviation used by some RV Parks in their park literature or websites to identify utilities by space.

White water: Fresh water in the fresh water tank.

Winterization: Process necessary to ready a RV for winter storage; may include activities such as draining water lines, emptying the water heater, and adding RV anti-freeze to internal water lines.

Workamping: A growing segment of the overall RV community, Workampers are individuals, or couples, who combine RVing with some form of employment. There are a wide range of Workamping offerings, but the premise is similar: an offer of free space and utilities is made in exchange for some agreed-upon number of hours worked. Some examples include folks working at RV parks as hosts;

folks who travel seasonally and work for Amazon during holiday rushes; Motorsports events; or State and National Park attendants. An August 2016 Google search for "workamping" returned over 150,000 hits for Workamping opportunities.

The Tin Can Tourists, named because they heated tin cans of food on gasoline stoves by the roadside, formed the first camping club in the United States, holding their inaugural rally in Florida in 1919 and growing to 150,000 members by the mid-1930s. They had an initiation; an official song, "The More We Get Together;" and a secret handshake. (Source: www.smithsonianmag.com)

Chapter Two

Getting Started

My wife and I always look forward to getting away in our RV, which now has become the source of some of our most enjoyable memories. We absolutely love the RV lifestyle. However, if you find yourself "on the fence" about RVing, then you're doing yourself a great service by reading this book and everything else you can to inform yourself about what RVing really entails. Making the decision to purchase a RV, then making the commitment to use it, is a major undertaking. I often see couples seemingly trying to talk themselves into the idea. You shouldn't have to convince yourself. Equally, I see too many examples where folks jumped headfirst into RVing and are still suffering, or paying the consequences.

You see it at RV dealerships all over the country. Motorhomes or trailers on the used RV sales lot, virtually brand new, possibly with some minor backing damage or a crease or tear along the side. What happened? Simple. People jumped in—then bailed out! Too often folks embarked on the purchase of their RV without having conducted absolutely any research on the subject beforehand, apparently holding the belief that RVing was as easy as staying in a hotel with wheels. They didn't visit any RV Parks or talk to any folks experienced in RVing—they just bought into the hype of those commercials on television and wanted to be a part of what, with proper resources and information, can become a wonderful American pastime.

For many of us, RVing is a wonderful pastime—absolutely incredible for families or those wishing to explore this great country of ours. RVing can be a great means to get away, and relax and unwind.

However, RVing does require some work and, again, it's a commitment. Even renting a RV requires some work on your part. RVs don't come with a staff of people to set them up, empty the tanks, or keep all the systems and functions operating smoothly.

So, as you're reading so far, does the tone sound as if I'm encouraging people to shy away from RVing in a book that professes to be about getting ready to go RVing? OK, maybe a little, but I take some pride in knowing that for as many people as I've helped get started in RVing, I've nudged an equal number away. My ultimate wish is that before you actually put hard-earned money on the table and ink the commitment for a RV, that you know you're making the absolute right decision. That knowledge is as important as the decision itself. That's why I think it's important to dedicate some space in this book to discuss making the decision. While RVing is a wonderful lifestyle for many, it's not for everyone.

You will need to balance many decisions along the way to make sure your investment serves you well. A major consideration is whether to buy your RV new, gently used, or a real fixer-upper? How handy are you with tools? Do you know the difference between a converter and an inverter? (Shockingly [pun intended] many RVers don't know, but they should.)

Over the years, I've heard people say that owning a RV is like owning an old house. It's true. With a RV, there is always some project to work on or something to fix. Not necessarily major items, but little things here and there along the way. Though the years, I've come to realize that the only RVers who never have anything to fix were those who didn't mind having things in their RVs that didn't work. Clearly, dragging a house up and down the highways of our great country is going to shake something loose, break something, tear something, dislodge something—well, you get the idea. If you're prepared to do a little work here and there, then most of the time, these little annoyances are just that—annoying—but easily resolved. For the bigger issues, there's always the mobile RV service/repair truck which we see in RV Parks quite often, stocked with all the goodies that years of service calls have prompted them to stock.

Without question, some RVs are made to more demanding standards than others. Your time spent on due diligence while preparing to get into RVing will demonstrate this fact over and over again. It's no different than the car industry. There are luxury cars that are incredibly well made and appointed, and there are real budget models that get you to your destination, without fanfare or the price tag.

Considerations

The RV lifestyle is not for everyone. For the amount of time my wife and I are able to get out each year versus the time and effort we expend maintaining and preparing our RV, would make some folks shake their heads in disbelief. To us however, it is money well spent—an investment in our happiness and sanity. It is our escape—our way to recharge—and we love to be extremely comfortable while doing so. It's a tremendous advantage to be in your own home-away- from-home, but it comes with a price tag.

There are many points to consider before diving into the world of RVs. The following items are some discussion points to get you thinking.

Type of RV

Deciding on what type of RV to purchase is a critical decision, and one that will impact the type of camping you do, sights you see, places you stay, etc. for as long as you own it. The point is, when it comes to RVing, size does matter! National Parks and State Parks have size limitations[2]. Mid 30-ft units seem to be "safe" in RV Parks and campgrounds just about everywhere, but you need to check first and know for sure instead of assuming or guessing before embarking on a trip or visit. I checked several National Park websites and found specific information on RV size limitations.

Do you want a motorhome, or do you need a motorhome? Just you? You and the wife? You and the husband? You and all the kids? Size matters because floor plans vary and options occupy space. Do you want private areas to sleep? Is sleeping on a convertible couch going to "jackknife" your back and make your trip a bust? Do the kids really care, or is this an adventure for them? Do you need room for food and supplies for a weekend, a week, or a month? Better look into this really carefully. Many RV refrigerators are smaller than you might think. Usually, only larger RVs come with huge refrigerators. RVing is all about trading space and the possible trade-offs and give-and-takes of what you want versus what you need to be comfortable. Don't assume you need anything; know you need it. We have had items in each of our RVs that got little use and we could have easily done without them.

Renting

I mentioned to a friend that I thought renting a RV from one of the national chains was an awesome way of determining how much of an RVing candidate he really was. He agreed and was off in search of options. After a few weeks, I ran into him again and he was astonished learning the costs associated with renting a RV— "astronomical," he said. Fees for this and that, and costs per mile and renting dishes, blah, blah, blah. I thought the discussion was somewhat telling.

If you're remotely undecided about whether you'd really enjoy RVing or what kind of RV you believe you want, then you should probably consider renting a RV at least once. If you think renting is too expensive, you likely have no business investing in a RV. The price of fuel is the same whether you own or rent. You need dishes, whether you rent them or buy them for your own rig.

Renting, in my opinion, remains a great way of learning the ropes without the ultimate financial risk. If you rent a RV for a couple trips and determine that RVing is too much like work, then you've come out way ahead. If you rent a few times and really enjoy the experience, but were annoyed with the price tag associated with renting, then maybe you've just proven that you're a candidate to buy your family a RV.

Renting is also a great confidence booster. If you've wondered whether you could handle driving a motorhome or towing a trailer, renting will prove the point to you one way or the other. Don't be quick to write off the possibility of renting a RV because of the fees. It's a great way to help make the right long-term choice.

Type of camping

The type of camping you'll do goes hand-in-hand with the type of RV you'll ultimately need. If you're just a weekend warrior, jetting off to the nearest lake and setting up for a couple nights, with moderate hookups, several RV types can meet your needs. If you're more into boondocking for a week or so at a time, your choices are more limited and your RV will require some additional equipment to make living off the grid possible. If you're into glamping, then your needs are slightly different yet. Your RV may need to have more power options and a larger floor plan.

Actual costs for camping locations vary greatly. Some Public Lands and Bureau of Land Management (BLM) camping locations are absolutely free of charge. While free, these spaces will likely have absolutely no hookups of any kind. On the opposite extreme are RV Resorts, where every amenity and desire is addressed by the Park. It's only money! Knowing what type of camping interests you will help narrow the field and necessary options.

Saving money on trips

This is a great discussion point and one that can grow into a fairly complex spreadsheet of expenditures versus savings. I've spoken to many families who are absolutely convinced that they have saved significant money using their RV for family vacations.

A recent study by PFK Consulting USA for the Recreational Vehicle Industry Association confirms this assertion[3]. In fact, their study indicates that a family of four, traveling in their own RV, could recognize a 23 to 59 percent savings when compared to the cost of other types of vacations. A vacation from Atlanta Georgia to Orlando Florida by typical Class C motorhome was 46 percent cheaper than getting airline tickets, a rental car, and a hotel. For a family of four, the average week-long vacation in the family travel trailer, staying at campgrounds and eating meals prepared at the campgrounds

48

averaged $1,997, while that same vacation with airline tickets, rental car, hotel, and dining out averaged $4,045.

A host of websites offer very complete comparisons for family vacations that include airfare, rental car, and hotel versus taking the family camper. These examples vary widely and admittedly, there are so many potential variables. I tend to agree with the majority of the examples and concede freely that the RV option in many of these examples is a far less expensive (and better, in my opinion) option. My only caution is that it's not an apples-to-apples comparison. What I'm getting at is you don't own the airline, or the rental car, or pay year-round for the hotel room. You do, however, own the RV and when trying to analyze what makes sense for you, one must address the cost of ownership.

Cost of ownership

The actual cost of ownership is a difficult calculation. The many folks I've talked to over the years get pretty animated about what counts and what doesn't count when discussing cost of ownership. At a minimum, you should consider these factors when determining your cost of RV ownership.

Purchase price. Remember, really get very serious about determining whether a gently used RV can fit your family's needs. The costs associated with gently used versus new are fairly significant. Later in chapter 5, this specific topic is discussed in greater detail.

Insurance. Some type of insurance is required, whether you own your RV outright or you're financing it. You can check the annual cost of insurance before you purchase. If you have a driving record with several moving violations (yes, you know who you are), insurance on a motorhome might be cost prohibitive. Check with your primary insurance provider about the possibility of getting a multi-vehicle discount, or any progressive rates that may apply. Ask the agent specific questions about discounts because they may not be offered without you doing a little prodding. Lastly, when you get the quote, cuss like a sailor and squawk that it's too high and ask them to go back to the well and run the numbers again. You just might be surprised.

Registration. Like insurance, registering your RV is mandatory. Some states offer very financially reasonable registration costs, while registration costs in other states are based directly on the purchase price or weight of the RV. It is easy to check on your state by simply visiting the appropriate state's motor vehicle division website.

Maintenance. On several occasions in this book, I mention that if you own an RV, you're going to need to fix things. Maintenance and repairs of issues inside the RV are really two separate issues. Maintenance includes tires, oil, brakes, electrical, plumbing, roof, batteries, and general upkeep. Replacing an appliance, like a refrigerator, that quits working is considered a repair and differs from maintenance, but an expense none the less, and is definitely a factor in cost of ownership.

In general terms, there is a direct correlation between the size and options of a RV and the cost of maintenance. Also, like anything else you buy as a consumer, there are broad differences in quality and workmanship in RVs. I'll make this point and ask you to consider it when contemplating a RV purchase. Spending a little more upfront on a better manufactured unit could potentially save you significantly in the long run. There is a lot of truth to the old adage "you get what you pay for" in the RV world.

TOAD or Dinghy. If your choice of RV is a motorhome, you may need a vehicle to tow behind the motorhome so that you can run errands, sight-see, or just generally get around without moving your house each time.

Towing a vehicle behind your RV is accomplished in two ways, depending on what type vehicle you wish to tow. Vehicles that can be towed with all four wheels on the ground are called TOADS (towed on all down). The many vehicles that cannot be towed with all their wheels on the ground and require a tow dolly are referred to as dinghies.

Be careful as some vehicles cannot be towed in either manner. Regardless of TOAD or dinghy, a tow dolly or towing bar and vehicle mount will be required. A supplemental braking system, if the vehicle is over 2,000 pounds, is also likely required. (See Appendix Four for supplemental brake information.)

Storage. A lot of folks I've talked to over the years did not investigate the expense of storing their RV until much after the fact of the RV purchase. Of course, your RV must be stored and parked somewhere when you're not using it. If you own property, this may not be an issue for you. If you live in an area with covenants or restrictions, you may not be allowed to park an RV at your home. If you live in multi-family units or apartments, it's unlikely that you'll be permitted to park your RV in their parking lot. Check into this before buying. RV storage can run several hundreds of dollars per month for a large, covered space.

Taxes. It's not all bad news. While tax rules change slightly from year to year, most RVs (that include a bed, kitchen, and bathroom) are considered by the Internal Revenue Service to be homes[4], potentially making the RV tax deductible.

Paying while parked. This goes to the heart of the discussion about whether RVs are cheaper for family vacations than traditional transportation and lodging options. Regardless of that discussion, the cost being discussed here is that you're paying for your RV, and all the costs associated with having an RV, while it sits between uses.

Let's say that, between weekends, holidays, and vacations, you can typically get away using your RV for 80 days a year. While those 80 days may be some of the most enjoyable of the year, the costs of ownership are still in effect for the remaining 285 days of the year while the RV sits, unused. For us, that's perfectly fine. Just make sure you address it and consider it.

Roadside assistance plan. This might be an additional expense depending on what type of RV you decide to purchase. For many trailers and smaller motorhomes, it may be more of a nicety than a necessity. On larger motorhomes, however, a road-side rescue plan is really not an option. I'm not implying that your regular RV insurance does not cover this; it may or may not. What I am saying is that, if you have a large RV and you have a flat tire, you can't deal with it yourself. You have to have a roadside service respond and fix the issue. Something else of which you may not be aware, larger motorhomes don't come with a spare tire. I therefore knew that if we had a flat on our 38 foot Class A, I was not going to attempt a tire swap on the highway by myself; we happily accepted the cost for a professional roadside service plan to replace the flat tire.

Winterization. Winterization is discussed in detail in chapter 11. If you store your RV over the winter, this might be an added expense that you need to balance. Winterization should not be a significant cost unless it's done improperly.

Tow vehicle upgrades. If your RV is a travel trailer or fifth wheel, don't forget to consider the costs of outfitting your tow vehicle to safely pull your trailer (e.g., fifth-wheel hitches, receiver hitches, sway controls, weight distributing hitches, brake controllers, air bags, etc.; the list can be daunting). Make sure you address the costs associated with outfitting your tow vehicle into your ownership equation.

The first RV was Pierce-Arrow's Touring Landau, which debuted at Madison Square Garden in 1910. The Landau had a back seat that folded into a bed, a chamber pot toilet and a sink that folded down from the back of the seat of the chauffeur, who was connected to his passengers via telephone. (Source: www.smithsonianmag.com)

Although several categories of expenses associated with RV ownership have been covered in this section, all of the categories have not been covered. Each circumstance is unique and you might experience additional expenses beyond our list. The keys to preparing yourself to make the ownership decision is data and details; the more you have, the more accurate and appropriate your decision will be.

Stress

Here's a scenario. You're pulling your Class A motorhome and your Mini Cooper convertible TOAD behind you on your way to a week of fun and sun at your favorite RV destination. Suddenly, some traffic accident-related issue requires that you back up half a city block to utilize a side street as an alternate route. In case you're not aware, you can't back up a TOAD. Tow bars and vehicle mounts aren't designed to work that way. If you have to back up more than a few feet, you have to disconnect the TOAD from the motorhome, and that's not necessarily a task than can be accomplished simply or quickly. Meanwhile, horns are honking, people are waving with a varied number of fingers and traffic is backing up.

Would this scenario cause you stress? How about backing a 32-ft travel trailer into a tight parking spot with tight shoulders and little maneuvering room while a line of other eager campers are trapped behind you...waiting, Waiting, WAITING! Do you and your spouse agree on what your hand-and-arm signals represent? Seems like every single camper in the park is now headed your direction for the simple reason of watching you attempt to back into this parking spot. You've become a Park attraction! Are you stressed out yet?

If your answer is "no," that these situations cause you no stress at all, then you're unique. Most people would rather talk in front of an audience of strangers than back a RV into a tight parking spot. However you personally deal with stress, figure it out beforehand. Backing maneuvers are a part of RV ownership. While it looked strange, my wife and I set up orange traffic cones in an empty

54

parking lot one afternoon and I practiced backing from various angles of attack and from differing depths. As they say, practice makes perfect.

Pets

You'd be amazed at how many folks admit to purchasing their RV so they could travel with their pets. My wife and I fit into that category with many others, and more folks yet are too embarrassed to admit it! It is not uncommon for pets to experience car sickness in motorhomes and that can be a real mess. For sure, traveling with pets presents some challenges and will require you to do some checking before you strike out.

Many RV Parks have pet restrictions of some form or fashion. We travel with three dogs and have been refused reservations at a handful of RV Parks that have a "strict" 2-dog limit. Many RV parks also have breed restrictions, and the number of parks with this restriction is continually growing (for insurance liability reasons, I surmise). Many RV Parks will not allow dog pens or dogs to be tied up on a leash outside your RV. To avoid problems with the unknown regarding pets in RV Parks, check with the RV Park before making reservations, and don't take anything for granted.

Also, keep in mind that finding a veterinarian while traveling outside your residential living area may be challenging and costly. If your pet requires medication or special diet, make sure you have plenty of everything packed before leaving.

Mail forwarding

An important consideration if you plan to be gone from home for extended periods of time is a mail forwarding service. While more and more bills and payments can be managed over the internet, other items like packages or official correspondence require an actual delivery location. Several offerings for mail forwarding range from commercial services to a willing neighbor.

Phones and internet

In this day and age, most "mobile" people have cell phones. If your plan is to travel, make sure your cellular plan can travel effectively with you. Virtually all do, but verify. RV Parks often have WiFi, but you can't count on it. We are mostly disappointed at the WiFi availability in RV Parks that we visit. If you need internet availability, make sure your cellular service and phone are capable of being a hotspot. A hotspot is a device that other WiFi capable devices can use to access the internet. It's easy to set up and use, and most plans offer data plans at reasonable rates.

Chapter Three

Types of RVs

So, you're still really thinking about buying a RV? What kind? Motorhome? Trailer? Slide-in? Once you've decided you want one, the real work begins—making sure you get the right one to meet your needs and, more importantly, your expectations. This chapter discusses each of the concepts, as they are often not in sync. Remember, you're going to be married to this decision, at least for a while, so do your due diligence, take your time, research, ask questions, and even consider renting one first before making a purchase. The bottom line here is that the more work you do on the front side, the better off you'll be on the back side.

Other chapters of this book discuss some of the trade space and options offered by the many styles of RVs. Discussions include price, financing, maintenance, and upkeep. Once you know the type of RV you really need, blending that information with what you really want will drive your buying decision. Before that can happen, you need to have a good sense of what types of RVs are out there. This chapter will help you in that effort.

There are three categories of RVs on the market, with two dominant styles: motorhomes and trailers; truck campers also have a faithful following. Each style is represented in this chapter. Once you decide on an RV style, the range of models and options available is almost staggering. In 2016 alone, more than a dozen manufacturers were building units of every conceivable configuration. According to the Recreational Vehicle Industry Association, sales of RVs exceeded 374,000 units in 2015, and 430,000 units in 2016—an increase of 15% in one year. Continued growth for 2017 seems all but assured.[5]

So, let's take a look at what's out there!

Motorhomes

Motorhomes are just as the name implies: homes built on a motorized chassis. There are three main classes of motorhomes.

Class A. Class A motorhomes are built on a specific motorized chassis and can be quite large and luxurious. Class A units can easily reach into the several hundred-thousand-dollar range, with some exclusive units tipping the $1 million mark.

The Ford F53 chassis, powered by the Ford V10 engine, is the most common chassis in use[6]. This front-mounted engine chassis has a gross vehicle weight rating of up to 26,000 lbs, and RV manufacturers offer units up to 38 ft in length.

The Freightliner chassis is the most common used in diesel motorhomes; the Freightliner XC chassis is currently installed in more than 80% of all diesel units[7]. The Freightliner chassis offers a gross vehicle weight rating of up to 47,000 lbs and lengths up to 45 ft. Diesel pusher motorhomes are very popular because of their expansive storage. The Freightliner chassis rails allow complete, pass-through storage slides, something rarely seen in any other type of RV.

There are other gasoline chassis besides the Ford F53 and other diesel chassis besides Freightliner. The Ford F53 and Freightliner offerings are specifically referenced here because they are, currently, the *de facto* standards. Smaller Class A units are becoming more and more popular with units such as the Forest River FR3 at 25 ft, and the Thor Ace at 27 ft (both priced at about $105,000); and the Winnebago Vista at 26 ft (priced under $90,000).

Class As can't be competed with for the ultimate in luxury—they are the flagship. Units like the Prevost H3VIP are sleek, modern, and priced at a mere $1.6 million. The Newmar King Aire includes technology like collision avoidance and is built on a custom Spartan chassis for a cool $750,000.

Bus conversions are also considered Class A motorhomes. Bus conversions run the spectrum from million-dollar custom buses (like those used by rock stars for travel) to actual bus conversions. You've seen bus conversions—old school buses that have been stripped out and customized for personal use. Bus conversions should not be mistaken with the old hippie rides of days past. Do some research on-line. You'll be amazed at what some clever craftsmen have done with old buses. There are even Class A Toy Haulers where an area of the unit is dedicated for loading your

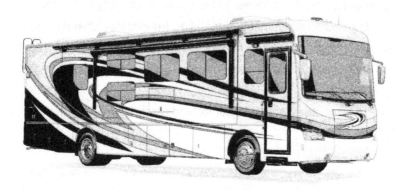

Figure 1 Typical Class A, Diesel Pusher

favorite toys.

Class A Pros: Motorhomes are very popular because of their turn-key-go availability. Class As are very popular because of their panoramic view from the windshield and access to your living area while motoring down the highway. Imagine your wife driving and asking you to make her a cool drink and a sandwich. Many Class A units offer this ability (including bathroom breaks for the passengers, of course). Many units are self-leveling (or automated leveling), and are considered to be pretty simple to set up. Slide rooms offer incredible room for you and your family with units over 14 ft wide when the slides are extended. Many Class A units have generators, which allow the units to be completely self-contained. On extremely hot days, the generator allows you to cool the coach by running a standard roof air conditioner. Diesel pushers also have air-ride suspensions for that "riding-on-air" feeling that makes traveling down the highway truly enjoyable. Air brakes complement the system with sure braking.

Class A Cons: The size of Class A units can be intimidating to some drivers and make maneuvering in tight spaces very difficult to accomplish. Most choose to pull smaller vehicles behind their Class As to use for grocery runs, sightseeing, and running errands (it's not really practical to make short trips in a full-size motorhome).

Backing up a Class A motorhome requires some patience, but the skill set is the same you've learned from driving your personal vehicle. The most common concern I hear regularly is true to all categories of motorhomes. Unlike a trailer, in the event you have a mechanical failure and your rig has to go for service, you're without your home. With a trailer, if your tow vehicle fails, a towing service will transport your trailer to a RV park (within reason) while your tow vehicle is repaired.

Fuel mileage is generally pretty low, but then you wouldn't expect a 40-ft motorhome to get comparable mileage to your personal car. Class A units can be very tall, making overhead clearance a concern. Some folks don't like the space that is wasted up front where the steering wheel and chassis controls are located.

Class B. Class B motorhomes represent a popular segment of the motorhome market and one that is very popular now with the addition of the Mercedes and Sprinter van chassis options. Class B motorhomes, the smallest of the motorhome lineup, are built using van cutaway or van chassis. These units may appear similar to Class C motorhomes, but one important distinction is the lack of the cab-over enclosure that Class C motorhomes have. Some of the larger Class B units with fiberglass bodies rival the nicest Class C units of similar size.

Figure 2 Typical Class B motorhome

Class B Pros: These units have a lesser cost than a Class A while still offering your family everything necessary to be comfortable on the road and for short trips. Some units will fit into standard garages and their size renders them manageable in confined spaces and easy to navigate in traffic. Some people call these units "SUVs on steroids." These units are designed for efficiency in every aspect. The fuel mileage for Class B's is best of all the motorized RV classes.

Class B Cons: Most Class B units do not have a defined bedroom; instead, sleeping arrangements are normally managed by dropping the dining table or reducing a jackknife-style couch. Probably best suited for two, some models claim sleeping for four. Entertainment systems are small, and bathroom facilities often combine the toilet, sink, and shower into one tight corner.

Class C: Class C motorhome units are very common and, in 2016, outsold Class A models[8]. Class C units use a standard cargo van chassis and come in lengths of around 35 ft. New "Super-C" units are becoming ever more popular. These units are built on medium- and heavy-duty truck chassis like Freightliner and International. As such, they offer units into the mid-40-ft range and boast incredible towing capabilities (often 20,000 lbs).

Class Cs share many of the same benefits of their Class A brethren, but the amenities are not usually as complete. Washer and dryers, for example, are rare in Class C units and, while they offer ample room, most installations (e.g., fixtures, cabinets, closets, dinettes, etc.) are smaller. Class Cs are easily spotted by the unique cab-over design, which is often used for a bed, but in some units is used for storage and/or entertainment systems.

Class C Pros: Many owners of Class C units appreciate their ease of maintenance. Chassis service is available from your local dealer, which is arguably much easier than getting a Class A unit serviced, and certainly less expensive. These smaller units allow more camping options and are easier to maneuver than their larger Class A siblings. Fuel mileage is slightly better and owners I've spoken to, enjoy the normal "van like cab" with traditional doors.

Figure 3 Typical Class C motorhome

Class C Cons: Class C units lack the larger open areas afforded by Class A models due to lack of slides or size of available slides. Longer floor plans suffer from extensive rear overhang. In our travels, we have seen this rear overhang "rear" its ugly head. Exiting a gas station in Colorado, we spied a Class C with a long floor plan stuck while attempting to depart a fuel station across the road. The roadway had a significant dip and sharp turn. As the driver exited, the rear of the Class C scraped the ground until the drive wheels simply had no traction. While this type of event is rare indeed, the rear swing of these units can be problematic.

Trailers

According to the Recreation Vehicle Industry Association, trailer sales outpace motorhome sales by a wide margin. In fact, in March 2016, RV dealers moved 35,632 trailers, while only moving 4,977 motorhomes.[9] Not necessarily surprising, trailers are often an economical way to begin RVing and come in an amazing array of sizes and shapes, with options abound.

Travel trailers dominate the trailer category with roughly two thirds of all trailer sales.[10] One of the most commonly cited reasons people choose to buy a trailer is that option leaves only one drive train to maintain: the tow vehicle. Trailers are enormously popular due to the extreme range of floor plans available. Both travel trailers and fifth wheels, as an example, offer "Toy Hauler" models. Toy haulers are units with a specific area of the trailer dedicated, or specifically enhanced, to haul toys (motorcycles, quads, bicycles, canoes—anything you consider a toy!).

Also in the trailer category are some unique offerings designed for a very specific clientele, like Pop-Up Campers and SURVs (Sport Utility RVs) flatbed trailers with an aft living quarters. These variants of toy haulers are rugged and can carry tremendous weights. Trailers range in lengths from just over 10 ft, to triple-axle monsters over 45 ft.

For people looking to get into RVing, trailers offer the potential to use your current vehicle as your tow vehicle. With the wide range of trailer options, some trailers out there can be pulled by virtually any passenger car or pickup truck. In fact, a quick Google search for "Smart Car towing trailer" will provide numerous examples of Smart Car owners pulling micro teardrop RVs. Pricing for trailers runs the gamut also, from a few thousand dollars to well over $200,000 (and beyond) for some well-appointed fifth wheels. Chances are, if you need it, one or more of the manufacturers is making it.

Travel Trailers. As stated earlier, travel trailers are the mainstay of the RV industry, and outsell every other type of RV, hands down. In fact, there are more sales each year of travel trailers than of all motorhome sales combined. Travel trailers are generally lightweight but durable, thanks to sturdy construction techniques. Travel trailer units come in a wide variety of sizes, shapes, and lengths, ensuring that most family vehicles stand ready in the driveway to become capable tow vehicles. A travel trailer is connected to a tow vehicle using the trailer's A-frame and ball coupler, which is attached to the tow vehicle's ball hitch. The several variants of these hitch assemblies and more information about hitches are discussed in chapter 14.

Figure 4 Typical Travel Trailer

Travel Trailer Pros: Travel trailers allow you to separate your trailer and tow vehicle, thereby allowing you a means of exploring, sightseeing, or running errands. Since the travel trailer and tow vehicle can be separated, a mechanical issue with one or the other does not take both out of operation.

Travel trailers have less mechanical issues that can go wrong than do motorized units. Average cost per unit is the lowest of all RVs while returning substantial investment or bang-for-the-buck. Travel trailers offer a lower profile so, for some folks, they are easier to get in and out of parking and other spaces.

Travel Trailer Cons: Larger travel trailers can be hard to maneuver when parking and backing up, and are also less stable than their fifth-wheel cousins. Some travel trailers can be sparse on space, and storage is often at a premium. Unlike a motorhome, you are separated from the living space in a travel trailer while moving. Your tow vehicle capacity may limit your purchase options or if you're set on a particular unit, it may require the purchase of an alternate tow vehicle. Most travel trailers have mechanical leveling jacks, which can requiring some effort to get the unit ready for camping.

Fifth Wheels. For total trailers sold in a given year, fifth wheels represent around one-third of sales. Fifth-wheel units are normally larger than their travel trailer siblings and, as such, their design is different.

Fifth wheels are connected to their tow vehicle by connecting the king pin on the trailer hitch to the fifth-wheel plate mounted on the tow vehicle. By design, a substantial portion of the trailers weight is then transferred to the tow vehicle. This fifth wheel attachment allows fifth wheel trailers to articulate differently than tow vehicles and travel trailers. Most folks agree that fifth wheels behave better while being towed, suffer from less sway, and are more stable in crosswinds.

Fifth wheels are available with various floor plans, including "Toy Hauler" models, where the entire back end is a dedicated garage. Some new luxury fifth-wheel models are in the $200,000 price range. Their larger size allows for larger living areas, sizeable kitchens, and storage galore.

Fifth Wheel Pros: Sturdy and stable while towing, fifth-wheel units suffer less from sway and wind than travel trailers. Easier to tow and back up because of the hitch location, fifth wheels can be articulated to about 90% for close-quarter maneuvers. High ceilings and spacious interiors provide ample living space. Fifth wheels generally have more interior and exterior storage than do travel trailers. A tow vehicle can be separated from a fifth-wheel unit and used for local commutes, sightseeing, and errands.

Figure 5 Typical Fifth Wheel - these units use a kingpin instead of ball hitch like travel trailers do.

Fifth Wheel Cons: Fifth wheels can be more expensive than travel trailers and, depending on the size you choose, may require a larger tow vehicle. By design, fifth-wheel units require a pickup truck or flatbed truck with fifth-wheel hitch capabilities. As with travel trailers, you are separated from the living space while moving. Larger fifth wheels can be difficult to maneuver in tight areas. Many campgrounds have 36- and 38-ft limits on RV length, thereby prohibiting accommodations for larger fifth-wheel units on the market. Fifth-wheels can be very tall, thereby making overhead clearance an issue for concern.

Pop-Ups. Pop-up trailers have a very celebrated past and date back to the early days of trailer RVs. Pop-ups are usually small, can be towed behind most any tow vehicle, and have a reasonable price tag. Pop-ups are really geared towards keeping you out of the weather and giving you a more comfortable sleeping environment. While some pop-ups have toilets and entertainment systems, they are not geared towards you "hanging-out" inside. Some folks say

Figure 6 Typical Pop-Up trailer. Pop-Up units are very popular and easy to tow.

that if you're using a pop-up, you can still claim you're camping, whereas if you're using a travel trailer, fifth wheel, or motorhome, you're "Glamping." Hard to argue when your Class A's wine cooler alerts you the doors been left ajar!

Pop-Up Pros: Pop-up units are inexpensive to purchase; easy to tow with virtually any tow vehicle; and easy to maneuver in traffic and tight spots. A pop-up's top folds down so as not to obstruct your vision while driving, and because of its low profile, allows your tow vehicle to maintain relatively good fuel mileage.

Pop-Up Cons: Pop-up units offer very limited space and are not really designed for use during long stays. Amenities are minimal (or compact, at the very least). A pop-up's soft sides allow you to keep dry, but cold weather can chill you, despite use of its built-in furnace.

Toy haulers

While toy haulers are really not a segment of their own, I've chosen to break them out because of their uniqueness and popularity in the RV industry. Toy haulers have gained so much popularity that they are now available in virtually all platforms (Class A, Class C, travel trailer, fifth wheel, and SURV).

Generally, toy haulers have special tie down points, or anchors, to secure your load. Some even have their own integrated gasoline tank and pump hose like those used at a gas station. Here are a few examples of toy haulers in this growing market:

Fifth-wheel toy haulers. Fifth-wheel toy haulers are extremely popular and offer their owners advantages not available with regular floor plans. Toy hauler owners can bring motorcycles, quads, small

Figure 7 Typical Fifth Wheel Toy Hauler - a large ramp, often in the rear, allows for loading of all your toys.

boats, bicycles—just about anything. Toy haulers usually dedicate the rear of the fifth wheel to the "garage," but don't think that space is useless once you get to your destination – because it's not. Once you take your toys out, the rear can be reconfigured. On some models, the area has couches mounted on the sidewalls that are extended once the "garage" is cleared. In addition, some have queen- size beds that can be lowered to allow for additional sleeping options. Regardless, while fifth-wheel toy hauler units may be a little more utilitarian than their fifth-wheel counterparts, you don't have to sacrifice any amenities.

Toy haulers have become so popular that manufacturers are really putting effort forth to design and build very capable units. There are Class A toy haulers in a couple designs but generally, just as in the fifth wheel variety, the garage is the rear of the Class A and the rear cap is replaced by a ramp door.

In one popular design, the Thor Outlaw, the bedroom is actually above the garage. It makes for a tight space, but then, RVs are all about giving you what you asked for by blending the obvious trade space. Class As can only be so long and so tall!

Figure 8 Side loading Travel Trailer Toy Hauler

Some fifth-wheel toy hauler designs are less garage-like, attempting to maximize the available living space. Examples of these include models that have side-mounted loading ramps into a forward garage to help with weight distribution while maximizing useable space in these fairly light toy hauler models.

Another interesting variant is units that have the ability to convert a slide room into a garage. While these units are more upscale (pricey), they absolutely maximize your living comfort while still allowing you to take your Harley Davidson Cruiser on vacation.

Still other examples of toy haulers exist! Some Class C toy haulers include some monster units built on large, Freightliner (or like) chassis.

Figure 9   Hybrid toy hauler, combines large flatbed with pop-up style camper (great for hauling quads, dirt bikes, and mountain bikes).

A newer category of toy hauler that dealers are showing off more and more is referred to as the SURV (Sport Utility RV). These units resemble more of a large flatbed with a camper added to the back as an afterthought. In reality, SURVs have well-thought-out designs and are substantial construction, which often means serious hauling capacity. This new offering is appearing more and more.

Truck campers

For purposes of defining some boundaries, I'm going to define the truck camper category as more of a self-contained, slide-in type unit, not the fiberglass or aluminum units that just bolt/clamp onto a pickup bed. For folks who think these units are too basic and lack any comfort creatures, then you've not really looked into these units. You may be surprised to find that some slide-in truck campers can cost upwards of $50,000; in fact, I've seen a few priced even higher. Some of these units really require a one-ton truck to be completely safe and still be able to tow a trailer of some kind. Truck camper units can have air conditioning, heat, refrigerators, entertainment systems, toilets, showers, dinettes, and large beds. With that said, the toilet may be a cassette type and you may have to straddle the toilet to shower. The refrigerator may be as small as some coolers you've seen at tailgating parties. Size in these units is everything. Clearly, these are niche units for a very specific segment of the market. You see a lot of these units in the wilderness, blasting across Alaska, or on secluded rivers and streams.

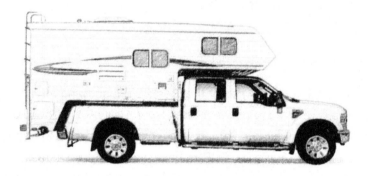

Figure 10 Slide-in truck camper.

There is no real need here to discuss specific pros and cons. These units are very specialized and fit a specific need in the RV community. I've talked to folks who are quite comfortable and would never consider trading to a different style. As with all the choices presented when deciding on an RV, the most important qualifiers are what you intend the RV to serve. If you get that question right, the rest tends to all fall into place.

Chapter Four

Pre-delivery Inspection (PDI)

A pre-delivery inspection (PDI) is a buyer's opportunity to check every aspect of your new (or new to you) RV—to physically check every system, component, accessory or option installed in your unit. It is your one (and perhaps only) chance to document issues with your RV that need to be corrected before actually taking delivery. The types of issues found during a PDI may indicate a red flag to not accept delivery and to not sign paperwork to complete the purchase.

The problem with not performing a thorough PDI is that once you have taken possession of your RV, many dealers become much less inclined to make repairs in a timely manner. Once a dealer or individual sells a unit, it is off their lot inventory and books. Of course, on new (and some used) units, a warranty is certainly a mechanism to get repairs made, but now you will have to navigate and manage the warranty process. A dealer will be considerably more "motivated" to have repairs completed quickly to get a unit sold than he will be to make warranty claim repairs after a sale. While the unit remains on the dealer's lot inventory and books, the dealer makes payments on the RV.

I devote a substantial amount of space to this topic in this book, and for good reason. PDIs are a critical, but unfortunately, widely ignored or completely misunderstood component of the RV buying process. Often, when buyers do conduct a PDI, it is completely inadequate and, therefore, of little true value to the new owner. In reality, after you've completed all your research and you've taken the plunge to get that new RV, your focus and investment should be getting prepared to complete your PDI. In the years we've been

RVing and talking to all the good people we've encountered, I can count only a handful who claim to have performed a complete and thorough PDI of their new unit even though everyone should. It would be virtually impossible to total the number of complaints on forums, angry letters to dealers, and frustration directed at manufacturers that could have been virtually eliminated or at least avoided if the buyer had simply completed a thorough PDI. A RV should be delivered ready to use; however, I have concluded from my experiences that is rarely the case. Your best and most direct route to getting a RV that is ready for you and your family is to complete an aggressive PDI.

Now, as with many things that seem obvious, there's a catch. Dealers are not interested in you performing a thorough PDI. Instead of an actual or useful PDI, they often schedule "walk-throughs" or "new rig orientation tours" in hopes that you'll accept these as adequate and sign on the bottom line. Too often, they get their way and only after you've left the lot with your shiny new RV do you realize something, or worse, lots of somethings don't work properly, if at all. It is a tired old story and one repeated all too often. The following section on problems discovered during PDIs could literally be a book by itself. Really, there is so much to do, check, and evaluate. The more you do, the better you're prepared; the more things you touch and test for complete functionality, the better off you'll be in the long run.

Why PDI? Some personal examples

Does conducting a PDI really make a difference? Absolutely, it does; and, I feel uniquely qualified to discuss the PDI process with you. Why? Because I've paid the price for not performing an adequate PDI and, subsequently, I learned the tricks and tools necessary to conduct one in an appropriate manner. Once informed, I've conducted thorough PDIs, helped others complete theirs, and written extensively on the topic.

For our first RV purchase, I was one of those people you see at the dealership: an overenthusiastic buyer who was "too excited" to purchase and own his first RV, and I allowed the dealer to determine the type of walk-through to be conducted and the time allotted for its completion. I totally surrendered to the dealer, and allowed them to talk their way out of conducting a complete inspection...and I paid for it (dearly). Literally, starting just hours off the lot, I began paying for it.

Our first RV was a gently used, 38-ft Class A diesel pusher. My lack of understanding about how to conduct a proper PDI culminated in me making a series of poor decisions. A proper PDI and a basic knowledge of the topics covered later in this chapter would have saved me considerable time, money, and frustration. In the following sections of this chapter, I provide examples of what I missed and a couple examples from people I've met along-the-way. These personal accounts should help focus on why a properly completed PDI is so important.

It was Friday morning when I arrived at the dealership, excited to see the new (to us) diesel pusher that I had made a tentative offer on over the internet. I thought I was ready and prepared. I was not. The dealership had seen many like me before and was well prepared with rehearsed answers to all my questions. In hindsight, they were masterful at their art, in the way they orchestrated the walk-through, in the ways they had items displayed and functioning or, more importantly, how they did not. Now, in the name of full-disclosure, I do not believe that any member of the dealership staff purposefully mislead me; however, there were many instances where I was not told everything.

So, what went wrong with my first PDI? Everything. From the beginning, the dealer ran the show and I was ill prepared to understand some of the problems that were staring me right in the face.

I had researched enough to know that I should ensure that the RV had newer, good-quality tires. Mine did not. I knew enough to demand that new tires be included as part of the deal and the dealer, after much back and forth, agreed. What I didn't know was that tires have date codes (chapter 15 discusses tires in detail.) New tires were installed and I felt large and in-charge. While the tires looked and smelled new, the reality was they were actually already five years old. I had them less than three years before they required replacement. The tires failed essentially from dry-rot, certainly accelerated by their age. Impact to me: $4,000 for new tires.

The dealer's service technicians had the two roof air conditioners running and the coach was cooled down prior to my arrival. I did not "exercise" the air conditioners nor did I check their output with a digital thermometer. If I had, I would have detected that the front unit was not effectively cooling. The rear air conditioning unit was working well and had struggled to cool the entire coach. Additionally, the front unit should have included a heat pump (it did not, or at least it wasn't wired into the thermostat properly). Impact to me: $650 to repair a pinhole leak and recharge the refrigerant for the forward unit. Even with repairs, the forward unit never cooled adequately, nor did we ever get the heat pump to function.

The dealer turned on the generator to prove that it started and worked. Starting and then allowing a generator to run for a few minutes proves nothing. I should have "exercised" the generator with a substantial load. Had I done so, I would have discovered that the generator had a faulty internal inverter, a not-so-uncommon issue with the Onan 7500 Quiet Diesel unit installed in our coach. The failed inverter would periodically report an error indicating "overcurrent fault" which, under load, caused the generator to stop running. Had I put the generator through a stress test on the dealer's lot, the problem likely would have surfaced there on the lot, not days after leaving the dealership, on the interstate, driving across the desert. Impact to me: more than $1,000 for parts and labor for the repair.

I watched the technician light a stove-top burner, carefully committing to memory the way you had to twist and turn dials, and throw switches to ignite the LP. Had I been more knowledgeable and prepared, I would have checked each of the three stovetop burners. In preparing for our first trip, going through the coach, ensuring I knew how to operate the various systems, I discovered that one of the three burners would not light. Regardless of what I tried, no flame. Impact to me: $62 to replace the defective burner. While the original burner seemed clean and looked factory fresh, it had some defect that prevented it from working properly.

I watched as the technician used the remote control to operate the bedroom television. The picture was crisp and clear and the small television seemed to work, and using the over-the-air antenna, it did work wonderfully well. It was not until I tried to watch cable television that some gremlin seemed to appear and then nothing appeared on the television screen. After a substantial amount of work, cable tracing, checking cable connections, replacing cable splitters, it was finally discovered, using a multi-meter, that the coax run from the basement to the bedroom coax amplifier-switch, was shorted. Likely an errant wall staple had pierced a coax run. Running replacement coax can often be a nightmare job in a RV. In our case, the run was short, through a hollow wall and into a bedroom cabinet. While it turned out to be a relatively simple fix, it took several hours over a couple of days to diagnose the actual problem. Impact to me: $45 in parts, but a lot of sweat equity invested to find a solution to the problem.

We replaced a small section of carpet in a slide room—carpet that had been damaged by water infiltration from a window leak that I did not detect because I didn't inspect any of the windows closely, nor did I get on my hands and knees to evaluate the condition of the carpet. Now here's a great buyer beware notice. Our motorhome had a "heavy plastic floor covering laid down on the carpet to protect the carpet from soil as prospective buyers walked through the coach," I was told by the dealer. Keep in mind that the plastic also hides issues with the carpet (including water damage). Impact to me: $340 to replace damaged carpet. Luckily there was only minimal damage to the subfloor, which was easily repaired. The leaking window frame was repaired using a standard RV screw and some silicone.

It was 99 degrees the day I accepted delivery of our coach. With the heat beating down from every direction and angle, I never thought to check the furnace or chassis heater. On our first trip in cooler weather, we discovered the chassis heater blower did not work. Our chassis had two blowers: one for the chassis air conditioning and defroster ducts, and one blower motor for the heater unit to force air out of the (large) lower dash vents. To repair the broken chassis heater-blower required removal of the entire front dash of the motorhome to access the blower motor. Impact to me: $94 for the blower motor, and 8 hours of labor at a cost of $75/hour to remove and replace the dash.

Our motorhome had a wonderful video monitor built into the dash radio system. The monitor would slide out of the radio chassis and then fold back to allow the driver to see the screen—perfectly! Really cool, high-tech, and something that would impress friends down the road. The screen provided clear video of the sides of the coach activated by the turn signal switch, then returned to the rear view mode for normal driving. For the first day of ownership, the video worked wonderfully, but I began to wonder why the screen didn't automatically retract into the radio chassis when not in use. Then I spied it: a small button on the radio facing marked "RETRACT." I pressed the button and, sure enough, the screen slipped effortlessly back into the radio chassis, never to be seen again. Seems this brand radio/video screen combination had a habit of developing this particular problem after a bit of use. The display motors quit moving the screen out. I'm not suggesting that the dealership knew the radio display was faulty or that it would fail if cycled. The problem was that I didn't try to cycle it. Had I done so, the failure would have certainly occurred right then and there and would have been an item I would have required them to repair before finalizing the purchase. Impact to me: more than $1,000.

What? For a radio with a monitor? Well, like so many things in the RV repair business, few things are simple. I'll be as brief as possible. Firstly, that specific brand of radio was no longer available, not even on eBay. Secondly, the radio was a 1.5 din radio chassis— there were slim pickings available in that size chassis and what I did find had worse-than-poor reviews and ratings. OK, I gave in and got a 2.0 din radio. How hard could that be? Trim the dash panel a little and I'll make it fit. Nope. Not the way the dash panel is made, no such luck. To solve this all and make the coach not look like a 5th grade science fair project, I'd need to order a new dash bezel with a 2.0 din radio opening. I had to remove each of the gauges and then replace them into the new dash bezel. I decided not to use a radio with a built-in display and instead opted for a dedicated video monitor that I could mount atop the dash, off to the side. That seemed easier to me and certainly less impactful should either the radio fail in the future or the monitor drop dead. All I could keep thinking was "Why didn't I just cycle it sitting there in the parking lot of the dealership?"

I had to replace a cracked roller on the kitchen slide. The roller worked "mostly" as designed when the slide was being retracted back into the RV, but made a terrible ruckus when the slide was extended out. When I arrived to check out the coach, the dealer had the slides already extended. I can remember the technician standing at the controls telling me that "since you've already got the slide out, to take it back in, just press this button," and he had me do it, just for my confidence. It never crossed my mind that I should operate the slide for at least a complete cycle. Had I cycled the slide completely, I would have immediately detected the roller failure. (*Note to reader: keep this example in mind; it will be revisited in the PDIs done well section with far different results!*)

In several more examples, in addition to the few mentioned above, had I been more informed, prepared and aggressive, I would have saved thousands of dollars and countless hours of labor, frustration, and aggravation.

These examples are specific to our first coach and my inadequate attempt at a PDI. I think these personal examples are impactful, each in their own way. Important as testimony to what can be wrong with that beautiful, shiny RV sitting right in front of you. These examples should reiterate the importance of taking your time and spark ideas of which areas to investigate. While not personal examples, I'm including two more from folks I've met during my travels because they highlight the complexities of these rolling homes and offer yet more examples of why getting serious about your PDI is so important.

A fellow RVer, Dave, purchased one of the newer, retro-looking Class A units and was excited to check it out and get on the road. The unit had a previous owner, but you couldn't tell. Dave conducted a fairly thorough PDI and caught numerous items that needed attention, all of which, however, were sufficiently minor that, by the end of the afternoon, the fixes had been completed and he was on his way from the dealership in San Diego to his home in Tucson. Getting a late start from San Diego, Dave thought that a noise he heard at highway speed seemed unusual. A fluttering sound that sometimes seemed quit noticeable, but alone, he was unable to pinpoint its origin. Dave was aware that during his trip, several passers-by made strange hand gestures to him as they passed but he assumed they were signaling their approval of his retro-looking purchase or that perhaps he was driving too slowly. David stopped for the night and then after a restful sleep, got after it again, early the next morning. Once on the highway, the fluttering returned, sometimes less so, sometimes more. Mid-morning, David spied a rest stop and decided to stop and stretch his legs. Behind Dave, a fellow RVer decided to stop and make sure Dave knew about his growing roof problem. As Dave stepped out, the Good Samaritan asked him if he knew that his rubber roof was billowing in the highway winds like a parachute. Seems the fluttering sound inside was created by a gash in the rubber roofing material (commonly used in motorhomes and trailers) and, as the RV's speed increased, more and more air got under the material, lifting and stretching it like a sail. Not a good problem to have and not a simple issue to fix. A call to a RV Roadside Repair truck revealed a long gash in the rubber roofing material just behind the roof air conditioner. Subsequent inquiry revealed that the dealer had replaced the front roof air conditioner under warranty and evidently, one of the service technicians had either cut the roofing material or failed to reseal the roof around the air conditioning mount.

A good PDI includes getting on the roof, assessing the roof materials condition and checking for potential water infiltration sources. In this case, Dave was not physically capable to do those checks himself. This is an area we'll discuss later but sometimes getting a PDI done correctly involves hiring a professional to do it.

Vince, a retired trucker and life-long RVer, told me about his new diesel pusher and the biblical mess he had and the remnant odor that reminds him about it to this day. Vince remembered being very pleased at the amount of time the dealer spent showing him and his wife their new home away from home. The one thing Vince said he didn't do, in fact never thought about doing, was to fill the fresh water, gray water, and black water tanks to some level and drain them. After everything was satisfactorily reviewed and inspected, Vince signed on the bottom line, took possession of RV, took the keys, and he and his wife pointed the rig down the highway and off they pressed. They camped for two nights in small parks before getting into a large RV Resort for their third night. For the first time since leaving the dealership, Vince hooked everything up completely. After two days, the black tank was nearing the 75% mark, so Vince decided to open the waste valve and dump the tank. He vividly remembered the hose jerking with pressure and the tank began to empty. Very quickly at first, then strangely slower and slower. It was not until the next morning that Vince's' wife convinced him something was wrong with their new home, based on the worsening stench throughout their coach. When Vince dressed and exited the coach, the problem was immediately evident. Waste water and debris were still draining from the basement side doors and there was a substantial mess on the ground. Without going into gory detail, his system failure, while uncommon, was catastrophic to Vince and quickly became a serious incident at the RV Resort.

Whether as a result of poor workmanship or improper installation, the black tank drain pipe and waste valve assembly were improperly configured and connected. The problem manifested itself with a combination of the weight in the tank and the pressure applied when Vince opened the waste valve. Those forces acting together created enough tension that the pipe separated, not completely, but enough to slowly start flooding one of the basement storage areas, destroying most everything inside.

I included this last example, not for impact, but to highlight how problems can compound quickly. While the damage to Vince's RV was terrible enough, Vince still had to pay for a "special" crew to respond to the RV Resort's pleas to clean the grounds. The dealership refused the unit back referring it to the manufacturer, claiming they didn't have the means or capability to repair it.

Just like my personal examples, these two problems likely would have been caught during the inspection phase of the PDI. Don't accept a dealership telling you they have no means to drain water, or that you're not allowed on the roof for "insurance" reasons. Clearly you have the right, and need to inspect your RV thoroughly before taking delivery and finalizing the purchase. If a dealer cannot permit an adequate inspection, you definitely should not purchase from them.

What do you need to conduct a thorough PDI?

I gained a tremendous amount of knowledge after our first purchase, often during the process of seeking assistance to fix problems that I encountered. While learning hard lessons of my own, I also began speaking with folks regularly at RV Parks that we visited, and began absorbing the wisdom of those who had learned many of their own hard lessons before me. What could or should I have done differently? From this, I learned that I could have been more prepared about the specific unit I was buying, and I should have demanded the time necessary to evaluate the RV completely.

It is interesting to me that if a person were buying a new home, he or she would not take the realtor's or builder's word that the home was in perfect condition. Likely, a person would pay for a home inspection to be conducted before making an offer or purchase or, at a minimum, go through the home with a very critical eye. Yet, few (very few) persons do the same when buying a RV. It really makes no sense as, in all honesty, your RV will likely have many more issues than your brick-and-mortar home ever will.

Why is that? Fundamentally, it's the constant vibration, jarring, bouncing, and extreme temperature cycles that your RV is likely to experience that increase the likelihood for higher maintenance and repair that issues with an RV's components. RVs cannot be constructed like traditional house; RVs have weight limits to which they must conform. Just try to imagine having a professional house-moving company move your house down the block. Do you think you might need to repair at least a couple of things after the move? I'd think so. RVs are meant to be hauled up and down roads, that's true. Just don't expect that they will be maintenance free. That's just not realistic.

If you decide that you're fully capable of tackling the PDI for your rig, consider taking some or all of the following tools and equipment with you. These items will help you check and thoroughly inspect your rig. If you weren't interested in doing that, you'd likely not be reading this chapter. So, pick and choose what makes sense to you but remember, RVs are complex machines and should be inspected as such. The more items you thoroughly inspect now during the PDI, the less likely you are to be surprised by something later.

What tools and equipment you ultimately end up taking to perform your PDI depends somewhat on your technical capabilities and background. It serves little purpose to take a multimeter with you if you don't know how to use one. If you don't own basic tools, conducting a PDI might not be for you. If you lack basic mechanical skills, then maybe performing a PDI is not for you. Again, the important thing is having a PDI conducted, not who performs it.

Lastly, of course, some folks will review this list and consider it as absolute overkill.

So, what should you take? The following are mere suggestions for items to take that, if you have access to and can haul them to the dealership, will make your inspection more productive. Again, like virtually everything I suggest in this book, the decision on how you ultimately perform your PDI is up to you. These suggestions are just that.

- Blu-ray or DVD movie to test your audio-visual equipment
- Camera to take pictures of problems found during your PDI. Pictures will go a long way in helping the dealership understand an issue, as well as to provide additional documentation for potential claims you may have down the road.
- Creeper or mat
- Crescent-style wrenches
- Electrical outlet tester
- Flashlight
- Freezer thermometer
- Hammer
- Ladder of sufficient height to enable you to reach the roof of the RV safely. Most RVs have built-in ladders, but they are not an option to help you look at awning attachment points or other areas near the RV's roofline. Also, some RV ladders have significant weight restrictions and limitations.
- Laser thermometer to check air temps at air conditioner vents

- Level
- Measuring tape
- Multi-head screwdriver (at a minimum, small, medium, and large Philip's head, flat blade, and the most widely used screw in RVs, the #2S square head
- Multimeter
- Pliers
- Rags or towels
- Rubber mallet to check floor substructures for integrity and stability. A tap here and there can tell you a lot about the condition of your RV flooring.
- Video source. Virtually all RVs have a coax input (for example, cable television). If the dealership does not have the capability to provide a cable source, then you should consider taking a portable video device that will produce a signal on a coax output. Attaching this device will allow you to check your coax cable runs in the RV. I've seen folks use old portable VCRs, DVD players, and even a television station test screen generator to test the functionality of a coax input. Again, the intent is to get a signal broadcast on the coax throughout the RV.
- Portable television. I've caught lots of gruff for suggesting this in the past, but I know of no other way to test coax outlets that don't already have a television attached.
- Coax continuity tester. If you can get access to one, this saves the need to take a television and video source.
- Tire pressure gauge
- Work gloves and Latex-style gloves

Even though I believe that this list is fairly complete, if you think of something else that you believe may be useful, by all means take it with you.

Now that you have an idea of the tools that will help you inspect your new rig, what do you look for?

PDI Checklists

To aid you in performing your PDI, I've assembled a series of checklists, broken down into several sections and provided in Appendix One. Review the checklists and become familiar with them prior to conducting your PDI. These checklists are purposely arranged so that you can focus on specific sections of the RV at one time and not become distracted or frustrated. You may find that you will not need every checklist as portions of some checklists may not apply to your RV class or model. Spend some time to assemble the checklists that you will need. If it is helpful, copy or pull the appropriate checklist(s) from the book or, for as long as this book is available for demand printing, you may download PDF versions of the checklists at _www.areyourvready.com_ and print them out for your personal use.

NOTE: If there are areas of the checklists that you do not understand or with which you do not feel comfortable completing, do some research into that topic or find someone that is knowledgeable to assist you. In nearly every market in the country, you can find RV technicians whom, for a small fee, will help you complete or, if you wish, will conduct the entire PDI and document the inspection with a warranty. In the event the technician's inspection failed to catch a problem or equipment failure, the warranty will pay for (or pay some portion of) the repair of that item or issue. Again, I'm not saying you need to hire a technician's services for your PDI; I'm saying that you need to do a complete and thorough PDI before taking delivery of your RV. If you cannot or do not feel comfortable performing it on your own, then definitely consider hiring a professional technician to assist or perform the PDI for you.

The checklist format is straight forward. The header section of each checklist describes the checklist focus area. Then, inspection items are identified with a description, if applicable. To the left of the item name is an empty box. Consider leaving that box blank for areas not completed. Enter a check mark for areas that are satisfactory, or enter a dash for areas that may not specifically apply. For concerns, consider placing an X to get your attention when compiling your notes at the end of the inspection. To the right of each identified area is a blank comments area. Use that space to enter notes so that when it comes time to report your findings to the dealership, you have good, detailed descriptions.

Checklist format example

	Inspection Item	Description	Comments
√	Review book intro	Provides prospective buyers some insight into RV purchase important to help make informed decisions	No way; this won't fly
	Read book twice	Make sure you don't miss any author dry humor	
X	Buy additional copies	Books make great Christmas gifts	

These checklists are also great for conducting your annual RV inspection before hitting the open road. Use the materials to your advantage; configure them and modify them to suit your needs.

PDI success story

By the time we reached our second RV purchase go-round, I was much more prepared for the new RV delivery dance. The dealer again tried to push his schedule on me, telling me, in fact, that the dealership could only allot two hours for a new RV orientation. When I told the dealer that I planned on being there early and might need the day to complete an appropriate review, I was told that I would not be permitted to do so.

You must be firm on this issue; wavering can literally result in thousands of dollars out of your pocket and total frustration that will ruin your RV experience before it even begins. So, after being very blunt and informing the dealer that I would not sign anything until I performed a thorough PDI, the dealer relented, but continued to make the process difficult.

I arrived at the dealership to perform the PDI, and was prepared to take as long as necessary to ensure that our new unit was indeed ready for the road. Upon my arrival, to my chagrin, the trailer was sitting in the parking lot of the dealership, slides opened, but no shore power, water, or coax signal of any kind was available. A dealership representative told me that she would be spending a couple of hours with me to make sure I understood everything there was to know about the unit. I then asked her if she thought her spending a couple of hours with me would be sufficient? She indicated that only a couple of dealership representatives were available and that a couple of hours was all the dealership could allot to me. I told her of my intent to perform a thorough PDI, and that I would gladly spend a couple of hours with her, but that I likely would be there several more hours, checking each and every system, component, switch, plug, connection, switch, lever, latch, and device. Clearly, not enough purchasers do this, as she was obviously quite surprised.

We began the orientation and the two-hour tour seemed more like Gilligan's six hour cruise that ended in disaster. While friendly and cordial, the dealership representative did not know more than the absolute basics and then, she was often mistaken during her presentation. Several times during our two-hour engagement, I corrected her on simple erroneous statements and errors. She made many claims about the unit that were simply overzealous or outright misrepresentations. At the end of the orientation, I asked for the unit to be connected to water and power. Originally, the dealership representative indicated that the dealership had no means of hooking the trailer up to utilities. After quizzing her about how the dealership could possibly make repairs without such capabilities, the trailer was towed to the rear maintenance area and hooked to water and shore power.

As I moved through the unit with electrical tester in hand, I could sense some of the staff were watching me as if I was a lost tourist. No matter. Voila! I found an outlet wired incorrectly. While testing the shower and faucets, I discovered a poorly connected J trap that immediately leaked as water ran through it. The refrigerator power would not work from the inverter (a plug seemed to have shaken loose). One of the wall light switches in the convenience panel did not seem to operate anything. A dealership technician stated that often additional switches were added at the factory but not connected. OMG! I protested and asked the panel be removed. Once we looked behind, once again, a slide connector either shook loose or was never connected. With a gentle push, eureka! The entry step light magically turned on.

During my PDI, I tested the televisions using the over-the-air antenna, amplifier, and cable inputs as these are often a source of problems, but was pleased to discover no issues. In fact, after almost five hours of intense inspection, I was about completed having only found what I consider minor annoyances, all of which were promptly corrected.

The last inspection criteria I had on my list to complete was to exercise the trailer slides. I ran each of the slides in and out three times. Our fifth wheel has a long kitchen slide, which includes a side-by-side residential refrigerator, and it's heavy, I'm sure. It was also the last slide to operate for the PDI. I was literally just minutes from being completed and heading into the finance office, but it was not to be. On the second iteration, extending the kitchen slide, there was an enormous boom, an immediate change in the sound from the hydraulic pump, and the slide was stuck. A quick visual inspection from outside revealed what the manufacturer referred to as a catastrophic failure in the hydraulic ram attachment point to the slide. In other words, the mechanism that operated the kitchen slide, which would allow the room to extend and retract, had completely failed. It had disintegrated into shrapnel and metal filings.

I don't know, and maybe don't want to know, how the dealership finally got the slide pushed closed. What I do know is that, fortunately for me, it had failed on the dealership's lot and before I had signed to accept delivery and agree to pay for the unit.

Exercising each of the trailer slides was a lesson I learned the hard way during the PDI of our first RV. This mechanical failure was significant and resulted in the unit having to be returned to the slide manufacturer for repair. We did not see the trailer for a full month. One can only wonder how long it would have been in repair had I taken possession of the unit. I shudder to think of the slide failing on our first voyage, as it certainly would have. What a nightmare scenario that would have been!

PDI Pledge

This long chapter has covered lots of information. I hope, without any doubt, that I have conveyed the absolute need for you to complete a thorough PDI of your RV unit. I hope I have made it crystal clear that, if you don't feel comfortable or don't have the time to complete a PDI, you have one performed by a fellow RVer who is knowledgeable and capable of performing it, or by a certified RV technician. The time, energy, and potential expense associated with a proper PDI absolutely pales when compared to the potential time, energy, and expenses of not performing a thorough inspection.

Use the checklists in Appendix One, make them work for you, and keep them handy as reference materials.

PDI Notes:

_____

_____

_____

Chapter Five

The Bottom Line

As stated earlier in this book, if you are contemplating RVing as a means of saving money, I believe that vision is a bit far-fetched. That said, some people are impeccable money managers and can stretch a dime further than mere mortals. Certainly, there are examples where a family can travel and pay for accommodations for a lesser cost than if that same family were to get airline tickets, rental cars, and hotel rooms. Those specific examples make it easy to justify having a RV. The catch is how often those extended trips occur.

I believe we fit firmly into the segment of RVers for whom the financial practicality is not a major concern. We very much enjoy the freedom and spontaneity that travel by RV allows and, even more so, the comforts of home, always.

This chapter is a reminder that the bottom line of RVing may cost a little more than you expected. After the honeymoon has ended, some of the expenses keep coming. As long as you're aware and prepared, I contend that RVing is one of the best life changes my wife and I have ever made.

MSRP and Fair Market Value (FMV)

We all know that one guy who, regardless of what deal he's working, manages the "best deal" ever! That one guy with stories about how he robbed the dealership, paid less than the dealership owed, was banned from ever coming back because he abused the salesman so badly. Again, we all know that one guy but, the reality is, he only managed the best deal the dealership was willing to accept on that particular day.

RV industry sales offerings are no different. Often, there are huge markups in new and used RVs and, if you have not done your homework to understand what those percentages could be, you're taking a risk and possibly wasting some of your hard-earned money. Timing is everything, too! Buying a RV at the end of the model year as new units are filtering in increases your odds of having the opportunity to work a fantastic deal. In preparing for our RV purchases, I scoured sites, reached out to recent buyers, read forum and blog articles, and posted questions to dealers at nauseam. When trying to determine a fair market value for the RV we wanted to buy, I spent weeks and weeks reading, researching, and internet trolling.

The Fair Market Value (FMV) for a RV is a simple formula, which includes nothing more than the amount of money a dealership has invested in a RV combined with the minimal margin they will accept to sell it. Reviewing sales information for like units sold in your area helps provide another basis for fair market value. Another helpful means of determining FMV on a new (or newer) RV is to search sales data for a similar used model and add depreciation back to the sales price. This method should get you pretty close to FMV.

Let's assume you're looking at a new fifth-wheel trailer model. You can't get any comparable new sales figures, but you can find examples of a same-model, three-year-old used unit that is being sold. Using the depreciation schedule below, we see that depreciation on three-year-old trailers is roughly 26%. If the used trailer sold for $50,000, adding the depreciation value back should give a reasonable FMV. (Example: $50,000 used fifth-wheel trailer model divided by 0.74 (the inverse of the 26% depreciation value) = $67,567. Through our research and simple stubbornness, I decided a good starting negotiating point was 30% off the advertised asking, or MSRP, price.

I'll use the sales data from our two purchases as examples. Our Class A diesel pusher was three years old when we bought it through a deal with a national chain. Our rig was posted on-line, at a sale price of $124,900. Even at that price, the dealership played hardball and made every attempt to make us believe this was a one-time, never-to-be-repeated-in-the-history-of-humanity, amazing deal. I made an offer to the dealership and, if memory serves me correctly, I was hung up on, or at least summarily dismissed.

While the art of the deal took a couple of weeks, in the end, I paid exactly what I originally offered: $88,000, or about 29% off their original price (and rest assured, the dealership didn't lose a dime). Like everyone else, I paid my share of the light bill, property taxes, salaries, etc.

My second example is our current fifth wheel. Our new rig had a MSRP sticker of $128,249, and was a custom order. Just like the Class A, we went around and around with the dealership for a few weeks and had to listen to all the standard rebuttals: "that's impossible," "we'll lose our dealership," and so on and so on. In the end, we paid $87,210, or 32% off MSRP, and could have done even better I'm thinking. By this time, however, I had honestly caught the fever.

The fever is what the dealerships are counting on. You get hooked and drawn in. The lights, the sounds, the smells—it's all overpowering and they know it. Sales staff are very clever and very good at reading people. They can smell a sell and (don't kid yourself), they have been up against the absolute best negotiators in the business. Not saying that sales people are bad, but keep in mind they pay their mortgage by making sales. In the end, the only way for you to "win" is to get what you want, at a price you're comfortable paying.

Before going to the dealership for the first time, you should already know what you want the deal to be. Make it and stick to it. You can "what-if" your buying interaction forever. If you have a fair deal in mind and you get that price, be happy with it and go start enjoying your RV.

Various means and tools are available to help you determine a fair market price for a RV that you're interested in purchasing. You can also internet window shop, which I find as a very direct means of identifying average sales prices. The internet can also help you distinguish regional influences on price. Several RV sales websites deal coast to coast and using these sites can help you identify the "direct-to-you" price versus the price at which a dealership may be listing a unit. These gaps can be several thousands of dollars.

Lastly, if you're one of those people who'd rather have major dental work done than deal with a RV salesman, consider a RV Broker. You can hire these folks to take all the drama out of the purchase and for a few bucks, they broker your best deal.

Depreciation

Depreciation is something no one wants to discuss, but it is a reality with most things mechanical, and very much a reality in the RV industry. In fact, RVs have some of the highest depreciation values of any major investment you're likely to make. How much depreciation you realize as a buyer depends on several factors, including whether you purchased your RV new or used, and is directly linkable to how prepared you were at the time of purchase.

In an effort to report some depreciation values based on real-world examples, I sent out requests for purchasing information from people who had recently purchased RVs, or sold them, either as trades or outright direct sales. I collected this information across several forums I frequent and a couple internet blogs that exist to help people make purchasing decisions. While the data are not scientific by any stretch, the data are telling and do line up closely with data from other sources that have undertaken more thorough analysis.

I collected data for several months documenting well over 100 sales and then culled the information down into two sections: motorhomes and trailers. I made no differentiation between gas coaches and diesel pushers, and made no distinction between travel trailers and fifth wheels. I used the data provided back to me and scoured internet and published resources for "like sales data" for comparison. I also used information from the NADA Price Guide and months of RV sales information from a national RV sales broker site.

My simple data collection activity provides at least some ground-truth when addressing depreciation and highlights two points. Firstly, unless you specifically want or absolutely need a new RV, buying one a few years old results in a savings of thousands of dollars from depreciation. Secondly, with few exceptions, people pay too much when purchasing a RV.

The depreciation calculations made below comprise the data I collected and include no less than 10 sales in each year category. The following table is a snapshot of select years and the amount of depreciation realized across the two RV platforms.

Table 1 Depreciation data using Internet RV sales information.

Age (Years)	Motorhomes	Trailers
1	20%	22%
3	27%	26%
5	36%	38%
8	45%	41%
10	54%	48%

Selling

Selling your RV can be a very trying proposition. While trading your RV into a dealership precludes the hassles of selling the RV yourself, a trade-off can represent thousands of dollars less in your pocket. It's the same as selling your personal car. You'll do better in the end financially by selling it yourself as opposed to trading it in toward another purchase, but that may not be practical for everyone. And selling a RV is certainly more involved than selling a car. You're not going to be inclined to just throw the keys to your $100,000 Class A diesel pusher to some stranger and tell them to take it for a test drive.

If you decide you want to sell your RV, a couple of options beat putting your RV out in front of your house with a "For Sale" sign taped in the window.

- Look into consigning your unit; a few nationwide dealers will consign your RV for a modest price. You get the exposure of a national chain and none of the hassles of people showing up at your house.
- Use specific RV Internet sales sites. There are a few very popular sites. We posted our Class A diesel pusher on *RV Trader.com*, and have nothing but good things to say, resulting in an excellent experience. We sold the unit within three days of posting it and for $20,000 more than we were offered in a dealership trade. You will still have to manage the sale in the end, but at least the site focuses people looking for a specific RV.

Insurance

Insurance seems like a pretty straightforward topic, and it really is. The key here is to research and shop around. Many traditional insurance companies do not cover RVs; others insurance companies don't directly insure them, but contract out coverage while keeping it under the original insurance company's name.

To get the best deal for your RV, shop insurance providers that deal specifically with RVs. An internet search will provide several examples. One factor to keep in mind as you shop RV insurance, it is sometimes not an apples-to-apples comparison. What this means is that sometimes, coverage from a company that deals exclusively in recreational vehicles may have a slightly higher premium. That fact alone might be slightly misleading as the RV-specific insurer may provide exceptionally better coverage than a standard auto policy company. As best you can, detail the coverage from all the companies you contact for quotes, including coverage types, deductibles, and exclusions. In the end, selecting a company that focuses on recreational vehicles may provide more thorough coverage, resulting in a better policy.

Warranty

A lot of frustration exists in the RV community concerning warranty issues. Devote some extra time when you're finalizing your RV deal to ensure that you thoroughly understand what your warranty actually covers and, possibly more importantly, what it may not cover. If after having the warranty rules and process explained it still does not make sense, don't ink the deal. Don't sign until you fully and completely understand the terms and limits. Why? One quick example.

 **Tired of small campgrounds? The Ocean Lakes Family Campground in Myrtle Beach South Carolina has 3,447 residential and transient pull through campsites. (Source: iRV2.com)**

I met a Class C owner who was working through some warranty issues and was denied a claim because his unit was over the original 12,000-mile mechanical warranty. The frustration was that when he took delivery of the Class C, the unit already had over 1,700 miles on the clock from delivery. His issues and problems started at 13,000 miles. His warranty should have started at the delivery mileage and been in effect to 13,700, not the original 12,000 manufacturer warranty. Bottom-line: make sure you get the facts on your warranty before finalizing the RV purchase.

Here's a scenario for consideration. You're working with a dealership and you mention that you can get a better price somewhere else. The dealership tells you "that's fine, but we will not service your RV if you don't buy it from our dealership." At this point, you should do two things: 1) get the individual's name you're working with at the dealership; and 2) then get the name of the dealership manager. Write a few letters. At a minimum, you should write the parent company of the RV you're contemplating purchasing and inform them how their dealer network is treating people.

While a dealership may have the legal right to refuse service, it is a terrible message to send and should start a series of warning bells and sirens going off in your head! If this happens to you, in my opinion, you should walk away and do whatever you can to not go back. The RV industry has enough credibility issues without nonsense like this being added. Show your displeasure with your wallet; write about your experience and communicate your experience to others.

Extended maintenance contracts and warranties

Extended maintenance contracts and warranties are another topic that gets a tremendous amount of attention from RV owners and users groups. Talk to folks that own RVs and you'll get the full range of sentiment on these extended warranties. Interesting arguments can be made support both sides of the debate. In the end, you must be comfortable with the decision you've made, as it can represent a significant expenditure.

When you boil this discussion topic down to its roots, there are really two options, to buy an extended warranty or not. How do you decide? What is an extended warranty and what does it really cover? How much is the warranty? All great questions and answers you should have and understand before you decide on what answer is right for you.

In fairly simple terms, an extended warranty is a protection policy you purchase to extend the original warranty of your RV if purchased new, or provide a warranty if your RV is used and the original manufacturer's warranty has expired.

Once you start looking into extended warranties, you will quickly discover there is nothing simple about them. Contracts for these warranties can be 20 pages of legal gobbly-gook, and the sections of exclusions and exceptions can be downright impossible to navigate and understand. Many types of warranties are available in the RV marketplace, and dealerships often push one that they have a vested interest in (meaning that if the dealership sells it to you, they get a cut of the deal).

A warranty may also cover (or not cover) a wide range of RV parts and components. Coverages may specifically apply to motorhomes and trailers. There are basic warranties and platinum warranties. You bear the burden of fully reading and understanding what your coverage includes. You CANNOT RELY on a member of a RV sales staff to explain a warranty with any level of accuracy as he or she is not an expert on these coverage plans and, again, may often have some incentive to sell them.

If you're interested, you need to ask for a sample warranty contract to take it, read, and mark up areas that you find confusing so that you can get clarification. It can be a little daunting. One of the large national RV chains has a company warranty that is widely advertised on television and in magazines, and is consider reputable. Their high-end policy claims "complete" coverage, yet has a full page of exclusions when you get to the fine print. Again, read, read, and re-read the policy and every word of the fine print. Many items in these policies are excluded from coverage or, if they are not excluded, are only covered after a deductible is paid.

Also, look very closely in the warranty contract for provisions that require you to demonstrate proof of a viable and continued RV maintenance program. Some policies require you to prove that you've kept up with all the manufacturer-required maintenance before they will pay a claim. Be informed!

Price is always an important consideration when looking at purchasing an extended warranty. Warranties can range from a few hundred dollars to several thousands of dollars. I've seen diesel pusher warranties that cost over $10,000. Warranties for trailers are less expensive than those for motorhomes (clearly there is no engine or drivetrain coverage included); however, that does not mean that trailer warranties are inexpensive.

When we closed the deal on our 2016 fifth wheel, the dealership originally wanted almost $6,000 to cover the trailer for a full five years ("$1,200 a year for complete peace-of-mind, no worries, no hassles"!). Sound reasonable? Hmmm. The unit came with a full two-year warranty from the factory, so the reality was to extend the manufacturer's warranty for three more years was going to cost us an additional $6,000. Does $2000 a year for complete peace-of-mind still sound like a good deal? It may, to you, and that's what you have to work through. Just like the purchase price, if you're happy with it, then it's a good deal.

The decision to purchase, or pass on, an extended warranty requires thought, analysis, and research. RV dealerships are going to push the warranty during your closing back in the finance office. I wish that they would not do that; there's too much already going on and too many numbers bouncing around in your head. But their argument is that it's best to roll the price of the warranty into the original deal so you'll almost not notice it. Many people do that without hesitation or concern. I'd recommend that you ask the finance people for "drafts" of all the paperwork a few days before closing so you have a chance to review and question the numbers. If they balk at that, then you should demand to know why. A RV purchase is a significant investment and commitment. The RV dealer should be bending over backwards to support you.

Here are a couple of my final thoughts on extended warranties. Like any other insurance policy, you're paying a provider to fix your RV in the event that something fails. The insurance policy provider is banking on you not needing the repairs so that at the end of the policy, they come out ahead. It is a simple and time-tested business model. If you're interested in an extended warranty, please do all the research you can before committing. Get on-line and search the company you're evaluating. I guarantee you'll find forum and blog posts from previous and current customers detailing their experiences.

Lots of rules accompany these policies. Getting pre-approval for service before having your RV worked on is virtually always required. For some repairs, the insurance provider requires that an underwriter review the repair work or agree with the identified repairs, potentially adding days to the repair process. Again, it's critical for you to understand what the rules of your policy state.

In closing, for some people, the need to roll the price of the warranty into the RV purchase is the only way they can afford, or justify, the added expense. Otherwise, consider taking that same amount of money and putting it away in a dedicated savings account and only touch it for the repairs for which the extended warranty would have been used. Statistically, you're likely to come out way ahead.

 The average RV owner uses their RV 28 to 35 days per year. (Source: RV USA)

Chapter Six

We Bought It; Now What?

You use it, that's what! Using your RV and enjoying your RV sometimes don't necessarily coincide. Getting use and enjoyment to complement each other should be an immediate goal of yours once you purchase a RV. To ensure success in this regard, you need to accept, learn, listen, explore, research, prepare, relax, and enjoy.

Accept

Accept that the RV you purchased—regardless of type, make, or model—is unique. What do I mean by this statement, and why is it important to accept?

Two models of a RV—of the same brand and with the same floor plan—can come off the assembly line, one right after the other. If you could magically open them up, remove the walls, and explore each, you'd find differences. In some cases (depending on the manufacturer), you may encounter fairly significant differences between the two RVs. By difference, I'm not implying that doors would be in different locations or windows would be reversed; I'm referring to what's inside the walls and where the guts of the RV are positioned during assembly.

In general terms, everything should be relatively similar, but you should be aware that tolerances on the assembly line can be pretty broad. For example, a red wire in your unit might be a brown wire with a red stripe in the sister unit. A bundle of ground wires may terminate directly behind a fuse panel in your unit, and be routed through the top and be neatly wrapped in the sister unit. Again, the take-away is to accept differences in "like" units. This is important as you grow into RVing and begin to realize these slight variances. You may also find yourself discussing tips and modifications with fellow owners, only to discover that their modification won't work in your unit.

Two quick personal examples. In our Class A diesel pusher, I wanted to add two satellite radio speakers—one each above the driver and passenger chairs. Through the course of discussing my proposed modification with several fellow owners, I was informed that the speaker wires for the stereo worked their way up the passenger side windshield pillar, where they were attached to the coach's surround-sound system. I carefully removed parts, pieces, clips, fasteners, screws, bolts, and looms, only to come up empty-handed. With many of these parts removed, I was more able to actually trace the wires out of the back of the dash-mounted stereo, discovering that the wires in my coach were routed up the driver's side, not the passenger's side.

In our current fifth wheel, I was frustrated that the Dyson vacuum seemed to shake loose from its wall mount after a few trips. My mount was simply screwed into a section of thin melamine board (common in most all RVs). When I questioned fellow owners on the manufacturers' forum how they were dealing with the annoyance, without exception, they responded that their mounts were attached with molly-bolts.

Enough on the topic; suffice to say that, like people, all RVs are a little different.

Learn

Learning everything you can about your RV will save you much frustration over time. Read the user manuals that came with your RV. If you purchased a used unit and didn't get user manuals, with few exceptions, they can be located on-line, either on the manufacturer's website or on brand forums and blogs. Read the manuals for the various appliances and systems in your RV. Don't be one that guesses how something works; understand how it works. That way, if a system is not functioning properly, you'll know it instead of assuming its working OK because that's how it always shook and coughed. RV owners' forums and blogs are a great place for information, but always remember the all-important "*Trust but Verify.*"

Listen

Listen carefully when RVers offer advice. In our years of RVing, we've found fellow RVers with whom we converse at RV Parks to be a very honest, sincere, and thoughtful group. While those traits are wonderful, sincerity does not make you an expert on RV suspensions. Listening with a critical ear is important, and this holds true not only with RVs, but with all subjects. Elsewhere in this text, I refer to those who will proffer advice that is absolutely contrary to manufacturer guidance. I often hear RVers provide guidance and advice based purely on their personal beliefs or luck to that point and this advice is often contrary to fact. Be critical and ask questions when discussing topics like RV weight, tires, and supplemental braking systems. These three areas specifically generate a lot of misinformation, provided as gospel. Statements like, "you can run over your gross vehicle weight rating because the manufacturers always engineer in some tolerance." (Yes, engineers may indeed over-engineer vehicles, and NO you should never run overweight!). Statements like, "I've been pulling a TOAD for years without a supplemental brake and nothing bad as ever happened to me" may be true, but are reckless.

Each state has laws concerning towing vehicles and the weights that require supplemental breaking systems (discussed in detail in Appendix Four) to be installed. Know the facts, not the legend. Listen for those key words that should cause you concern when someone is providing you with advice.

Explore

Your RV is yours now, so go ahead and explore the nooks and crannies of it. Explore each of the systems and how they operate. As you do, take the time to understand what you're looking at or what you've uncovered. As you're exploring, if something does not look right, ask! It might not be. Just because a RV is new does not mean there might not be something amiss. In used RVs, be aware that the previous owner may have added some components that are not documented in the literature you have for your unit. Explore those items and find out exactly what they are, what they do and how they operate.

Research

Research topics and systems that you're interested in adding or making changes to. One of the most common issues I see and try to help folks with in the RV forums I frequent are problems associated with satellite television systems and RV heaters. Previously, I mentioned learning the systems in your RV. In the case of RV heaters, you should understand how the system operates and learn how to use the system effectively. Imagine camping one cold morning and you've suddenly got no heat in your rig. You need to understand the system and its operation sufficiently to be able to research what has gone wrong. You can't Google "air flow sail switch" if you don't even know that the furnace has one! Most of all problems that can go wrong while you're trying to enjoy a quick trip in your RV can be researched quickly and addressed by you. Obviously some problems can't be resolved quickly and will require professional attention, but research will direct you.

Satellite television receiver cabling, hookup problems, or inability to get satellite signal are among the most common problems I see discussed. A little research reveals that coaches with rooftop satellite dishes and camp parking spots surrounded by mature tall trees are mortal enemies. A little research makes clear that RV coax cabling that includes splitters (which most all do) is a satellite receiver installation's worst nightmare. Researching the specific changes you wish to make in your RV will save you lots of time and frustration as compared to just diving in and trying to add something.

Prepare

Prepare for the unexpected and have some contingency plans in place. We discussed the possibility of your RV furnace acting up so you wouldn't be able to take the chill off the coach in the morning. With a little forethought and preparation, you can be ready for some of these surprises as they arise. Carrying an oil-filled radiator heater in your storage bay would not take much room or consume much precious weight, but could save a camping trip if your furnace crapped out. A small gas grill could backup a failed stovetop.

Certainly you can't plan for every potential failure, but being prepared to deal with a wide range of possibilities requires only a few extra parts and pieces. Few things are worse than losing a weekend with the family because of a system hiccup.

Relax

Now that you're an RV owner, you'll be better off if you're able to relax and accept those little challenges and annoyances as they occur. Being able to relax is really dependent on how seriously you took the preceding points. The more prepared and knowledgeable you are of your RV systems and operations, the more likely you can react to issues and deal with them. That determination and preparation, in the long run, is key and will serve you well.

Enjoy

Enjoy your RV with your family. You've paid good money for your RV; now, start claiming a return on your investment. The memories you'll create in your RV will be lasting ones that will arise in discussions for many years to come. Enjoy this great country, your state, and our National Parks, and relish meeting those folks along the way that without choosing to RV, you would have never met.

Make it comfortable

This is really one of those areas that you should have considered and agonized over before deciding to purchase your RV. While shopping, if you thought, "this is a great RV, but I'll have to change everything about it," then in the end, it's not a great RV at all!

That said, I'm continually amazed at how many RVers have just resigned themselves to accept their RV as it is. Don't do that! Your RV is a virtually endless canvas to create your perfect RV. Think of modifications that you'd like to make, and research the possibilities. Don't accept things that don't work for you. If the mattress is not comfortable, there are a tremendous number of other options out there. If you don't like the recliner, change it. Again, within reason, you can change the RV you purchased from being one in a thousand, to being yours.

Have an RV set

This specific topic has led to some colorful interactions with folks and, at a minimum, I usually get called a Rockefeller before it's all over! However, I remain steadfast, at least in the concept. Having a set of virtually everything dedicated just for use in your RV will reduce the stress of preparing for a trip, and will certainly put an end to the "oops, I forgot the "*list any item here*.""

Your RV likely came with most of the big-ticket items, so the "set" I'm referring to are of more common, day-to-day items and conveniences. If you like waffles on the road (and who doesn't?), don't try carting the waffle iron back and forth from your house. We've met folks who bring their bedding from home. Don't make getting ready for a RV trip so cumbersome and difficult that it's not enjoyable to go!

With few exceptions, we've met folks along the way that bring whatever they use at home on the road with them. This includes just about everything—pots, pans, vacuum, DVD player, mattress cover, pillows, sheets, towels, silverware, glassware, all the way down to the family's electric toothbrush.

114

Don't do that! At the risk of being chastised or labeled uppity, once you buy a RV, you need to develop and implement a plan to get your RV "outfitted" and ready to hit the road at a moment's notice. To get this right, your goal should be to do nothing more than put food in the refrigerator and pantry before striking out on your next adventure. Regardless of what some may believe, we didn't whip out an American Express Diamond Platinum Anniversary limit-free spending card and have a concierge stock our RV. We did it a few items at a time, over the course of a couple camping seasons, but we did it, and we're glad we did!

For us, the first items we wanted duplicated in the RV included things like dinner plates, flatware, pots, pans, bedding, and bathroom items. Some of these items we just went and purchased specifically for the RV. However, it's not practical for everyone to go out and buy a RV full of goodies, especially having just laid out the money to buy the RV. I get that.

One of the ways to get your rig stocked with all those things you need, is to begin a deliberate "upgrade" plan for those items you have at home. Before waiting on the waffle iron to die, buy a new one and transfer the old unit to the RV. Since it was still in working order and will now see more limited use, it should last you for many outings. We did that with several items and over a fairly short period of time, with no insult to our pocket book, we had a RV ready to pull out on the open road at a moment's notice.

Getting your RV ready for you and your family takes some effort and resources. Make a plan and slowly add items to your rig that make it turn-key, ready-to-roll. It's a great relief to not have to worry about packing or unpacking.

Chapter 7

Managing Your Weight

In the years I've been associated with RVs and, after meeting many fellow RVers at RV Parks and in the course of our various travels, I've come to the conclusion that weight management is one of the most, if not THE most, overlooked, misunderstood, and/or completely ignored aspects of RVing. The problem with this conclusion is that not managing your weight can be deadly. Literally.

I've met more folks than I can count who either don't understand, or don't care to understand, the importance of knowing their RV's weight distribution, axle weights, and combined weights. It is frustrating to speak to RVers about their rigs, only to learn that they really misunderstand the physical dangers associated with overloading their RV.

You may recall a Toyota Tundra television commercial where the truck was shown pulling one of the Space Shuttles to its permanent display location. I've actually spoken to RVers who cite that very commercial as real-world testimony of how powerful their tow vehicle engine is. These people assert their tow vehicle "can pull anything out there with power to spare." They are absolutely correct in that engines are amazingly powerful and can pull most any vehicle out there. The issues come into play when you're trying to stop or the complete failure of the vehicle structure. Ignoring weight management may never cause you any issues at all or, before you know it, could lead to disastrous consequences. Remember, the tow vehicle and trailer essentially create an articulated vehicle assembly; therefore, weight considerations are critical to safe towing. The tow vehicle must be a proper match for the trailer.

All new RVs are required by law to have a series of placards or manufacturer labels that detail specific weights and allowances. Older RVs should have this information available as well, but it may be a little more difficult to locate. For tow vehicles, the information should be readily available, either on the vehicle, in the vehicle owner's manual, or in the trailer towing summary guide. As you are becoming an informed RVer, spend the time to understand what weight variables your RV actually has. You may be surprised.

Keep in mind one of the many recurring themes used throughout this book: *do your own research*. Salesmen are great at selling, that's what they do. When it comes to no-kidding facts and stats, some are lacking, undereducated, or are simply trying any line necessary to get you to commit and make the sale. *Trust, but verify*!

While researching our first motorhome, I actually looked at a few units that I thought would more than fit our needs. What I found seemed to almost defy logic and common sense. One Class A motorhome spec sheet showed the front axles within a few hundred pounds of their gross weight right off the lot! What does that mean? Besides a poor design, it means that, after loading all the things the typical RV family would want to take along (like a spouse, fuel, some food, etc.), your RVs front axle already would be significantly overloaded. At a RV show, we toured a mid-size toy hauler fifth wheel. The salesman showed us where our motorcycles would be loaded and the spacious garage with its infinite possibilities. The weight placards quickly told another story. This unit empty had just 2,100 pounds before hitting its gross rating. The salesman went to great lengths to explain how the balance of the fifth wheel was affected by loading the garage, and explained the pin weight formula. Although that information was all true, it did not change the gross weight rating of the axles.

You don't have to be a rocket scientist to figure out that loading two nice cruiser motorcycles in the garage of this fifth wheel would eat up the majority of your available weight budget, and would leave little room for helmets or cool leather jackets! This is precisely why several RV experts say you should "weigh before you pay." Get the weight facts on your new RV before you make the deal so that you know exactly what kind of weight overhead you have remaining. Think about all the "stuff" you and your family would pack into your RV for a week-long vacation and, before you know it, you've added 2,000 pounds of cargo to your rig (literally, a ton of stuff!).

Not understanding your rig's weight and available capacity is where folks get into trouble. They either never take the time to understand about weight capacities, or they simply ignore them. In some cases, I surmise that folks purchase what they believe is a great unit at an affordable price and, by the time they figure out what weight management is all about, it's too late. At that point, having heard the weight naysayers talk about towing overweight for years without issue, they often choose to do the same.

It's the wrong decision to make for a host of reasons. Simple statistics would allow that some percentage of RVers have been overweight, without incident. Others have been overweight for years, without incident. Still another percentage have never weighed their rigs. Perhaps not knowing somehow lessons the risk? Unfortunately, some RVers went about their trips and the statistical Gods were not on their side. Their overloaded RV caused a tire failure driving down the highway. This scenario can play out with a wide range of dramatic ends. Often, the ends include substantial damage to the RV, or worse.

One of the most blatant examples I've encountered about someone being oblivious to RV weight limits occurred one spring, while we were enjoying a long weekend at a RV Park. I was mesmerized as I watched a young man loading up a dual-axle travel trailer toy hauler with what appeared to be most, if not all, of his worldly belongings. After a while, I couldn't help myself and I walked over to see what the young man was doing. He indeed was loading up everything he owned, preparing to leave and excited for the new job he had accepted. When I reluctantly asked if he didn't think he was overloading his trailer, he replied, "Oh no, I've got lots more room," at which time he pointed to some void spaces in the upper corners of the trailer where he could fit a few more things.

Cargo capacity in a RV is not like the US Post Office Priority Mail slogan, "If it fits, it ships!" Cargo capacity can be, and most often is, reached well before all visual empty storage space is consumed.

Understanding the weight limitations of a RV requires a bit of time and effort. The end result is an informed RV owner and the confidence and comfort of knowing that you're operating within the design limitations of not only your rig, but the law, as well. (Oh, the "L" word.)

To help highlight the importance of this topic, let's walk through a scenario. Let's say you were on a trip in your "overloaded" RV and you're involved in a crash where there are injuries. For the sake of the example, let's say you just rear-ended someone because you couldn't stop. Do you think that law enforcement personnel could figure out that your RV was over loaded? Do you think some slick insurance investigator might figure out that you were overloaded? If you answered no to either, I'd inject the mental game-show buzzer sound and in my best television voice say, "Oh, wrong answer—but thanks for playing!"

In all seriousness, I ask that you reconsider and maybe do a little more research about weight management before making your RV purchase. Ask your insurance company. There are countless examples where good, honest, hard-working people ended up on the wrong side of the settlement table because they didn't spend the time reviewing and understanding their RVs weight ratings.

The following pages contain discussions about some of the weight variables; some real-world examples of vehicle weight identification labels; and how to appropriately weigh motorhomes and tow vehicles with trailers.

So, when it comes to weight, are you RV ready? Not sure? Then have a calculator and a piece of paper available so that we can get busy doing some calculations to help you be sure. The calculations themselves are not difficult; it's more how the industry has confused the weight issue over the years by changing acronyms or burying details where they are difficult to find.

What do you weigh? Certainly within a handful of pounds, you probably know. And that's good, because to most accurately determine the gross weight of your motorhome or tow vehicle and trailer combination, you need to know what you weigh and add it to the gross weight calculation. Better gingerly ask your spouse, too. What did the vet say that Fido weighed last trip in for shots? Don't think that giant cooler full of ice and sodas counts? Think again.

Let's refresh on some of the most frequently used, common terms when discussing and determining RV weights. Others may be found in the chapter 1, "Definitions".

Gross Combination Weight Rating (GCWR): The *__maximum__* weight of a tow vehicle and <u>everything</u> it is towing. The GCWR is the absolute limit. It cannot be exceeded.

Gross Vehicle Weight Rating (GVRW): The maximum weight allowed for any vehicle; determined by the manufacturer of the vehicle. All vehicles have a GVRW. Sometimes finding out what the GVRW actually is can be a bit of a challenge, but it is critical that you know what it is. Once again, the GVRW cannot be exceeded.

Gross Axle Weight Rating (GAWR): The maximum weight that an individual axle of a vehicle can support. This rating is often misunderstood. A trailer, for example, could be under its GVWR, but over on its GAWR because of improper loading.

Cargo Carrying Capacity (CCC): The CCC value is provided by the manufacturer to give you an understanding of how much cargo can be added to your RV. This value is established by the manufacturer and is determined before adding any options and after-market goodies.

Unloaded Vehicle Weight (UVW): The weight of the vehicle as originally shipped from the manufacturer.

I've been pretty determined in getting the point across that weight, does matter. Be determined when working on these calculations. Ignore those who say the issues of weight are over-exaggerated by those trying to sell bigger units, or an insurance industry ploy to suck the last hard-earned dollar from your wallet. Weight is directly attributable to safety. Simple as that; end of story.

Now determining all these weight calculations will require some work, possibly even a calculator, but it can be done and you CAN do it. The mechanics of "how" to get it done, and done correctly, vary a bit.

Near the end of this chapter, a discussion of the various type of hitches and weight classes is provided. For now, you need to focus on the type of RV that you have, and understand the subtleties of the various methods to weight your RV. You may wish to glance ahead to the weight worksheets appendix to see the various worksheets available. This will help you decide the "how" based on scale options available to you. I do address weight-distributing hitches because, when you are weighing your RV, if you have one of these hitches, getting the most useful weight figures will require that you weigh with the weight-distributing hitch both connected and disconnected.

Now that you're determined to be an informed RVer, how exactly do you weight your RV? That depends on what type of RV you have. The technique used to weigh a motorhome is slightly different from weighing travel trailers and fifth wheel units. So, we'll look at each variant. There are also a few ways you can obtain your RVs weight; some ways are better than others.

Where do you go to weigh your RV?

That depends on several factors and where you might be at the time. Perhaps the most convenient location to weigh your RV is at a CAT Truck scale. The CAT Company is the largest truck scale operation in North America, with over 1,725 locations.[11] Often, you can find certified CAT scales at large truck stops. For a specific location, you can refer to their website. Other weighing options are

Figure 11   CAT Scales are located across the United States

available, too, like certified public scales, state motor vehicle departments, moving companies, grain elevators, and more. Perhaps the best place to get your RV weighed is at a RV Rally. Many RV brands and clubs host RV Rallies across the country. More and more, these events include RV weighing as a benefit for attending. Vendors attend these rallies with certified portable scales and can check your weight with little effort and without trying to navigate your RV through some unfamiliar truck stop. I like this option because it offers weight for each wheel (the most accurate and informative weighing option available).

For less than the price of a nice family dinner, you can get your rig weighed by wheel position. Some notable groups schedule offerings around the country, and more and more RV Parks are offering the service. Some popular services include the RV Safety and Education Foundation (RVSEF)[12], RV Weigh[13] , Escapees RV Club Smart Weigh Program [14] and Weigh To Go, LLC[15].   Check out these sites and learn about their specific methods and availability in your area. This is one of the best investments you can make.

Ways to weigh

Ideally, you want to measure the weight of your RV at each wheel. This can be done by various means. Portable certified scales will allow individual wheel measurement, and some platform scales, like truck-axle scales, may allow you to maneuver your rig as necessary to get a wheel at a time. If that is not possible, large, big-rig truck scales (like CAT) that use three separate pads to measure weight are a fantastic alternative. Some big-rig truck scales use a single axle pad that requires you to move the RV and position one axle at a time. Lastly, some scales (like at freight yards, refuse centers, or grain elevators) use a large, single platform scale that captures the entire RV configuration at one time and provides the total gross weight. If this is all you have access to, then use it!

Knowing your weight is infinitely better than wondering how much you weigh. Ideally, spend the time necessary to obtain and record both empty and loaded weights. Specific information and procedures are provided for weighing motorhomes, fifth wheels and travel trailers. Review the specific section for the type of RV you have or are interested in or discover the subtle differences by reviewing each.

Motorhomes

As we learned before, motorhomes can come in a variety of shapes and sizes but the good news is that they are common in the process for weighing them because they are all chassis based vehicles.

Best: The ideal method is to weigh the motorhome by wheel. Remember, there are services that do this, including vendors who attend RV rallies. Some of the larger RV sales centers can weigh your RV this way. Spend some

Figure 12 RV Weigh uses special portable scales to get very precise weights.

time researching what weighing options are available in your area.

Better: For segmented scales (like CAT scales at big-rig truck stops), drive your motorhome onto the scales so that each of the RV axles are centered as much as possible on each platform. These scales usually have three measured sections. For your motorhome, center the front axle on the front pad, and the rear axle on the middle

Figure 13 On segmented scales, place each axle on a separate scale pad, as centered as possible.

125

pad. Once you're satisfied with how your rig is positioned on the pads, have the scale operator register your weight.

If the scales allow (meaning that the scale operator and the physical orientation of the scales permit), drive off the scale, loop around, and drive back on the scales so that only the right- or left-side wheels are on the scales. Try to center the motorhome on the edge of the scale, half on, half off. Using the weight from the first pass, subtract the second weighing and this will give you a pretty accurate "by corner" weight.

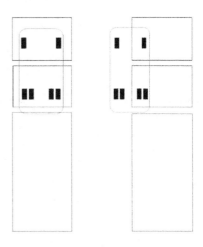

Figure 14 If the scales permit, weigh half of the RV.

Better: For scales with a single, axle-type pad, drive the motorhome onto the scale, centering the axle as best you can. Get the weight confirmed for the front axle, and then pull forward to the rear axle, centering on the pad as best you can. For multiple axles, if possible, try to position the vehicle to get the weight of each axle independently.

Notes:_____

_____

_____

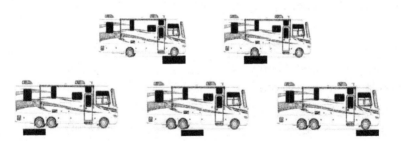

Figure 15   For single axle scales, center and weigh each axle. At automated scales, you'll be signaled to move to the next axle. Weighing only takes a few minutes.

If the scales allow (meaning that the scale operator and the physical orientation of the scales permit), drive off the scale, loop around, and drive back on the scales with only the right or left side, front or rear axle on the scales. Try to center the motorhome on the edge of the scale, half on, half off.

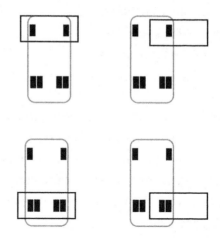

Figure 16   If scales permit, make a second pass, weighing only half of the RV.

Using the weight from the first pass, subtract the weight result from the second weighing. This should provide you with a pretty accurate "by corner" weight.

Good: The last option would be to weigh on a single-platform scale, which really only provides you with a total vehicle weight, but with this, you're still well ahead of many RVers on the road.

Fifth wheels

Getting an accurate weight on a fifth-wheel system is a bit more complicated than getting one on a motorhome because it requires that you get an additional set of axles onto the scale pad. Additionally, for the most accurate representation, it requires you disconnect your trailer and get your truck weighed separately.

Best: The ideal would be to weigh the fifth wheel trailer, wheel by wheel—both for the truck and trailer. As previously mentioned, there are services that do this, including vendors who attend RV rallies. Some of the larger RV sales centers can weigh your RV this way. Make sure to spend time researching what weighing options are available in your area.

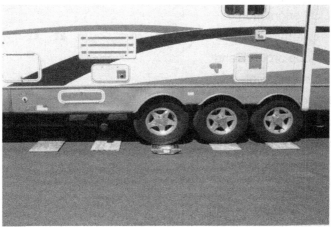

Figure 17 RV Weigh uses special portable scales to get very accurate weights per wheel. An excellent value and something you should consider investing in.

Better: For segmented scales (like CAT scales at big-rig truck stops), drive your truck and fifth wheel onto the scales so that each of the truck and trailer axles are centered as much as possible to each platform. These scales usually have three measured sections. For your truck, center the front axle on the front pad and the rear axle on the middle pad. The trailer axles should align over the third scale pad. Once you're satisfied with how your truck and trailer are positioned, have the scale operator register your weight.

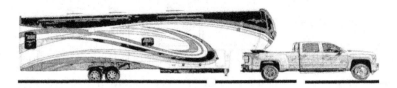

Figure 18   For segmented scales, center the axles on the appropriate scale pad.

If the scales allow (meaning that the scale operator and the physical orientation of the scales permit), drive off the scale, loop around, and drive back on the scales, with only the right or left side wheels on the scales. Try to center the truck and trailer on the scale, such that one half of the truck and trailer are on the scale, while the other half is sitting off the scale pads.

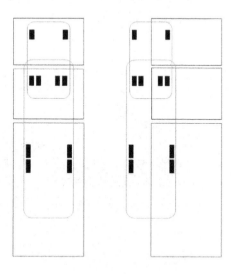

Figure 19   If the scale permits, weigh half of the tow vehicle and trailer.

Using the weight from the first pass, subtract the second weighing and this will give you a pretty accurate "by corner" weight.

Better: For scales with a single axle-type pad, drive the truck and trailer onto the scale, centering the axle as best you can. After the weight is confirmed for the front axle, pull forward to the rear axle, centering on the pad and confirming weight, then pull completely forward and position the trailer axles on the pad. For multiple axles, try to position the vehicle to get the weight of each axle independently, if possible. If that is not practical, obtain the weight with all of the trailer axles centered.

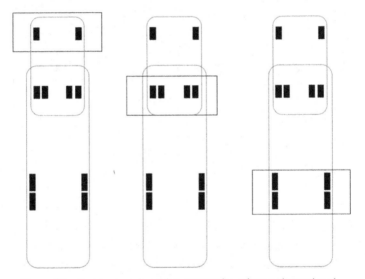

Figure 20   For single-axle scales, center the axles on the pad and move to the next axle once the weight is recorded. In this illustration, the pad is wide enough for both trailer axles to fit on the scale. Scales are configured differently, so evaluate the available options when you select a scale.

If the scales allow (meaning the scale operator and the physical orientation of the scales permit), drive off the scale, loop around, and drive back on the scales, with only the right or left side, front, rear, or trailer axle on the scales. Try to center the truck and trailer on the edge of the scale, half on, half off. Using the weight from the first pass, subtract the second weighing and this will give you a pretty accurate "by corner" weight.

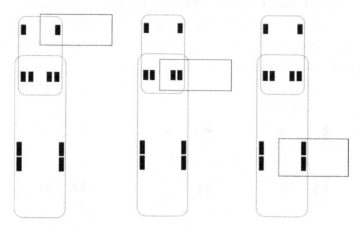

Figure 21 If the scales permit, make a second pass, weighing just half of the tow vehicle and trailer.

Good: The last option would be to weigh on a single-platform scale. While this really only provides you with a total truck-and-trailer weight, understanding your total weight is critical for safe operation.

Notes:_____

_____

_____

Travel trailer

The method for getting an accurate weight on a travel trailer is similar to that for weighing a fifth wheel. It's a bit more complicated than a motorhome because it requires you get an additional set of axles onto the scale pad and, for the most accurate representation, requires you disconnect your trailer and get your tow vehicle weighed separately.

Best: The ideal method would be to weigh the tow vehicle and trailer combination wheel by wheel. As previously mentioned, there are services that do this, including vendors who attend RV rallies. Some of the larger RV sales centers can weigh your RV this way. Make sure to spend time researching what weighing options are available in your area.

Figure 22   RV Weigh uses special scale pads to weigh each wheel of your RV configuration. Knowing the specific weight of your RV by wheel position is ideal.

Better: For segmented scales (like CAT scales at big-rig truck stops), drive your tow vehicle and trailer onto the scales so that each

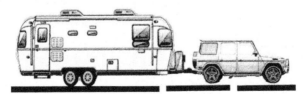

Figure 23   Center each set of axles on a scale segment.

132

of the tow vehicle and trailer axles are centered as much as possible on each platform. These scales usually have three measured sections.

For your tow vehicle, center the front axle on the front pad and the rear axle on the middle pad. The trailer axles should fall somewhere in the third scale pad. Once you're satisfied with how your tow vehicle and trailer are positioned on the scales, have the scale operator register your weight. While this type of weighing is a preferred method, depending on the length of your tow vehicle and trailer, it may not be appropriate for you.

If the scales allow (meaning that the scale operator and the physical orientation of the scales permit), drive off the scale, loop around, and drive back on the scales with only the right or left side, front, rear or trailer axle on the scales. Try to center the tow vehicle and trailer on the edge of the scale, half on, half off. Using the weight from the first pass, subtract the second weighing and this will give you a pretty accurate "by corner" weight.

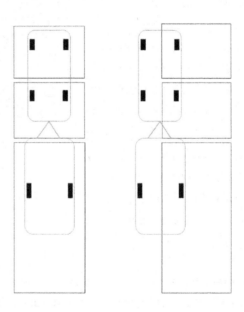

Figure 24 Tow vehicle and travel trailer centered on CAT style scale pads. If the scales permit, take a second pass, weighing just half of the tow vehicle and trailer.

Better: For scales with a single axle-type pad, drive the tow vehicle and trailer onto the scale, one axle set at a time, centering the axle as best you can. After getting the weight confirmed for the front axle, pull forward to the rear axle of the tow vehicle, centering on the pad and confirming weight, then pull completely forward until the trailer axle(s) are on the pad. For multiple axles, try to position the vehicle to get the weight of each axle independently if possible. If this is not possible or practical, center the trailer axles on the pad and obtain the weight reading.

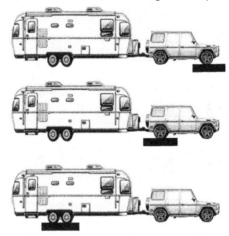

Figure 25 For single pad scales, center your axles on the pad and record each weight.

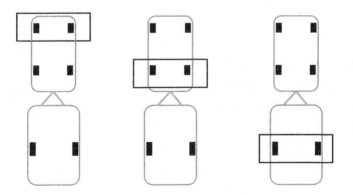

Figure 26 Center each axle on the pad and obtain recorded weight.

If the scales allow (meaning that the scale operator and the physical orientation of the scales permit), drive off the scale, loop around, and drive back on the scales with only the right or left side, front, rear, or trailer axle on the scales. Try to center the tow vehicle and trailer on the edge of the scale, half on, half off. Using the weight from the first pass, subtract the second weighing and this will give you a pretty accurate "by corner" weight.

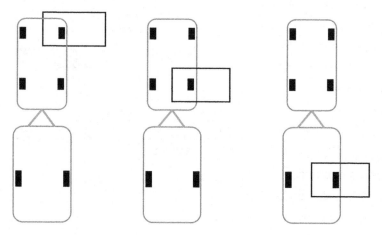

Figure 27 If the scales permit, take a second pass with the tow vehicle and travel trailer, and record weights for half of each vehicle.

Good: As with the fifth wheel, the last option would be to weigh on a single-platform scale. While this really only provides you with a total tow vehicle-and-trailer weight, understanding your total weight is critical for safe operation.

Weight-distributing hitches

A quick note to those using weight-distributing hitches. To maximize the amount of information available to you and to ensure your vehicle and hitch are setup properly, weigh with the weight-distributing hitch connected, and then weigh again with the weight-distributing hitch disconnected. Using both of these weights will assist you in getting your weight-distributing hitch aligned properly, and will ensure that the distribution of weight across the RV is appropriate.

Weight-distributing hitches are wonderful safety enhancements, but only if used properly. They can be a little work to get installed properly, but they are amazing when properly balanced. A lot of confusion exists out there about when weight-distributing hitches are really necessary. *eTrailer*, a leading supplier of trailering and towing components, offers very straightforward advice: *"Weight-distributing systems should be used any time the trailer weighs more than 50 percent of the vehicle's weight."*[16] Right to the point. If your tow vehicle weighs 5,000 lbs. and your trailer weighs 3,000 lbs, you should have a weight-distributing hitch. Chapter 14 provides a detailed discussion about hitches.

One size does not fit all

As I've stated throughout this book, your fuel mileage may vary! One size does not fit all. The above weighing information is critical

Figure 28 While knowing your weight is very important, it would be difficult to weigh this configuration at a CAT scale.

for your safety and you should make every effort to weigh your rig. However, if your "adventure" rig coupled together is shorter than most traditional pickup trucks on the market today, the segmented scales detailed in these instructions will likely not benefit you substantially. If your rig is on the smaller size, weighing for individual wheel weights is best; otherwise, you might be better off at a single-platform scale.

Getting weighed

So now that you know where you can go and the various methods you can use to get your RV weighed, get out there and do it! To get the most useful data out of your trip to the scale, there is a little prep work to do first.

How are you going to weigh?

In the previous sections of this chapter, I provided several options available to you to weigh your RV—from fairly simple, single-pad scales to individual wheel-weighing methods. Access to scales in your area may be a major consideration—if not **the** determining factor in the weighing option you choose. I'm a believer that the more information you have, the better prepared you will be; however, I'm also a realist, and even minimal data is better than none at all.

Once you determine the method you will use to weigh your RV, select the most appropriate weight worksheet from Appendix Two, where you can select from very detailed worksheets that I've provided there for the following RV configurations.

Individual wheel weight worksheets:

- Class A
- Class B
- Class C

- Pickup Camper
- Tow Vehicle (unattached)
- Fifth Wheel and Tow Vehicle
- Travel Trailer and Tow Vehicle

Segmented (CAT-style) weight worksheets—both single-pass scales and scales where a second pass can be completed with half the RV scaled:

- Class A
- Class B
- Class C
- Pickup Camper
- Fifth Wheel and Tow Vehicle
- Travel Trailer and Tow Vehicle

Single-axle scale weight worksheets—both single pass scales and scales where a second pass can be completed with half the RV scaled:

- Class A
- Class B
- Class C
- Pickup Camper
- Fifth Wheel and Tow Vehicle
- Travel Trailer and Tow Vehicle

Once you're armed with the appropriate worksheet, you'll need to complete a little more legwork before the actual weigh-in.

Manufacturer weight data

For the weight worksheet you select to be completely useful, you need to find the manufacturer weight data labels specific to your RV configuration. If you have a motorized RV, the manufacturer weight data labels are often in an overhead cabinet near the driver compartment. For fifth wheel and travel trailers, the data labels are often at the front of the trailer, near the hitch apparatus or located inside one of the baggage doors. If your RV configuration includes a tow vehicle of some type, don't forget to collect that weight data as well. Often, the gross vehicle weight rating for your tow vehicle can be found on a sticker inside the driver's door. If you can't locate the label, consult your owner's manual or the manufacturer web site for the most accurate numbers.

The following actual examples of weight labels are provided so that you can get an idea what to look for and what information to expect. As you can see (unfortunately), each one is a little different. While the information they are to convey is fairly set, the manner in which each of the various manufacturers go about it varies substantially. Once you collect your specific weight data, keep it handy as you will be entering some of the numbers onto the weight worksheet.

Example Weight Stickers

2011 Ford F-350 Super Duty

The Ford pickup is an incredibly popular line, and the F350 is a very capable truck. The 2011 example we'll use comes equipped with the diesel engine options and single rear wheel. This setup is very common in the fifth-wheel world.

Note that, in the picture below, the vehicle data sticker is attached very close to the door hinge attachment point. Also note that the vehicle has a 10,000-lb gross vehicle weight rating; 5,600-lb front axle weight rating; and a 6,290-lb rear axle weight rating. The vehicle data sticker tells you a little more about the vehicles as well, including the full VIN number (partially redacted here), manufacture date, and original tire and wheel sizes.

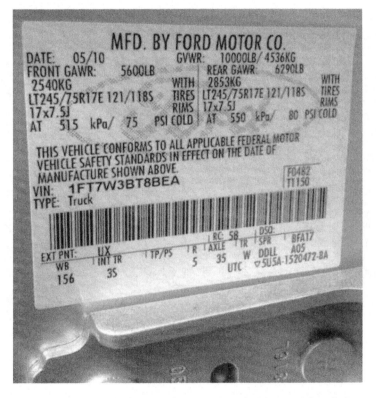

Figure 29   2011 Ford F350 Super Duty, Diesel Pickup Weight Label. The F350 is a very common and very capable tow vehicle, often seen pulling some of the largest travel trailers on the road.

2012 Newmar Class A

Newmar produces high-end, well-made recreational vehicles. Shown below is an example of a Newman Class A coach vehicle weight label. Note that it is similar to the Ford Super Duty vehicle data sticker. In the Newmar coach, this sticker is found in the overhead cabinet area, above the driver's seat. Note that, for this Newmar coach, the front gross vehicle axle weight is 9,000 lbs; the rear gross axle weight rating is 17,500 lbs; and the coach has a gross vehicle weight rating of 26,000 lbs.

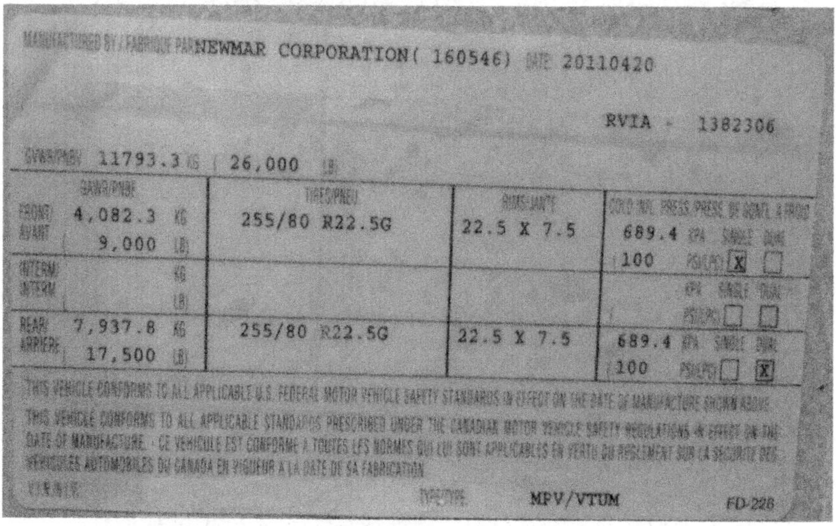

Figure 30 The 2011 Newmar Class A weight label
(normally located in the upper cabinet area, above the driver's seat).

2016 Newport Landmark Fifth Wheel

Shown below is the vehicle weight label for a 2016 Newport Landmark fifth wheel, which is located on the street-side of the fifth wheel, near the front. The label includes the VIN number; manufacture date; gross axle weight ratings of 9,000 lbs each; and the gross vehicle weight rating 18,000 lbs.

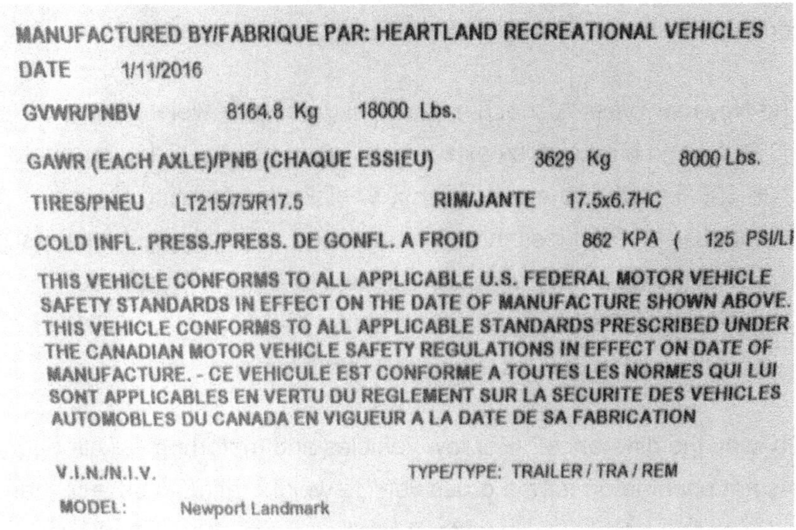

MANUFACTURED BY/FABRIQUE PAR: HEARTLAND RECREATIONAL VEHICLES

DATE   1/11/2016

GVWR/PNBV   8164.8 Kg   18000 Lbs.

GAWR (EACH AXLE)/PNB (CHAQUE ESSIEU)   3629 Kg   8000 Lbs.

TIRES/PNEU   LT215/75/R17.5   RIM/JANTE   17.5x6.7HC

COLD INFL. PRESS./PRESS. DE GONFL. A FROID   862 KPA (125 PSI/LI

THIS VEHICLE CONFORMS TO ALL APPLICABLE U.S. FEDERAL MOTOR VEHICLE SAFETY STANDARDS IN EFFECT ON THE DATE OF MANUFACTURE SHOWN ABOVE. THIS VEHICLE CONFORMS TO ALL APPLICABLE STANDARDS PRESCRIBED UNDER THE CANADIAN MOTOR VEHICLE SAFETY REGULATIONS IN EFFECT ON DATE OF MANUFACTURE. - CE VEHICULE EST CONFORME A TOUTES LES NORMES QUI LUI SONT APPLICABLES EN VERTU DU REGLEMENT SUR LA SECURITE DES VEHICLES AUTOMOBLES DU CANADA EN VIGUEUR A LA DATE DE SA FABRICATION

V.I.N./N.I.V.   TYPE/TYPE: TRAILER / TRA / REM

MODEL: Newport Landmark

Figure 31 Landmark Manufacturer Weight Label - often located on front of coach near the hitch.

These numbers don't add up?

After reviewing the three examples above, you may have figured out that the numbers don't always add up. For example, the 2011 Ford F350 has a front gross axle weight rating of 5,600 lbs and a rear gross axle weight rating of 6,290 lbs, but the gross vehicle weight rating is only 10,000 lbs—1,890 lbs less than the axle weights combined.

The Newmar Class A coach has a front gross axle weight rating of 9,000 lbs and a rear gross axle weight rating of 17,500 lbs, for a total of 26,500 lbs, while the actual gross vehicle weight rating is 26,000 lbs—500 lbs less than the combined axle ratings. In the last example, the Newport Landmark has two axles with gross axle weight ratings of 8,000 lbs each, while the trailer gross vehicle weight rating is 18,000 lbs, or a full 2,000 lbs more!

So, why the difference? For tow vehicles and motorhomes, although it is not uncommon for the gross vehicle weight rating to be less than the sum of the two axle weights, it can't be more. This difference may contain some of that "engineering margin," often referred to by old-timers, but more accurately, the gross vehicle weight rating is simply the maximum weight that the vehicle chassis can safely carry and bring to a safe stop.

In the fifth-wheel realm, the confusion often stems from the combined gross axle weight ratings being less than the gross vehicle weight rating. Look at the Landmark fifth wheel example. There are two axles rated at 8,000 lbs each. If you thought the trailer gross vehicle weight rating could be no more than 16,000 lbs, that would have been a fair assumption, but nevertheless wrong. In the

Newport Landmark example, the gross vehicle weight rating is actually 18,000 lbs, or 2,000 lbs more than the combined gross axle weight ratings. If that's the case, then why aren't the axles overloaded?

Trailers load balance some of their weight across, or through, the hitch. In the Newport Landmark example, it simply means that at least 2,000 lbs of the fifth-wheel weight is being managed (or carried) by the pickup truck tow vehicle. When it's parked, that load is being carried by the landing gear.

Pay attention to the numbers

It's critical for your safety and the continued mechanical well-being of your equipment to pay attention to what the information and numbers on the weight labels actually mean. Don't rely on a salesman who tells you that your truck will pull anything on the road. The Ford F350 example is key. Remember, the truck had a 10,000-lb gross vehicle weight rating. Empty, the truck weighs about 7,600 lbs, which leaves you 2,400 lbs to load into the truck before reaching your gross vehicle weight limit. This point is one of the most argued weight issues around the campfire. Why? Because the F350 has an empty rear axle curb weight of 3,019 lbs. Many are under the misconception that they can load another 3,271 lbs in the bed, thereby resulting in a rear axle weight limit of 6,290 lbs. Sounds simple enough but, if you add 3,271 lbs in the bed, the gross weight of the truck would be 10,871 lbs, or 871 lbs over the F350 gross vehicle weight rating.

It is your responsibility to understand the weight limits and restrictions of your specific vehicle, and ensure that you operate your equipment within their documented weight ratings.

Weight worksheet examples

I've been told by a few folks whom I've asked to critique my weight worksheets that, after reviewing them, they concluded that I must have been a reincarnated IRS worker trapped in tax-code purgatory. I guess the worksheets were either too busy or they had the look and feel of tax forms. Regardless, get over the initial "you-can't-be-serious" feeling, and let's walk through a couple of real-world examples.

To be thorough, we'll weigh the Newmar Class A coach on a CAT-style, segmented scale using two passes. Then, we'll weigh the Ford F350 and Newport Landmark fifth wheel on a single-pad scale. I don't include an example here using individual wheel weighing as the data are strictly understood, and these services usually have a series of folks helping at every stage of the process.

Newmar Class A coach

For this example, let's assume that we're going to weigh the Newmar Class A coach at a local neighborhood scale (similar to a CAT scale). This scale layout provides us the opportunity to weigh the coach half-on and half-off, so that we can get a really accurate snapshot of our coach loaded for trips.

To get the information we need, we'll need to weigh twice and, therefore, get two weight tickets. Using the method identified earlier in this chapter, let's go weigh.

Your Favorite Local Truck Scale
Hometown, America

STEER AXLE:	8,324
DRIVE AXLE:	15,796
TRAILER AXLE:	0
GROSS WEIGHT:	24,120

Certified Weight: *Joe Weight Guy*

Figure 32 Sample certified weight ticket for
Newmar Class A coach example, totally on the scales.

Your Favorite Local Truck Scale
Hometown, America

STEER AXLE:	4,098
DRIVE AXLE:	7,745
TRAILER AXLE:	0
GROSS WEIGHT:	11,843

Certified Weight: *Joe Weight Guy*

Figure 33 Second certified weight ticket for Newmar
Class A coach example, half-on, half-off the scales.

Using these two weight tickets, we now have enough information to complete weight worksheet #7.

WORKSHEET #7 - WIDE SEGMENTED SCALE WEIGHT
For Class A, Class B, Class C, Unattached Tow Vehicles and Pickup Campers

INSTRUCTIONS	
Position Vehicle so that axles are centered on separate scale segments. This worksheet is used for scales that have sufficient room to allow you to reposition the vehicle so that only half the Vehicle is on the scale. This will allow calculation of Vehicle weight by corner.	
VEHICLE ONLY WEIGHT – COMPLETELY ON SCALE	
Enter Steer Axle GAW.	1. *8,324*
Enter Drive Axle GAW.	2. *15,796*
Enter Tag Axle GAW (if equipped).	3. *N/A*
Calculate Tow Vehicle GVW: Add Steer Axle GAW (line 1), Drive Axle (line 2) and Tag Axle (line 3) and Drive Axle (line 2): (1+2+3=4).	4. *24,120*

VEHICLE ONLY – HALF VEHICLE ON SCALE		
LEFT *4,098*	Enter appropriate side of Steer Axle on the scale. Subtract that value from line 1 and enter the opposite side axle weight.	RIGHT *4,226*
LEFT *7,745*	Enter appropriate side of Drive Axle on the scale. Subtract that value from line 2 and enter the opposite side axle weight.	RIGHT *8,051*

147

| LEFT

N/A | Enter appropriate side of Tag Axle on the scale. Subtract that value from line 3 and enter the opposite side axle weight. | RIGHT

N/A |
|---|---|---|

CALCULATIONS	
Enter the Vehicle Steer Axle GAWR as listed on the Vehicle MWL.	5. *9,000*
Steer Axle GAW (line 1) MUST be less than GAWR (line 5).	**STOP** Verify
Enter the Vehicle Drive Axle GAWR as listed on the Vehicle MWL.	6. *11,500*
Drive Axle GAW (line 2) MUST be less than GAWR (line 6).	**STOP** Verify
Enter the Vehicle Tag Axle GAWR as listed on the Vehicle MWL.	7. *N/A*
Tag Axle GAW (line 3) MUST be less than GAWR (line 7).	**STOP** Verify
Enter Tow Vehicle GVW (line 4).	8. *24,120*
Enter the Vehicle GVWR from the Vehicle MWL.	9. *26,000*
The GVW (line 8) MUST be less than the GVWR (line 9). If not, the Vehicle exceeds its GVWR and this MUST be resolved.	**STOP** Verify

For our Newmar Class A example, the worksheet calculations indicate that we're in excellent shape. After completely loading this motorhome, we've still got a fairly sizeable margin remaining to pick up some souvenirs along the way!

We first weighed the coach totally on the scale. For our second pass, we centered the coach with the left side wheels centered on the scale pads. Using these weights and our worksheet, we determined that the right side of the coach is a little heavier than the left. This could be attributable to numerous reasons, including to include a heavier slide on one side or off-center loading. As long as the disparity is not too much, you're in great shape. Based on the weights recorded at the scale, we now know we still have about 1,880 lbs overhead remaining. That's great news.

Ford F350 and Newport Landmark Fifth Wheel

We're going to weigh the Ford F350 Super Duty pickup (tow vehicle) and the Newport Landmark fifth wheel at a local scale that utilizes a single scale pad. Unfortunately, this scale is located in an area that will not allow us to make a second weighing with the tow vehicle and fifth wheel half-on and half-off the scale. That's alright. We'll still obtain plenty of useful information. Based on the type of scale we're going to use, Weight Worksheet #11 is appropriate. We'll need to weigh twice—once with the tow vehicle disconnected from the fifth wheel, and once with the tow vehicle and fifth wheel connected.

Using the method identified earlier in this chapter, let's go weigh.

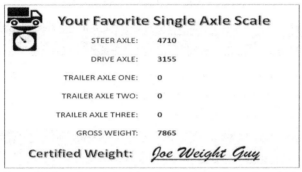

Figure 34 Sample weight ticket for Ford F350 Super Duty Pickup.

Your Favorite Single Axle Scale

STEER AXLE:	4885
DRIVE AXLE:	5895
TRAILER AXLE ONE:	8145
TRAILER AXLE TWO:	7955
TRAILER AXLE THREE:	0
GROSS WEIGHT:	26,880

Certified Weight: *Joe Weight Guy*

Figure 35 Sample weight ticket for Ford F350 Super Duty and Newport Landmark Fifth Wheel. There's trouble in these numbers!

Now that we have weighed the Ford F350 Super Duty pickup by itself, then attached it to the Newport Landmark fifth wheel and weighed those together, we have enough information to begin completing Weight Worksheet #11.

For purposes of this example, pay particular attention as the numbers are calculated, as there are a series of issues with this configuration that you would not know had you not taken the time to obtain your RV's weight.

WORKSHEET #11 - SINGLE AXLE SCALE
Fifth Wheel Trailers and Tow Vehicles

INSTRUCTIONS
Position the Tow Vehicle and Fifth Wheel on the scale platform, one axle set at a time, so that each axle is centered on the platform as best possible. Once a weight is established, move to the next axle.

TOW VEHICLE ONLY WEIGHT	
Enter Steer Axle GAW.	1. *4,710*
Enter Drive Axle GAW.	2. *3,155*
Calculate Tow Vehicle GVW: (1+2=3).	3. *7,865*

COUPLED TOW VEHICLE - FIFTH WHEEL TRAILER ATTACHED	
Enter Steer Axle GAW.	4. *4,885*
Enter Drive Axle GAW.	5. *5,895*
Calculate Coupled Tow Vehicle GVW: (4+5=6).	6. *10,780*
Calculate Fifth Wheel Pin Weight by subtracting Tow Vehicle GVW (line 3) from Coupled Tow Vehicle GVW (line 6): (6–3=7).	7. *2,915*
Enter Fifth Wheel Axle One GAW.	8. *8,145*
Enter Fifth Wheel Axle Two GAW.	9. *7,955*
Enter Fifth Wheel Axle Three GAW.	10. *N/A*
Calculate Trailer Total GAW: Add Trailer Axle One (line 8), Trailer Axle Two (line 9) and Trailer Axle Three (line 10): (8+9+10 = 11).	11. *16,100*

CALCULATIONS	
Enter Tow Vehicle Steer Axle GAWR as indicated on the Tow Vehicle MWL.	12. *5,600*
Tow Vehicle Steer Axle GAW (line 1) and Coupled Tow Vehicle Steer Axle GAW (line 4) MUST each be less than Steer Axle GAWR (line 12).	**STOP** Verify
Enter Tow Vehicle Drive Axle GAWR as indicated on the Tow Vehicle MWL.	13. *6,290*
Tow Vehicle Drive Axle GAWR (line 2) and Coupled Tow Vehicle Drive Axle GAW (line 5) MUST each be less than Drive Axle GAWR (line 13).	**STOP** Verify
Enter Trailer GAWR as indicated on the Trailer MWL.	14. *8,000*
Each Fifth Wheel Axle GAW (lines 8, 9 and 10) MUST each be less than the Trailer GAWR (line 14).	**STOP** Verify
Enter Trailer GVWR as indicated on the Trailer MWL.	15. *18,000*
Calculate Trailer GTW. Add the Fifth Wheel Pin Weight (line 7) and the Fifth Wheel Trailer Total GAW (line 11): (7+11=16).	16. *19,015*
Trailer GTW (line 16) MUST be less than the Trailer GVWR (line 15).	**STOP** Verify

Enter Tow Vehicle GCWR from the Tow Vehicle MWL.	17. *23,000*
Calculate GCW. Add Coupled Tow Vehicle GVW (line 6) and Total Trailer GAW (line 11): (6+11=18)	18. *26,880*
GCW (line 18) MUST be less than the Tow Vehicle GCWR (line 17). If not, the Tow Vehicle and Fifth Wheel exceed their designed combined maximum weight rating and this MUST be resolved.	**STOP** Verify

The news is not so good for our Ford F350 tow vehicle and Newport Landmark fifth wheel combination example. A few issues will have to be addressed to ensure compliance with the weight ratings of our vehicles. The Ford F350 has a front gross axle weight rating of 5,600 lbs, and we weighed under that loaded. The Ford F350 has a rear gross axle weight rating of 6,290 lbs, and we are under that figure by 395 lbs. Sounds great!

Not so fast. This is where the devil shows up in the details. The Ford F350 has a gross vehicle weight rating of 10,000 lbs. With the fifth wheel attached, the tow vehicle weighed in at 10,780 lbs—780 pounds overweight. The Ford has a gross combined weight rating of 23,500 lbs. Adding the tow vehicle and fifth wheel together, we exceed that weight rating by 3,880 lbs. Looking specifically at the fifth wheel, the trailer has gross axle weight ratings of 8,000 lbs. Our forward axle was 145 lbs over the maximum weight limit, while the trail axle was 45 lbs under the maximum weight limit. The fifth wheel has a gross vehicle weight rating of 18,000 lbs. Our calculations show that the trailer weighs in at 19,015 lbs—1,015 lbs over its maximum allowable weight. Using these weights and the calculations provided on the worksheets, we've got some work to do. In our specific case, we need to shed some weight from the fifth wheel and get these weights down to acceptable limits.

As previously mentioned, weight is a complicated component of RVing. On any given day, you see tow vehicles like the example above pulling large fifth-wheel trailers and toy haulers. Now that you've completed these examples, how many of those do you believe are pulling over their weight maximums?

There are always options when obtaining weight. What would the difference have been if we weighed using a Segmented (CAT-type) Scale and used Weight Worksheet #5?

TOW VEHICLE AND FIFTH-WHEEL TRAILER COUPLED WEIGHTS – COMPLETELY ON SCALE	
Enter Steer Axle GAW.	4. *4,885*
Enter Drive Axle GAW.	5. *5,895*
Enter Fifth-Wheel Trailer GAW.	6. *19,015*
Calculate Coupled Tow Vehicle GAW.	7. *10,780*
CALCULATIONS	
Calculate the Fifth Wheel Pin Weight. Subtract the Tow Vehicle Uncoupled GVW (line 3) from the Tow Vehicle Coupled GVW (line 7): (7 – 3 = 8)	8. *2,915*

Figure 36 Illustration of how weights are presented differently using various weight worksheets.

Had we chosen to use Weight Worksheet #5, the end result would have been the same. We would not have been able to determine which fifth-wheel axle was overloaded, but we would have known that the trailer's gross vehicle weight rating was exceeded.

The "Weighting" is over

No, I didn't stay up all night working on that clever section title (it just came to me like so many other bad ideas do!). The good news is that we've completed walking through some useful examples of weighing RVs. I hope that I've made clear that taking RV weight seriously is critically important to your safety on the road.

Your RV has been designed by talented engineers, and was manufactured by a company whose goal is for you to enjoy your RV so much that you want to buy another one from them; tell all your friends about them; and continually show off your RV, park to park. It is also the manufacturer's goal to keep out of courtrooms and minimize their exposure to lawsuits. So, while some diehards out there will continue to try and convince you that there is tolerance in every specification related to your RV, don't allow yourself to fall for that sleight-of-hand. The reality is, there is tolerance in RV design to address and mitigate physical demands and forces not usually present in normal RV use. Those design tolerances are not there for you to consume with an extra week's groceries and every piece of hiking gear you own. Know what the weight specifications of your RV are and manage your RV experience within them. If you simply can't, then start shopping for your next RV. While challenging the weight gods may work for some, it may not work out well for you.

Chapter Eight

RV Care

No one buys an RV with the intent of turning it into a money pit. However, if you're not interested in performing routine maintenance on your RV, that's likely what it will become. An RV can be very complex and, as such, requires a commitment to its care. Whether you do the work or have the work performed by a RV shop or garage does not matter. What matters is that you have the work done. Doing so ensures that your RV is ready to go when you are, and helps protect its value to the maximum extent possible.

Maintaining your RV depends a great deal on what type of RV you have. As an example, if you have a large, 45-foot Class A, tag-axle motorhome, it's unlikely that you have the appropriate equipment at home to rotate the tires. While some diesel pusher owners indeed change their own oil, most owners don't go through the effort or have the necessary means or tools to perform a 24-quart oil change.

There is a great saying that sometimes the most important tool in your toolbox is your credit card. Maintaining your RV requires that you decide what work you are willing to do yourself, and what you'll use your credit card to get done. As mentioned previously, it doesn't matter who does the work, as long as the work gets done.

Determining what you need to do to maintain your RV properly can be a bit of a challenge. If you've purchased a RV, then you should have received the various owner's manuals that came with the RV; these are a great resource. Often, manufacturers create their own, more generic owner's guides with instructions on how to care for your investment. If, for some reason, you do not have these manuals, guides, or instructions, it's time to evaluate what's in your RV. Then, hit the world-wide-web to download the necessary manuals or instruction sheets. Many manufacturers have on-line resource areas where you can get manuals for RVs from many years past. In the event you have a system for which you just can't locate the necessary reference materials, it may be worthwhile to schedule an appointment with a Certified RV Technician. During the visit, have them explain to you what you what actions you need to perform to keep the system in question in tip-top shape.

Exercising systems is something you're going to see referred to over and over in this book. Engines, transmissions, batteries, hydraulics, and some electronics need to be exercised to maintain peak performance. Starting an engine and letting it run 10 minutes is not considered exercising the engine and, in many cases, is even worse than just leaving the engine sit. Running a generator for a few minutes without putting the generator under a load serves no purpose either, and again can be more detrimental than just leaving it sit. Batteries need to be exercised to maintain their longevity.

Motorhome chassis are well documented, both by the engine and chassis manufacturer. In some cases, that manufacturer is one in the same (like the Ford RV chassis). Ford, as the original equipment manufacturer (OEM), provides very detailed maintenance schedules and instructions in their owner's manuals. The same is true for Freightliner, one of the larger chassis manufacturers for diesel pushers and Cummins, the predominant diesel engine found in diesel Class A models.

Motorhome care

Because motorhome engines and chassis are so well documented, this section will be fairly brief as there is not much point trying to replicate what's provided in those OEM manuals. What I will do is provide some key points and reminders to jog your memory and get you started down the right path.

Engine

Just like your primary mode of transportation, the engine in your RV requires continual service. Depending on the size and type of the engine, this service can become fairly complex and expensive. To keep an RV engine in optimum shape, it needs to be exercised. If you can't take the RV on a trip for six months, then a couple of times during that period, you should at least take it out for a drive down the highway for half an hour and at varying speeds. This exercises the engine, but also the cooling system, brakes, alternator, steering, suspension, and more. Keep the maintenance intervals in mind. Inspect the engine compartment regularly. In an RV, you'll be amazed at what you might find. Keep the air filter clean. Check belts, hoses, and wiring harnesses for signs of damage, leaks, or corrosion.

Oil

Your daily-driver vehicle likely has about 5 quarts of oil in the engine, about 20 quarts less than some large diesel engines. Regardless, the oil needs to be monitored and changed per manufacturer's instructions. Don't get caught up in the miles-versus-age debate either. That good-quality engine oil you purchased that said it was good for 5,000 miles does not mean it will be protecting your engine for 10 years because you only drive 500 miles a year. Oil deteriorates from use and from sitting. Your RV engine also deteriorates from use and from sitting. Seals and internal parts and pieces of an engine need to be lubricated, and this occurs when the engine is running.

Cooling system

Your cooling system, like the engine oil, should be considered the life blood of your engine. Your engine can not survive without either. To keep the system clean from rust and contaminants that can lead to clogs, the system should be properly maintained, which means periodic draining and flushing. Refer to your engine owner's manual for the specific timelines involved and follow them carefully. Physically check the radiator, radiator cap, overflow reservoir, and all hoses for signs of leaks and damage. If you find a spongy hose, this can be a sign that the hose is ready to fail. Weak points in hoses are no match for a coolant system under pressure.

Transmission

Depending on the type of motorhome you have, this might be an area that requires zero attention from you—meaning that some RVs have sealed, maintenance-free transmissions, while others have traditional dipsticks for you to check the actual transmission fluid level. Some larger diesel pushers have transmissions that require monitoring and have smart interfaces that can advise you of their condition with the press of a few buttons on the gear selector panel. Not to allude that you would perform actual maintenance, but it's important that you monitor what's going on. Just like the engine, you need to exercise the transmission periodically.

General RV care

Unlike the topics discussed above, the following areas are general to all types of RVs. Hopefully, your RV was bundled with owner's manuals for every device, component, and appliance installed. If so, great. If not, hopefully the following section will serve as a reminder to further your research specific to your RV so that you can locate all the appropriate information that will keep your RV serving you well into the future.

Suspension

The suspension is a critical set of components necessary to ensure the safe operation of your RV. All types of RVs, with the exception of slide-in truck campers, have some form of suspension. The suspension can include axles, shocks, coil springs, leaf springs, air bags, tie rods, and other various components. With a flashlight, get on the ground and inspect the underside of the RV (specifically, the suspension components). Look for signs of damage, loose parts, missing bolts, or anything that looks out of the norm. Inspect for signs or indication of components rubbing. This might be indicated by areas where metal parts appear shiny or scuff marks, and may be an indication of a loose or failing component.

Brakes

Maintaining your brakes is critical to ensuring safe and entertaining RV adventures. Whether it's the brakes on a motorhome or a trailer, improperly adjusted or malfunctioning brakes will make your RV impossible to handle during an emergency.

Large diesel pushers have air brake systems and very specific maintenance and adjustment procedures. Special features in the air lines keep water out of the brake system and bleed off valves keep the pressure from exceeding set limits. These brake systems have specific instructions from the original manufacturer regarding service and inspection before trips. Find this information, read it, and ensure that you understand how air brake systems work. Don't be surprised one day if your state requires a license to operate rigs with air brakes. There is a lot of discussion in the industry and at the state level, so keep an eye out for rule changes where you live.

More traditional brake systems in smaller motorhomes and trailers are no less critical or complicated. Trailer brakes and trailer brake controllers in tow vehicles have very specific setup functions. It is critical to follow these instructions to set the trailer brakes correctly. It is important when towing trailers that the brakes don't come on late and with too little braking force as it would make it exceedingly difficult to stop. Inversely, it's critical the trailer brakes don't come on too quickly and with too much force as it could cause the trailer brakes to lock up and jackknife the trailer and tow vehicle. Follow the setup instructions carefully and TEST the trailer brakes before getting out on the road. Just like on your daily-drive vehicle, brake's systems, fluids, and pads need to be inspected for serviceability.

Roofs

All RVs have some form of roof structure and roofing material to keep your RV safe from the elements. Most RV roofs are either Ethylene Propylene Diene Monomer (EPDM)—most commonly referred to as rubber, fiberglass, or some form of metal (likely, aluminum). Know what type of roof you have because each has specific care instructions and maintenance needs. You cannot allow your roof to be out of sight, out of mind. To keep your roof in good shape, you need to inspect it periodically. Personally, I think twice a year is reasonable; however, consider conducting roof inspections more often if the RV roof is exposed to the sun year-round or to lots of rain. Also, an immediate inspection should be conducted if you scrape the top of the RV with a low-hanging tree branch or other obstruction. An inspection might reveal a tear, puncture, or damage to other roof appliances, like the air conditioning. Any discovered damage should be addressed immediately.

Caution! Be careful. You must exercise great care and caution whenever you're going to inspect or work on your RV roof. A fall could lead to serious personal injury. Like so many other things we've discussed, if you don't feel comfortable or safe climbing up on the roof to check it, don't! Use that tool in your toolbox we've discussed so much: your credit card. Hire the work done, or perhaps have a friend or fellow RVer help.

If you're able and choose to inspect the roof yourself, the first step is to determine if the roof is meant to support the weight of a human. Not all are. If your RV does not have a rooftop ladder, it is entirely possible your RV was not designed to have someone traipsing around on the top. Assuming you've checked and your RV roof is structurally sound to walk on, carefully ascend to the top and gently position yourself on the roof. I suggest soft-sole tennis shoes as they provide good grip and have no hard-sole edges to potentially damage the rubber material. Once on top, you should notice sealing material generously used across the roof of your RV wherever there is something mounted, like air conditioners, skylights, antennas, etc. This is common and indeed useful protection. It can also be a real pain to track down a leak, but the material does come off fairly easily with the proper tools and some elbow grease.

Cleaning the roof and keeping it clean should be a priority. A clean roof makes it easy to spot problems, often before they become big problems. Check all of the roof surface and seals. If you discover gaps in the sealant, or cracks or splits in any of the roofing materials, patch the roof with the appropriate material based on roof construction. Clean and dry the specific area and apply the patching material, allowing sufficient time for the material to cure before exposing to the elements. In the industry, it is impossible to discuss roof repairs without referring to Dicor. The Dicor Company makes many RV products; their roofing materials, patches, and sealants are industry standard; their products are widely available; and they provide sealants and materials specific to any type of RV roof.

Rubber roofs should be cleaned a couple of times per year. If you reside or store your RV in an area where tree sap, leaves, and debris collect on the roof, creating rot and that green and black mildew and mold, then you need to clean the roof more frequently. The cleaning materials you use to complete the work depend specifically on the type of roofing material with which your RV is constructed. For rubber roofing material, it is widely agreed that you should stay away from any cleaning products that use petroleum solvents or harsh abrasives. A soft bristle brush or microfiber mop are great for applying the soap and helping break up grime and grit that have collected on the roof. While there are many commercial rubber roof cleaning soaps and additives, warm water and a mild detergent work well and pose no risk for damage. For stains or mildew, you may need a more specific cleaner from a RV box store.

After you've cleaned the roof, consider applying a coat of UV protectant. Choose one that is specifically designed for RV, rubber roofs. Lastly, try to avoid allowing the soaps or UV protectant from spilling over the sides of the RV. If it does, it can dry quickly and be troublesome to scrub off.

Metal roofs, like aluminum or panel seamed roofs, can be thoroughly cleaned using water and a mild detergent. A soft bristle brush or microfiber mop, like on the rubber roof, work well here too. For metal roofs, washing the roof does not require as much care as the materials are a little more durable. Pay particular attention to seams and seals as you work.

If, while moving across the roof of your RV you feel a little give, that may be quite normal, but avoid the area. Carefully inspect that area for any signs of previous leaks or a current leak. If you discover a leak, like a split seam or missing roof sealant, the soft spot may indeed be significant water damage and you'll need to effect repairs. If there is no evidence of an issue, that just may be a softer spot in the roof, in-between roof members.

Fiberglass roofs are not as common as rubber, but are considered more robust and easier to maintain. Again, water and a mild detergent make cleaning a fiberglass roof very easy. A regular floor mop or microfiber mop make the job even easier. When cleaning is completed, it is a good idea to apply a UV protectant. Many owners of fiberglass roofs use a marine wax that contains UV inhibitors. There are options on the material to use, but applying a UV product will help the roof last many years. Cracks in solid fiberglass roofs often appear during the cleaning process as brown or black lines that don't seem to clean off. That's is because the dark lines are dirt trapped inside the cracks. Repairing fiberglass roofs appropriately takes special processes and materials. Should you discover cracks in a fiberglass roof, consult a Certified RV Repair Specialist with expertise in this area of repair. It is not as simple as sealing over as the fiberglass area will continue to move and flex, ultimately allowing the crack to grow and worsen.

Protecting your RV roof

On RVs with rubber or fiberglass roofs, applying a specific UV coating to the roof during the cleaning process is a great benefit. The ultimate treat for a RV roof, however, is to keep it out of the elements while not in use. If you live in or use your RV full-time, clearly this does not apply to you. However, there is nothing worse than using your RV for 6 weeks out of the year, and then leave it to sit out in the elements during the remaining 46 weeks of a year.

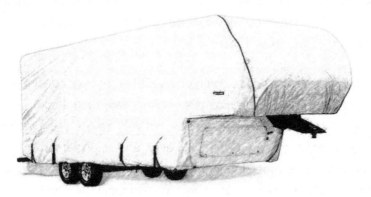

Figure 37 Illustration of fabric RV cover, which provides protection for RV roof from sun's damaging UV rays. Although they can be a pain to install, a cover can provide significant long-term savings.

You can greatly increase the service life of your RV by keeping it out of the direct sunlight while it is being stored. Keeping it out of the elements all together is ideal, but just by providing a cover over the roof will add tremendous benefit. No single option works for everyone in this regard so do your own research and determine what works best for you and provides the best cost/benefit analysis. Options include renting a covered storage facility, erecting a canopy cover, or purchasing a fabric cover for your RV.

Tires

Where the rubber meets the road—figuratively and literally. There are many ways to RV "on the cheap;" in fact, there's a series of books on that very subject. Safety-related items are not one of the areas where you should try to pinch pennies. Having good tires on your RV could be the difference one day between adventure and disaster. Your tires are your footprint on the road. In fact, your tires are your **ONLY** contact with the road, so they deserve and demand that particular attention be paid to their condition and serviceability.

Before every trip, check your tires for signs of damage, cuts, bulges, etc. Check each tire's air pressure, making a note if a tire requires air. If that tire requires air next time you check it, the tire has a problem that must be addressed.

Check each wheel for signs of damage, dents, scrapes, or rust, as well as the lug nuts for proper torque. To some, that may sound over-the-top, but trailer wheels are put through enormous stresses and lug nuts can work themselves loose over time. It takes five minutes to check and ensure your safety, and every manufacturer suggests this check in their manuals.

Lastly, tires, like your RV roof, hate exposure to the sun. Tires are actually manufactured with UV inhibitors in the rubber compounds but, over time, nothing is a match for the sun's harsh rays. Tires exposed to sunlight and ozone deteriorate at a much faster rate than those stored in cool dry areas or under protective covers. While it seems counter-intuitive, avoid using tire dressings. These products contain petroleum bases and other chemicals that actually will accelerate a tire's aging process. While in storage, using tire covers is an outstanding and inexpensive means to safeguard your tires. Chapter 15 provides additional information on tires.

Seams and seals

RVs, because of their increased size and production methods, may contain many seams across the sidewalls, roof line, floor, and other areas. RVs contain hundreds of seals of every conceivable size and shape that safeguard everything from antenna penetrations to side windows and doors. These seams and seals need constant attention to keep them from drying out and leaking as they naturally degrade over time.

Sidewall seams can be filled with outdoor and marine-quality sealant, which will ensure that water is not penetrating the sidewall panels. Seals and swipe seals on RV slide-outs should be lubricated continuously. Either a good-quality dry lithium spray or a graphite spray works very well. Aside from keeping the seals pliable, lubricating them periodically keeps them from heating up and adhering to the RV slide as it slides out to deploy.

Water infiltration is about the worst thing you can allow to happen to your RV. Check frequently and maintain window and door seals, panel joints and seams, baggage or service door and connector penetrations, or anywhere else sealant may have been applied.

Lubrication

Keeping the various moving systems and components on your RV lubricated is an important step. Knowing how to lubricate all these parts and pieces is just as important. Machine shop types will tell you that a little lubrication goes a long way. Too much lubrication simply creates a mess and attracts dust, debris, and grime. Don't over lubricate. Also, ensure that you use the correct type of lubrication. Many RVers like dry silicone-type lubricants because they are easy to use, and contain no oily residue to attract dust and grime.

Slide room mechanisms, gears, and roller plates all need to be lubricated to keep them operating smoothly. Your hitch is another, often overlooked, component that needs lubrication. Whether it's some hitch ball grease or greasing the zerk fittings on a fifth-wheel plate, don't forget to keep them lubricated per the manufacturer's instructions and guidelines.

Safety items and plan

Your RV should be equipped with a series of safety devices to keep you and your family safe while living in your RV. These include smoke detectors, LP Leak Detectors, and Carbon Monoxide Detectors. In some RVs, these detectors may be combined in some fashion. Check your detectors every trip. If they have a test function, test them. If they are battery operated, change the batteries at a set point at least once a year. Batteries are cheap!

168

Consider purchasing a LP Leak Detector Wand. These battery-powered wands can detect gas leaking from LP tanks, pipes, hoses, and appliances. You can also check for LP gas leaks by using spray-on leak detector fluid, or even soapy water.

Regularly check your fire extinguishers. Do you know how to use one? If not, find a fire station that offers a training class. They do it all the time, often for free, and many times will do it on the spot if you just ask. I'm from the school that you can't have too many fire extinguishers. Our fifth wheel unit came with two and I added two more. We also keep one of those aerosol kitchen extinguishers right next to the stove top. Cheap insurance and peace-of-mind.

If you pay attention to nothing else in this book, decide to not accept any of the advice, refute the stats and stories, please at least take and heed this simple offering: ***develop an emergency evacuation plan***. Even if it's just you alone, come up with a plan. Practice the plan. How would you get out of your coach if there was a fire between you and the door? Do the kids know what to do? Do the kids know where the fire extinguishers are? Do they know how to use them? Does your spouse know how to open the emergency window exit? Do you?

People are injured (and worse) every year in RV incidents that involve fire. Have an emergency plan. Decide where you all will meet during an emergency. Practice opening emergency windows. Know how to stay alive.

Slide-outs

If your RV has slide-out rooms, they need to be exercised, and the control drives, gears, or hydraulics need to be maintained per manufacturer's instructions. The awnings on the slide rooms (if equipped) need to be checked for proper operation as well. If you rolled up your awnings wet because it was raining when you departed your last camp site, as soon as you can, open up the slide and allow the awning materials to dry. Sweep debris (such as leaves and twigs) off before rolling up awnings. Slide seals, slide sweeps, and slide room seals need to be well lubricated to help prevent leaks and seal deterioration.

Batteries

Batteries take a lot of abuse and are integral to the RV working properly. Take care of your batteries so they can take care of you. If you have flooded wet cell batteries, check the electrolyte levels and add distilled water as necessary. Keep the batteries clean and the terminals treated with anti-corrosive conditioner. Monitor the battery cables for signs of damage or corrosion and replace as necessary. If you're going to store your RV over the winter, consider removing the batteries and storing them in a more controlled environment. Batteries have a finite life that, depending on how you use them, can be shortened considerably. Chapter 12 provides additional information on batteries.

Generator

Exercising your generator is important to keeping its operation in tip-top shape. Letting a generator sit for long periods, especially gasoline variants, is hard on the internals. Gasoline does not store particularly well, and within 30 days of purchase, gasoline begins breaking down[17]. Carburetors and fuel systems get varnished and fouled and will require maintenance (or even replacing parts) before the generator is able to perform to its intended purpose. Like other motors, generators need to be exercised, not just run. Refer to your generator owner's manual for complete details and specific guidance for your model. If possible, at least monthly, run your generator. Once it has warmed up, place the generator under a load by turning systems in your RV on to force the generator to work. Run the generator this way for at least half an hour and your generator will continue to be ready when you are.

Plumbing and tanks

Maintain your plumbing by following a few simple rules. Keep your water tanks (fresh, gray, and black) as clean as possible. Do not store your RV without cleaning the tanks. It is imperative that you clean and rinse the black tank before storage to ensure there are no solids or debris left in the tank which can harden to a "concrete like" consistency if left in the tank over time. Make sure to use single-ply, RV-specific toilet paper (chapter 11 provides additional information).

Clean your fresh water tank thoroughly before use each camping season by using a mixture of ¼ cup bleach to every 15 gallons of fresh water. Never rinse food off your dinner plates into the gray tank. Scrape your plates as clean as possible into the trash before washing. Food debris and grease will collect over time in the gray water tank and become nearly impossible to clean. Once this happens, the smell coming up from your gray tank will make you wish you had taken the effort!

Flush your water heater per the manufacturer's instructions. If you have a model with an anode rod, check the rod periodically and change as necessary. These rods are inexpensive and will keep your water heater from being attacked by harmful minerals.

171

Exercise

I've referred to exercising the various systems in your RV since this book's beginning chapter. The exercise concept is important to ensuring you have a RV that will provide rest and relaxation instead of continual repairs and grief. Don't let any system in your RV sit for too long. If you store your RV for long periods, visiting your unit once a month for half an hour to exercise the RVs systems will pay dividends in the future.

Windows, doors, and screens

It takes only minutes to do, but can certainly save you frustration later. Check all your windows for signs of damage. Make sure that windows open, close, and latch properly. Check for fog or moisture if you have double-pane window systems. Check your screens and make sure they are not torn or damaged. Check your main entry door often to ensure that the latch and deadbolt work properly and that the alignment is correct. Give your main door a good tug to ensure the deadbolt engages correctly.

Electrical

Not everyone owns or knows how to use a multimeter. And that's ok. It does not, however, mean that you're off the hook for checking out your RV's electrical system. At a minimum, you should carry an outlet tester. These little devices are great to confirm that you have an electrical issue. Learn the difference between your AC and DC electrical systems (more in chapter 12), and know the locations of your circuit breaker and fuse panels. Learn the difference between the two. Get in the habit of carrying some spare fuses and light bulbs. Understand your RV charging system and the location of converters, inverters, and transfer switches.

Winterization

Winterization is a process that you must complete before putting your RV up for storage over the winter. Winterization ensures that no fresh water is trapped in the fresh water system which, if left to freeze, would cause significant damage.

Each RV has a specific winterization process, but there are options to the actual methods used. Many RVers use RV antifreeze and by using the on-board RV pump, force RV antifreeze through the entire water system, running it through the faucets, showers, and toilets. Doing this also ensures that antifreeze is forced into the J traps of the plumbing. Don't forget to drain the water heater as a freeze with water in the tank could be disastrous.

Interior care

This section is a bit of a catch-all but is, nonetheless, important. Keep in mind that your RV is just a mobile version of your permanent home. In fact, for many folks, their RV is their permanent home, so all the more reason to take impeccable care of it.

Every time you move your RV, consider the enormous forces and pressures exerted on it bouncing up and down the highway. It is a testament to their construction that they survive the trip at all. When you do move your RV, you should expect that something may need attention when you get where you're going. The trip may well have shaken something loose. It is important to attend to these things every time they are discovered. Don't allow something to remain loose; tighten as needed.

As an example, a light sconce that is slightly loose will continue to vibrate and shake more rigorously until it shakes itself right off the wall. Keep a screwdriver and a square RV bit handy, and tighten as you go. This also is true for items on the outside of your RV, like ladders, light fixtures, and awnings. Pay attention to everything mounted in and on your RV.

Hitches

Don't overlook your hitch assembly. Visually inspect the hitch each and every use. Check for damage and signs of stress. Inspect any chains and cables to ensure that they are in serviceable condition. Lubricate any portions of the hitch that requires it. Teflon™ plates work well for fifth-wheel plates, and you avoid the greasy mess. Inspect ball mounts for damage and rust and lubricate as necessary.

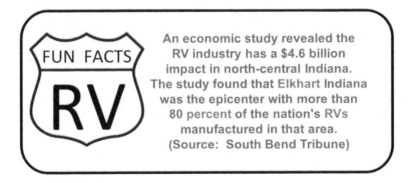

FUN FACTS RV

An economic study revealed the RV industry has a $4.6 billion impact in north-central Indiana. The study found that Elkhart Indiana was the epicenter with more than 80 percent of the nation's RVs manufactured in that area. (Source: South Bend Tribune)

Chapter Nine

Safety and Security

When it comes to RVs, the topic of safety and security is an awfully broad subject. In this chapter, covered topics include everything from keeping your RV safe at a campground, to keeping you safe while enjoying your RV. Awareness of all your RV systems—electrical, propane, water, and even chassis—are all key to ensuring a safe, enjoyable RVing experience.

More focused discussions of other issues, like RVs and firearms, are provided later in this chapter, and are intended to provide you with insight about knowing areas where you may wish to continue your research and find answers. As stated throughout this book, RVs are complex systems. The more you know about your RV, the more enjoyable your RV experience will be.

Safety systems

New RVs come filled with safety devices and appliances to ensure that you and your family are protected against often hidden dangers. If you have an older RV, you need to understand what your RV is equipped with and, if necessary, retrofit your unit to current standards. Never, ever compromise on safety. It is essential that you check your safety devices regularly and practice a few simple procedures designed to help protect you and your family. What safety devices should you be checking?

Smoke detectors

If your RV is not equipped with at least one smoke detector, then it is unsafe. Every RV should be equipped with at least one smoke detector in the bedroom area. For larger RVs, there should be at least one smoke detector in every living area that is separated by a door or partition. Smoke detectors should be battery powered (or battery backup powered) and mounted centrally and at ceiling height in the spaces they are intended to monitor. Smoke detectors come in essentially three varieties: ionization, photoelectric, and dual-sensor.

Ionization units normally contain Americium-241 and a small, air-filled chamber that includes two electrodes. A small current passes between these electrodes which, when disturbed by smoke particles, triggers an alarm. Ionization alarms are very popular and are excellent at detecting even the smallest amounts of smoke.

Photoelectric units contain a chamber that includes a light-emitting source and a sensor. When smoke enters the chamber, the light source is disturbed, triggering the alarm. These systems are generally better at detecting fire in its earlier, smoldering stage—the moments before actual flames appear.

Dual-sensor detectors contain both ionization and photoelectric units.

Some folks are annoyed by the sensitivity of the smoke alarms that are used in some RVs as they seem to always go off when you're cooking breakfast. Too often, people remove the alarm batteries with the intention of replacing them later. Never do that! If your smoke detector alarm annoys you when cooking, consider replacing it with a model that has a "silencing feature," a button that will allow the alarm to go into standby mode for 10 minutes or so before fully resetting.

Carbon monoxide detector

We've all heard of carbon monoxide, the tasteless, odorless, colorless killer. According to the Center for Disease Control (CDC), carbon monoxide is "found in fumes produced any time you burn fuel in cars or trucks, small engines, stoves, lanterns, grills, fireplaces, gas ranges, or furnaces." Carbon monoxide can, with little to no warning, build up to dangerous or deadly concentrations[18]. By design, RVs are fairly compact spaces where there are inherently several sources of carbon monoxide, including LP appliances, grills, coach or tow vehicle engines, and generators, to name just a few.

Fortunately, there are carbon monoxide detectors, and your RV should have one. Carbon monoxide is lighter than air, so carbon monoxide detectors should be mounted fairly high on a wall or on the ceiling. It is always best to follow the manufacturer's instructions.

Propane gas leak detector

Propane gas leak detectors provide the occupants of a RV with a warning when propane gas is detected in the sensor chamber. Some LP leak detectors simply emit an audible warning, while other units physically cut off the flow of LP gas through the use of a dedicated solenoid attached to the LP tank. Unlike carbon monoxide, LP gas is heavier than air, so the detector should be mounted fairly close to the floor. It is always best to follow the manufacturer's instructions.

LP leak detector wands are a handy appliance to have in your tool kit. They can be used to detect leaks at hose connectors and in tight spaces, are about the size of a small pen-light, and are available at all home box stores.

All detectors

Regardless of what type detector you have or choose to install, periodic maintenance is key. Each detector should have a process to test the unit. Using the instructions, test each device often. It takes only a moment, so test, test, and test again!

Most detector sensors have a limited life expectancy. Many brands now include a "replace by" date stamped on them. Make note of that date, and ensure that you replace the sensor before that date arrives.

Detectors must be kept clean from dust. To clean a detector, wipe it down, but never clean it by spraying compressed air or with cleaning products. Don't paint it or in any way obstruct its housing or chamber openings.

For LP leak detectors near the floor, periodically check for pet hair and carpet fibers. Come up with a schedule to change the batteries. Add changing batteries to your winterization checklist, and make sure to do it at least once per year. Consider changing all of your batteries on your first trip of the season, or on the same date (e.g., your birthday) every year. Read the directions for your device very carefully as they will contain the detail descriptions s for use, testing, and replacement.

Each of the specific sensors discussed has an Underwriters Laboratory (UL) specification for your reference. It is important to note that the product you choose should be designed for RV use.

UL References

- Smoke Detectors, UL 217, Standard for Smoke Alarms[19]
- Carbon Monoxide Detectors, UL 2034, Standard for Single and Multiple Station Carbon Monoxide Alarms[20]
- Propane Detectors, UL 1484, Standards for Residential Gas Detectors[21]

Weather radios

I consider a National Oceanic and Atmospheric Administration (NOAA) weather radio as a mandatory piece of RV safety equipment. A NOAA weather radio is simple to use and has preloaded channels for NOAA radio sites across the country. More importantly, once connected, it sits dutifully and listens in the background for emergency weather conditions, and provides an emergency alarm should a dangerous storm be approaching.

When arriving at a RV Park or campground, ask the camp hosts for the name of the county in which the park or campground is located as well as surrounding counties' names so you're at least familiar with them. Phone apps for NOAA alerts are available, many of which include live radar data so you be informed about any storms in the surrounding areas.

Fire safety

I mention elsewhere in this book that I'm from the school that you can't have too many fire extinguishers. Our fifth wheel unit came with two, and I added two more. We also keep one of those aerosol kitchen extinguishers right next to the stovetop.

Often, the manufacturer will provide a fire extinguisher adjacent to the main entrance door. That's great, but not enough. At a minimum, add fire extinguishers to your bedroom area and kitchen. If you're in a trailer, add one to the tow vehicle or basement of a motorhome. It's important to have one easily accessible from the outside. This will serve well for an emergency with the BBQ, generator, or neighboring RV.

National Fire Protection Association (NFPA) publication 1192, *Standard on Recreational Vehicles*, Section 6.4.1, "Provisions for Portable Fire Extinguishers," states that, "at a minimum, motorhomes shall be equipped with a 10-B:C extinguisher, while all other RVs are required to have a 5-B:C extinguisher"[22]. So now that you know what you need, what does that all mean?

Fire extinguishers are not one-size-fits-all. You should understand the differences and limitations of the different types of fire extinguishers. Fire extinguishers come in several classes, three of which are commonly found in RVs.

Class A extinguishers are for use with ordinary combustible materials, such as paper, wood, cardboard, and most plastics. Water or monoammonium phosphate are the most

Figure 38   Class A fire extinguishers are marked with green triangle.

commonly encountered materials used in these extinguishers. Exercise great caution when using a water-based extinguisher. Never use a Class A extinguisher on flammable liquids or kitchen fires as the water will simply spread the fire. Also, never use a water-based Class A extinguisher on an electrical fire or you run the risk of electrocution. Class A extinguishers are marked with a green triangle (Figure 38).

Class B fire extinguishers are for use with flammable or combustible liquids, such as cooking fluids, gasoline, grease, and oils. Class B fire extinguishers often contain either monoammonium phosphate or

sodium bicarbonate, which are both very effective in fighting fires involving combustible liquids. Class B extinguishers are marked with a red square (Figure 39).

Figure 39   Class B fire extinguishers are marked with red square.

Class C fire extinguishers are effective at combating fires involving electrical components, wiring, breakers, and outlets. Class C fire extinguishers use both monoammonium phosphate and sodium

ELECTRICAL

EQUIPMENT

Figure 40   Class C fire extinguishers are marked with blue circle.

bicarbonate together and are very effective in simply smothering a fire involving electrical components. Class C extinguishers are marked with a blue circle (Figure 40).

Multi-purpose fire extinguishers are now very common. Type B:C extinguishers are very common in the RV industry because of their ease of use and limited cleanup after use of the extinguisher. An extinguisher with an ABC rating would be considered suitable for use with fires involving ordinary combustibles, flammable liquids, and energized electrical components. A multi-purpose fire extinguisher should include a symbol for each hazard type.

Regularly check your fire extinguishers. Do you know how to use one? If not, find a fire station that offers a training class, which are conducted frequently, and often at no cost. Many Fire Stations will provide training on the spot if you just ask. To ensure that your extinguisher is ready in case of an emergency, periodically give your multi-purpose fire extinguisher a shake to loosen any dry-powder chemical material that has become packed down.

Now that you know about fire extinguishers, here's advice that seems contradictive. In case of fire or the smell of smoke in your RV, before you think about grabbing a fire extinguisher, first get everyone out of your RV! Don't think about using a fire extinguisher until you know for certain that everyone is out of the RV and in a safe location.

Fires in RVs can travel quickly with devastating results. Having fire extinguishers readily available for use in your RV is critical in the event of certain fire emergencies, like a fire on your stove or your outside grill, or other examples where your immediate intervention likely means the ability to safely extinguish a fire. Otherwise, if you encounter a full-blown fire emergency (e.g., fire is quickly consuming bedding, walls, furniture, etc.), don't try to fight the fire (a couple of hand-held extinguishers will be no match).

Some fire experts tend to classify fire extinguishers as tools to provide a safe corridor to help you escape, and advise you to leave the true firefighting duties to the professionals. Regardless, once safely out, stay out! Don't re-enter a RV that is on fire. There are too many hidden dangers, chemicals, batteries, fuels, and the list goes on. A fire can be traversing the basement area and not yet totally evident in the main living compartment. If you re-enter a RV in that situation, you run the risk of the floor failing and becoming trapped. The risks involved with attempting to save material things are definitely not worth re-entering a burning RV.

Pets pose a unique problem when discussing fires and evacuating a RV during an emergency. Pets can sense problems and anomalies and can become scared and seek their own safety by hiding in the RV. Imagine you're awakened by your fire alarm in the middle of the night with smoke, flame, and no lights. Your pooch, sensing that something was wrong, became scared and is hiding behind the jackknife sofa. You're disoriented, but you go about the work of getting your family safely out. What about the dog?

As a dog owner and lover, I'm going to simply tell you that fire experts, fire fighters, and safety professionals who have addressed the issue, without hesitation, say not to re-enter the RV to attempt a rescue. It may seem that the risk is slight, but again, when RVs burn, they can be engulfed with blazing speed. Also, combusting materials can put off toxic chemicals that can incapacitate you in short order. You should get clear of the burning RV and wait for emergency services to respond. Do nothing more than call for your pet from the door or window from which you escaped.

Pay attention to housekeeping and the manner in which you store chemicals, solvents, oils, charcoal, paints, and general cleaning materials. Some materials in storage can become dangerous when stored in proximity to other items. Simple charcoal used in the grill can spontaneously combust if the charcoal is put away damp. Cleaning rags and rags used to wax or detail your RV or perform engine maintenance should be discarded or stored elsewhere than in your RV.

Emergency evacuation plan

Have an emergency plan and review and test it often, especially if you RV with children. Make sure everyone knows how to get out of your RV in case of an emergency. Know where the emergency windows are and know how to use them. Consider testing how you would actually crawl out of a window in an emergency. It may sound a little dramatic, but interviews with families who have survived devastating fires in their RV's often include the acknowledgement that the family had an evacuation plan and that they tested it.

Ensure that everyone, including guests, knows how to work the door latches and locks. Have a rendezvous or rally point selected everywhere you stay. If the RV Park has an emergency storm shelter, make sure everyone knows its location.

Evacuating to an emergency shelter would be an intimidating experience, but would be less stressful the more prepared you are. Consider a "Bug-Out" bag—a small waterproof laundry-style bag that is preloaded with a few essential items which, in the event of an actual emergency, you could grab and "bug out." If you're taking any medications, consider keeping a pill case stocked with a few days' fresh supply. Keep a small flashlight in the bag and at night, put your keys and wallet in it. Then, in the morning, you know exactly where these items are; better yet, in an emergency, you know you have those items.

Electrical system safety

Remember that your RV is subjected to a lot of physical forces that are exerted on it while traveling from site to site. As such, it is not terribly uncommon for electrical wires to chafe or vibrate loose, or for electrical connections to fail. That makes it important for you to always be on the lookout for electrical anomalies. Ensuring your safety includes your RV's battery system and 120-Volt AC system. Check 12-Volt DC connections often as shorts in their wires are a source of a great many RV fires.

As mentioned in chapter 12, most RV Parks have 120-Volt AC power pedestals, which normally have connections that support the range of RV power requirements. Your RV will have a power inlet that is specific to the electrical capacity of your RV. This inlet may be located on the side of your RV under a spring-loaded cover, or it may be in a storage bay in the basement of your RV.

You will also have a power cord. To power your RV, you simply plug one end of the power cord into the RV power inlet and the other end into the electrical power source. Before plugging the power cord into a RV Park power pedestal, ensure that ALL circuits are in the OFF position. Inspect the pedestal for signs of damage or indications of burn or scorch marks. If you detect any signs of damage on the pedestal, I'd highly recommend asking a park attendant to verify the pedestals functionality before plugging your rig in. Testing the pedestal is NOT something you should do unless you specifically understand electrical circuits and the proper use of voltage meters. Remember, these pedestals carry enough electrical current to cause significant injury or death. If the pedestal appears in good condition, plug your cord in and switch on the appropriate circuit breaker.

Three popular items in RVers' tool kits are multimeters, outlet testers, and proximity testers. Multimeters require some understanding of electricity and electrical current and are invaluable for use in testing or troubleshooting electrical components. However, having a multimeter serves little purpose if you don't know how to use it.

Figure 41 Typical outlet tester.

Outlet testers on the other hand, require no electrical expertise at all. Simply plugging an outlet tester into an outlet will indicate whether the outlet is properly wired or if there is a wiring issue. Armed with this information, you could seek the appropriate electrician support.

Lastly, a proximity tester is a pen-like device that can detect the presence of AC electricity. This is a very useful device if you are concerned about the appearance of an RV Park's electrical pedestal and want to ensure that there is no stray electricity running through it. Open grounds, reversed polarity, or damaged electrical cords can wreak havoc with your RV, even allowing AC current to run across the metallic skin of an RV. **Important**: If you test the pedestal or other electrical hookups and find something wrong, do not continue to connect your rig. Immediately contact the RV Host to arrange for an electrician to check out the situation immediately. If the issue is on your side of the RV, contact a Certified RV Technician or electrician familiar with RVs. Never forget: electricity can be dangerous and if not respected, deadly. If you're not sure what you're doing or have limited background, never forget the most important tool in your toolbox: your credit card.

Propane system safety

Propane is a flammable gas, and you should exercise all due care and caution when dealing with it. Only fill your LP tanks with gas supplied by a certified LP vendor. This ensures that knowledgeable technicians fill your tanks properly and to the appropriate level.

There are two types of LP tanks in RVs: American Society of Mechanical Engineers (ASME) tanks (most often found in motorhome applications); and Department of Transportation (DOT) tanks (most common for use in travel trailers and fifth wheels. Newer LP tanks are equipped with an Overfill Prevention Device (OPD), which prevents tank overfilling. [23]

A DOT Pipeline and Hazardous Materials Safety Administration publication details the requirements for tank inspection and recertification. Currently, horizontally mounted ASME tanks (usually found in motorhomes) require that that the tank be visually inspected for damage every time the tank is filled. DOT-style tanks (commonly found in trailers) also require a formal inspection and recertification. The specifics for tank recertification are detailed in 49 CFR §180.205, which require DOT 4-series propane cylinders be requalified 12 years after their original manufacture, and every 5, 7, or 12 years thereafter, depending on the actual process used to inspect the tank at the 12-year mark[24].

Never use your LP stove to heat your RV, and never leave your stove or cooktop, unattended. **Open propane flames can create dangerous levels of carbon monoxide, so you should be constantly vigilant.**

Other components in the LP system that should be visually checked on a regular basis include the regulator, hoses, and connections. These components should be formally tested periodically by a Certified RV Technician, but certainly at any time there is a failure in the LP gas delivery system.

Travel safety

Before you set out on your next RV excursion, make sure you are prepared with the tools necessary to support you in the event of a breakdown. You can never have too many

Figure 42   A reflective triangle kit is useful for warning approaching motorists of a potential road hazard.

188

flashlights and keep batteries on hand in every size. Whether you have a trailer or a motorhome, you should have a set of collapsible warning triangles. Traditional flares, or the new generation LED flares are excellent choices as well. In the event of a breakdown, you need to be able to warn oncoming traffic at sufficient distance for them to slow and pass you safely. You should invest in a high-visibility mesh vest as well. A few dollars can mean the difference between being seen and being injured.

Maintain an adequately stocked tool kit, and make sure it includes a set of jumper cables. Weight is everything in RVing, so be creative when stocking a tool kit. Adjustable tools and multi-bit drivers can reduce the size and weight of your toolbox drastically.

Consider carrying a laser thermometer. This great tool is inexpensive and can provide an early warning to things like dragging brakes or bearings that are in the early stages of failure. To gain an instant temperature reading, simply point a laser thermometer at an object and pull the trigger. A laser thermometer is also handy for determining if your RV air conditioner is blowing cold air within specifications.

Be alert! Sounds simple, but it's more involved than you think. Focus on what you're doing. Clear your head of distractions. Don't allow yourself to be distracted while performing an inspection or operation. Distractions can possibly lead to situations such as electrical cords being ripped out; sewer hoses being dragged for miles; TV antennas being removed from the top of the RV by a tree branch; or worse. One of my favorite examples involves a friend who became distracted while connecting his TOAD to the back of his motorhome. While getting everything hooked up, he became distracted and, hours later, while stopping for fuel, he discovered his TOAD idling. Don't get distracted! Focus on the work at hand.

RV Security

Unfortunately, this is an area that is becoming more of a concern for RV owners. The stories of RVs disappearing from storage facilities and even from RV Parks or campgrounds are becoming alarmingly more frequent. Whether in storage or enjoying your favorite RV Park or campground, there are simple things you can do to limit your potential of becoming a victim.

Keep your RV locked and use the best locks you can get. Regardless what type RV you have, strongly consider upgrading the entry door lock, at a minimum. If you're not aware, the RV industry for some inexplicable reason (money) has chosen to use fairly simple locking mechanisms and with very few key combinations. The reality is that, your baggage door key likely fits a good number of other RVs in your RV Park or campground. I've seen too many examples to count where people have misplaced keys and asked a neighbor to open their door. There are companies that sell replacement entry door latches and locks. Again, consider upgrading yours, it is money well spent.

Get in the habit of locking your hitch, regardless of the length of your stay. Use a kingpin lock or a ball hitch coupler lock. Buy a good lock and try to purchase one that can't be cut with traditional bolt cutters.

I'm seeing more folks "boot" their RVs. These boots are just like the ones you see used in metropolitan areas for parking offenders. They are not very expensive and offer tremendous security for your RV. If you choose this route, ensure that you get a unit that fully covers the lug nuts for the wheel to which you choose to apply the boot.

Have your RV marked, and have the windows etched. Many police departments and insurance companies use various means to etch windows and other components with information that is easily identifiable to police in the event of theft.

For trailers, consider taking a wheel off and use a lug lock to prevent another wheel from being put on. This would require some effort, but it's an inexpensive and relatively sure solution.

Consider investing in an alarm system specifically designed for use in motorhomes and trailers. Motorhome alarms are very similar to traditional car alarms with a few more features, where trailer alarms are more like a brick-and-mortar alarm system. Regardless, alarms are a very effective means of deterring a criminal from hanging around your RV.

Make your RV unique in some way. In the event of theft, it is easier for police to spot something that stands apart from the normal. I've seen special murals painted on the rear caps of motorhomes and special-order paint schemes to ensure a RV's unique appearance.

These options are fairly expensive, and many don't want to alter the appearance of the RV because one day, they may wish to trade it in. So, there are other inexpensive ways to personalize a RV's exterior but still offer a level of personalization that just may make a would-be thief keep on walking.

On both our motorhome and fifth wheel trailer, we used custom decal graphics placed around the entry door area, which I think is a simple, but effective level of personalization.

Motion lights are great for illuminating the area while folks are standing outside your RV, and would make a would-be thief feel nervous. Motion lights are a no-brainer for when you're camping, but require a little more thought for a RV while in storage. Self-contained, solar-charged battery systems can be placed on the roof of your unit while in storage, and require no drilling or involved installation.

High-tech solutions abound in this age of gadgets; pretty much, if you can think of it, chances are you can find it. Becoming more and more popular and reasonable from a price point are GPS tracking technologies. A self-contained GPS unit can be mounted in a number of places on a RV while still remaining hidden from a potential thief. Cloud-based cameras can be installed that capture high-definition photos of a thief and post them immediately to the cloud for later retrieval and viewing.

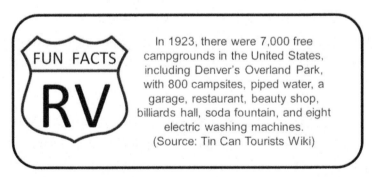

FUN FACTS RV

In 1923, there were 7,000 free campgrounds in the United States, including Denver's Overland Park, with 800 campsites, piped water, a garage, restaurant, beauty shop, billiards hall, soda fountain, and eight electric washing machines. (Source: Tin Can Tourists Wiki)

I've recently read of an individual who leaves an old cell phone hooked up in his RV that sends an SMS text message if it senses motion. As mentioned, in the high-tech category of theft prevention, you're pretty much limited only by your imagination.

Firearms and RVs

As a retired law enforcement officer, I'm fortunate to be covered under the National Law Enforcement Officers Safety Act (LEOSA), which allows me (with some restrictions) to carry a firearm across the country. I'm a gun owner and advocate that folks with the appropriate training (and whom otherwise qualify) should be permitted to own a firearm.

Owning a firearm comes with tremendous responsibilities. Firearms are extremely dangerous and, if used improperly, can result in devastating consequences. In my opinion, no person should own a firearm until he or she has been trained in its safe handling and the legal implications of its use.

With that all said, traveling in a RV with a firearm presents some challenges. By nature, the RV lifestyle is a mobile one, crossing city, county, and state lines with little effort. Laws concerning firearms and their legality for use in RVs vary from state to state. It is incumbent on you to understand the laws in the jurisdictions in which you travel. The old adage that ignorance of the law is no excuse certainly prevails as does the rule, "know before you go."

Some folks will defend their right to own and use a weapon to their last breath, and that's fine. I'm going to move on with this final thought. If you use a weapon, even if you do everything right and in full accordance with the law, you'll likely still find yourself facing many legal challenges and years of litigation. It's the world we live in.

By definition, carrying a loaded firearm and transporting a firearm are two completely different things, and you need to understand the difference. While it is absolutely necessary for you to research the laws of the areas you will travel, it is generally understood that you can "transport" an unloaded weapon from one location to another as long as you are lawfully allowed to possess the weapon to begin with. Here is the text from Title 18, US Code, for the Interstate transportation of firearms:

> *Notwithstanding any other provision of any law or any rule or regulation of a State or any political subdivision thereof, any person who is not otherwise prohibited by this chapter from transporting, shipping, or receiving a firearm shall be entitled to transport a firearm for any lawful purpose from any place where he may lawfully possess and carry such firearm to any other place where he may lawfully possess and carry such firearm if, during such transportation the firearm is unloaded, and neither the firearm nor any ammunition being transported is readily accessible or is directly accessible from the passenger compartment of such transporting vehicle: Provided, that in the case of a vehicle without a compartment separate from the driver's compartment the firearm or ammunition shall be contained in a locked container other than the glove compartment or console.*[25]

It is important to differentiate between **carrying** a loaded firearm or weapon and **"transporting"** a weapon. Because laws vary so widely and, in some areas, change so quickly, it is not practical or reasonable to try and explain loaded firearms rules of the road in this text. Some references exist that state that your RV is the same as your permanent brick-and-motor home, and that you have the same provisions and protections as a permanent dwelling. Admittedly, I'm not an attorney, but I have stayed at a Holiday Inn and, from my research, if you're not hooked up to utilities at a RV Park, then (with very few exceptions) your RV is considered an automobile. The laws that cover carrying a loaded firearm in an automobile are vastly different from those that cover having a firearm in your home. In all seriousness, do your due diligence, research and read the latest laws for the areas in which you're going to be travelling.

Remember, your right to possess a firearm does not trump jurisdictional or private rules established to preclude firearms. If you're staying at a RV Park that has a no-firearm policy, and you have a firearm in your RV, you're simply wrong. Period. I can't stress it enough.

Firearms pose very unique challenges to the Rving community. In a survey by RVTravel.com[26], 40% of those folks who were interviewed on the topic reported having a firearm available in their RV while traveling. That's an amazing statistic, but I'm guessing it's actually higher as many folks will not discuss the topic of firearms and RVs when asked. Again, the consequences for getting this wrong can be extreme, so research, read, and research some more.

Two excellent sources of information on the subject are the website, gunlawsbystate.com, and the *Travelers Guide to the Firearms Laws of the 50 States*, which is updated and published annually.

Chapter Ten

Personalization—Making it Your Own

This chapter was not originally one that I thought would be important to include but, over the past year, the number of folks I've talked to about ways to personalize their RV led me to add a few thoughts here.

Deep down, I think most people want to be at least a little unique and not just disappear into the landscape of what's around them. Standing out in the world of RVs, where so many RVs tend to look just like the one parked next to it, can be more than a little challenging. We've visited several RV Parks where, if you told someone "stop by, we're down the way in the Keystone Montana," they might have a hard time finding you among half-a-dozen other Keystone Montana's parked nearby. That's certainly a consideration when you purchase a very popular model of RV. This very reason is why so many ask about what's involved with personalizing their coaches.

There are limitless options available to assist you in truly making your RV one-of-a-kind. We've seen families dress their coaches in beautiful digital wraps (like those you see advertised on big city buses), and we've seen some coaches hand-painted by folks that are either artistic geniuses or legally blind. We've been passed on interstate highways by a diesel pusher that looked like a pack of wild horses running, and a fifth wheel painted to look like an old World War II bomber.

Sure, there are lots of ways to personalize your RV, but I'm going to limit my discussion to slightly less imposing options. Remember, one day you may wish to sell or trade your current rig, so whatever changes or modifications you make now may have to be "appreciated" by a future potential buyer.

Personalizing your RV is a very personal endeavor and a challenge that can be very entertaining to pursue. Making it yours does not necessarily mean spending a bunch of extra money either. Making your coach "home" may not even require any monetary expenditure at all.

Inside

The inside of your coach should be comfortable, homey, and represent your personal preferences. Sure, there are little trinkets and doodads that the RV manufactures use to hold parts, pieces, and panels together that may not be to your fashion at all, but they are important for holding things together nonetheless.

Pictures

Pictures and picture frames are very personal and add a very personal touch to the coach. The shape or size does not matter—just that they're included. We removed

Figure 43 A canvas collage of family pictures becomes a conversation piece for visitors.

a hideous cardboard print from a wall in our fifth wheel and replaced it with a canvas print that I had made at Costco. The print was a collage of 70 family pictures (arranged in no specific order or manner) which, when added to the coach, has received comments from every single person who

Figure 44 Family pictures in frames along plain walls makes your RV more like home.

has stepped foot inside our RV. Other pictures throughout our RV help personalize it to us as well. Pictures don't have to be mounted to the walls, either. Have a few free-standing frames or picture magnets for the refrigerator door. Recycle one of those digital picture frames you had sitting around your home office. Dust it off, add some recent photos, and set it up next time you set up camp somewhere. We used an old piece of scrap wood from another project and roughly cut it out in the shape of our Class A motorhome.

Figure 45 Custom picture frame we made to resemble our motorhome using photos we printed on our inkjet printer.

Using a little paint and some photographs, we made a custom piece of artwork that was fun and cost virtually nothing. There's no limit to the creativity you can embed here.

Table Space

Most RVers are always looking for more table space. Consider adding a fold-up counter extension in your kitchen area to add a little more prep space. In our diesel pusher, I made this round table to fit on the steering wheel when we got

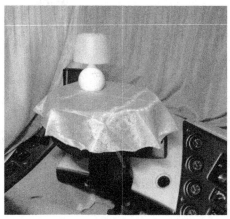

parked and set up. It turned out to be an ideal place to add a small table

Figure 46 Homemade tabletop that fit atop the coach steering wheel added convenient space for keys, and phones.

lamp, keys at the end of the day, and a place to put a flashlight for those early-morning "nature's calling" dog walks.

Pillows and decorations

Pillows and throws are a great way to add creature comforts to your RV but, with a little bit of effort, you can add something unique and fun. We added these travel trailer-themed pillows, which spark a lot of comments from guests.

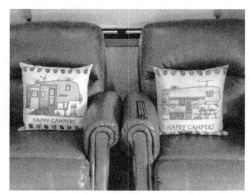

Figure 47 Have fun with your RV! We picked pillow covers that captured our mood.

Storage

Storage is always a commodity in RVs. For most folks, there's never enough. Big box and home improvement stores sell all kinds of plastic tubs, bins, and organizers, which can really help with the clutter and organization skills that I know all us RVers have. One of the best things we ever added to our motorhome didn't cost us a nickel. We converted a closet shoe storage organizer by mounting it on the back

Figure 48 A converted shoe organizer helped us store those small goodies that otherwise would be lost in a drawer somewhere forever.

wall of our bathroom. The individual clear pockets were a wonderful place to store small items, making it easy to locate them at a glance.

Fridge Magnets

I know you've all seen those decals on RVs where you add the State sticker for all the places you've been. I think a great variant on that is to collect refrigerator magnets for the places and sights you've seen. Can't find a magnet when you visit the World's Largest Pencil in Casey, Illinois? Then go to one of the office supply box stores and get either a roll of magnet tape, or an 8.5 X 11-inch magnet sheet, which are very thin and can be trimmed with standard household scissors. Take a photograph from your trip and make a refrigerator magnet. You can get magnetic pins, clips, and even fake picture frames.

Have fun with it

When it comes to personalizing your rig, your imagination is your only limiting factor. Keep in mind that your RV is just an extension of you, so have fun with it! Also, don't get it in your craw that you have to spend a lot of money to personalize your space. Much of what we've done over the years has been absolutely free, aside from some sweat equity. Take time when you're camping

Figure 49 This is our fifth wheel trash can. Seen any like it? Have fun fixing your rig up.

and pay attention to what other folks have done. Remember, imitation is the most sincere form of flattery. Take the ideas and concepts of things you see that you like and turn them into personal treasures.

Outside

Personalizing your RV on the outside may not necessarily enhance any of your creature comforts, but it is where you start distinguishing your coach from the ones parked next to it. Personalization should not equate to a capital outlay of funds, but it does require some planning and thought.

Signs and decals

Signs and decals are really easy to make and are a great way to distinguish your rig from the 30 others that look an awful lot like it. We had a graphics shop make the Boyer decal so that it looks like frosted glass, and we attached it to the small window next to our entrance steps.

Figure 51 Decal made to look like frosted glass.

Figure 50 We highlight our home state of New Mexico and have each of our dog's name on a bone.

Wooden signs are common around RV Parks, and we attach ours to the hitch of our fifth wheel with simple magnets. During our travels, we see murals, hand-painted decorations, and personalized artwork of just about every shape and variety. Again, it's whatever you want to do and however unique you want to make it.

Flags

When it comes to flags, we've seen just about every kind imaginable. Country flags, State flags, military flags, historical flags, sports team flags, and fun flags. We've seen some really creative flags, too. We saw one that was sewn to look like the motorhome it flew in front of and included the owners' names. We've seen dog paw flags and flags that we, frankly, never figured out. Flags are an easy way to personalize your rig and there are many simple ways to attach or hang them.

Lights

Lighting is becoming more and more of a "thing" these days. With the advent of LED rope lighting, which can be programmed with just about any color imaginable, these lights are showing up everywhere. LED pathway lighting is very popular and adds a little something outside your door, as well as helps you see at night when it's time to take the puppies out. I think the most interesting lighting attraction we've seen was a fellow who had programmed his lights to music— very impressive and, if you've got the time and talent, why not?!

Lawn statues

A lot of folks carry small statues with them. Some have names engraved or carved, and some simply say "welcome" or "home is where you park it." There are gnomes, elves, pets, and other various figures to admire. Frogs seem popular and, on a trip to the Arizona desert, we saw a giant buzzard that was rocking back and forth on top of a longhorn skull—as clever a lawn ornament as I've ever seen, and that's the point. Everyone who passes their rig will likely commit that buzzard to memory!

Personalizing your RV should not be something you dread doing. If it is, then pass up the effort and move on to something else. If you are indeed one of those that wants to stand out (even just a little), then this is a great place to make that happen. Again, it does not take a mortgage payment to be creative. It takes you deciding what it is you want to show and making it happen, in your own unique way.

Personalizing your rig is also specific to those things that make you comfortable on the road. Just because something came with the RV when you purchased it does not mean that it must always remain in the RV, with some exceptions of course. Virtually any and everything in your rig can be tailored to your needs and wishes. Have fun with it. Remember, it only needs to work for you.

April is the most popular camping month followed by August, September, June and July.
(Source: RVEscape.com)

Chapter Eleven

RV Plumbing

Plumbing in RVs is very similar to plumbing in traditional homes. There are, however, some notable differences and things that you need to know to keep your RVing experiences pleasant. This chapter focuses more on traditional RVs (i.e., travel trailers, fifth wheels, and motorhomes). This is not to say that camper slide-ins or pop-ups don't have plumbing of their own; it's just not to the scale of more traditional, larger RVs. For many folks, the appeal of RVing is the ability to travel virtually anywhere and be self-contained. Many RVs offer the ability to "get off the grid" and be disconnected from the hustle and bustle, while still enjoying the conveniences to which we've grown accustomed—conveniences like refrigerators, cooktops, showers, and toilets.

Most RVs are configured to support this ability to "be one with nature," at least for a while. At some point, you have to "plug-in" to some degree.

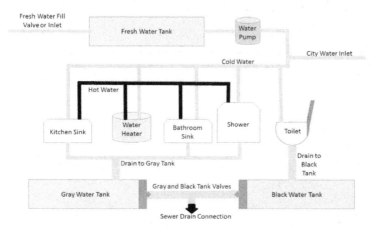

Figure 52 Typical RV plumbing system.

Figure 52 is an illustration of a very generic RV plumbing system to help prime your questions and allow a point of reference to come back to as we get further along.

(Note: When trying to diagnose a specific plumbing problem in your RV, it is important to have an actual plumbing schematic specific to your RV make and model for reference.)

Water

Water: We all need it! So where in your RV does it come from? Where does it go? Where is it stored? How much is available?

Fresh water

There are two ways to get fresh water into your RV.

City Water Inlet

Often, RVs are connected to a water spigot, either at a RV Park, storage facility, or other location; this type of connection is often referred to as the "City Water" connection, or inlet. To use the city water inlet, you simply connect a DEDICATED fresh-water hose from the spigot to the city water inlet of your RV. Why did I capitalize dedicated? Because it is critically important that you use a clean water hose—

Figure 53   City water inlet on outside wall of RV.

one specifically produced for drinking water—and that you use it ONLY for this purpose. There are many uses for hoses in and around your RV, and some of those uses are for dirty jobs (use your imagination). Don't run the risk of cross-contamination and making you or your family ill.

Dedicate specific hoses for specific tasks, and have at least one fresh-water hose that is used only for fresh water. When you're connected to a city water inlet, your fresh water is provided through that fresh-water source. In this configuration, you essentially have an unlimited supply (I say unlimited for a couple of reasons). Some RV Parks utilize well water and are not connected to municipal supplies, so water availability (specifically, water pressure) can become an issue at times.

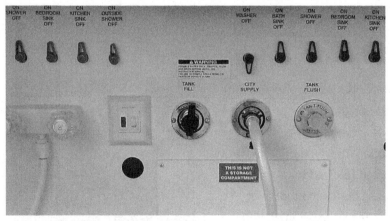

Figure 54   Plumbing command center in a Class A diesel
(note individual manifolds, tank fill, city feed, and sanitary flush inlet).

Fresh-Water Tank

If you're not connected to a specific water source, then you must have the water you're going to need and use, onboard. Prior to departing on your trip, you'll need to connect to a city water source and fill your fresh-water tank, which becomes your fresh water supply while you are on the road.

City water systems are pressurized. When you're using your fresh-water tank, you'll need an onboard water pump to supply that needed pressure. Most likely, somewhere in the bowels of your RV, you'll have a 12-Volt DC water pump connected very close to the fresh-water tank. When you turn on a faucet or flush the toilet, the water pump will engage and pressurize the system. When the demand for the water stops, the pump should stop. This is a very basic example using a water pump. Many RVs have an air accumulator that keeps an eye on the water pressure and cycles the pump as necessary to keep the water pressure very stable.

Gray water

Gray water refers to the "used" water in your RV that comes from everything except your toilet. Gray water is from your kitchen sink, bathroom sink, shower, dish washer (yes – some RVs have them), and washing machine. Gray tanks are normally fairly close to the size of the fresh-water tank, depending on the available space.

The gray-water tank is molded specifically with a low point to ensure that the tank drains quickly and completely. The gray-water tank is equipped with a waste gate valve—usually a valve that has a handle that you pull to open the gate and drain the tank.

Black water

Black water is the one part of RVing that no one wants to spend time dealing with or discussing. If you've ever known an RVer who would admit to having an accident while dumping a black-water tank, you'll immediately understand. If you've ever seen the Robin Williams movie, "RV," you'll certainly understand. If neither apply now, one day you'll understand.

Black water refers to the waste specifically from a RV toilet. Like the gray-water tank, the black-water tank is molded with a low point and have its own specific waste gate valve. More and more, black-water tanks are equipped with a fresh-water cleanout inlet, which is a hose attachment that allows you to connect a hose (**NOT YOUR FRESH-WATER HOSE**), and use fresh water to rinse out your black water tank. This is an important feature to help ensure that "sludge" does not build up and damage your tank or tank level sensors.

Plumbing

The actual plumbing in a RV is most often some combination of PVC pipes and PVC (or Pex) flexible lines. It's important for the system to have some "flexibility," keeping in mind that these portable homes have to travel up and down our road system. Smaller RVs often have very simple water connection points for both fresh water and sewer.

Larger RVs often have more dedicated water management systems, which may be located in dedicated basement bays. These systems may include complex manifolds to control which water lines are charged, and may also include multiple dump valve controls.

Anderson valves are also common in these universal docking centers and are normally located with the city water inlet.

Figure 55 Typical Anderson valve; allows City water source and has tank fill, tank use, and sanitize settings.

Sinks

Sinks are pretty straightforward in the grand scheme of things, but they vary wildly based on the RV in which they are installed. Mini RVs, like slide-ins and some pop-ups, share a single sink for all needs. This single sink may be a small, stainless-steel bowl with a small water spout and a hand pump for the water.

Large, luxury diesel pushers may have several sinks, including porcelain sinks in the bathroom with extravagant faucets and elegant fixtures.

Kitchen sinks often include farm-sinks with pull-down faucets; some kitchen sinks even have touch controls. With few exceptions, sinks drain into the gray water tank. I've stated this warning before, but it bears repeating: **do not place food into your kitchen sink drain**. Scrape whatever food or items remain on your plate into the trash. Food that does go down the sink drain often solidifies in the gray-water tank and, over time, an unpleasant odor will begin. Once any food or other items go down a sink drain into a gray-water tank, they can begin to build and solidify. Getting it cleaned out can become a very laborious task.

Shower

Like your RV sink, the shower, for most, is fairly straightforward. In mini-RVs, the shower may have a seat in it which, upon closer inspection, is actually the toilet. Yes, in some designs, all the bathroom fixtures are in the shower! For everything above the minis, the shower is pretty much the same as your shower at home, with the exception that the showerhead may have a trigger control on it to start and stop the water flow. This is a wonderfully useful feature for those boondocking, as it saves a tremendous amount of water (more on boondocking later). Just like sinks, the shower water drains into the gray-water tank.

Toilets

The toilet is the fixture that is most different from what you're accustomed to at home. There are a handful of different designs available for RV toilets: gravity toilets, electric flush macerator toilets, cassette toilets (removable waste tanks), and composting toilets. Each system is different and the type system you need greatly depends on what type of RVing you do.

Gravity toilets

The most common of these is the gravity flush system. Unlike sinks and showers, the toilet is connected to a separate tank (appropriately known as the black tank). Very often, the black tank physically sits directly below the toilet so that when

the toilet is flushed, the contents travel through a short pipe directly into the black tank. Seems simple enough. These gravity RV toilets do

Figure 56   Common gravity flush RV toilet system (flushed by pressing down on level with your foot).

differ from residential toilets in a few ways. Most notably, RV toilets do not have a water tank to flush the contents of the toilet. Instead, most gravity RV toilets use a foot pedal attached to a water valve and a ball valve in the bottom of the toilet bowl. When the foot pedal is depressed, the ball valve opens, allowing the contents in the toilet to drain into the black tank, and the water valve opens to rinse the toilet bowl. Once the bowl is rinsed, releasing the foot pedal closes the toilet ball valve and stops the flow of water. By depressing the foot pedal only slightly, you add a little water to the toilet bowl to ensure the ball valve seal remains wet, thus ensuring a good seal and preventing sewer gas from entering your RV. This design has been around for many years and is amazingly robust and reliable. These toilets are also very water efficient, which is, again important for boondocking.

Electric flush macerator toilet

Some higher-end RV units are equipped with electric flush mechanisms and a macerator, which is an inline blender (poor description) that takes the waste and blends it (worse choice) into a more manageable end product before dumping it into the black tank. Macerator toilets are not the same thing as macerator sewer lines, although they are based on similar concepts.

Cassette toilets

Cassette toilets are often installed in truck slide-in campers and some smaller towables. A cassette toilet is essentially a hollow bench with a self-contained toilet, which allows a "cassette" to

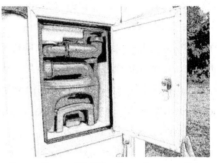

be plugged in from the outside of the camper. This cassette is the same as the black tank in other RVs. When inserted, the

Figure 57 Side view of a cassette toilet system. These usually mount to an exterior wall that allows the waste cassette to be removed and dumped.

cassette lines up to the bottom of the toilet bowl and captures each flush. These cassettes vary a little in size, but are generally about 5 gallons. Also inside the bench is a water tank (also about 5 gallons) that is used to flush the toilet. When the cassette is full, you simply remove it, wheel it to an appropriate dumping location, and empty it. Once emptied, you slide the cassette back into place and you're back in business.

Figure 58 Outside view of cassette mounted into cassette toilet base. When full, simply remove cassette and dump.

The 5-gallon water tank is also normally filled from the bay where the cassette is located. The beauty of this water is that it can be actual city water, bottled water, gray water, RV antifreeze (for those hardcore boondockers), or about any other liquid that is not corrosive to plastic, which is one of the reasons these are popular for those hell-bent to get off the grid.

Composting toilets

Composting toilets have been around for a very long time in various forms. These toilets are gaining some popularity in the RV world as they are ecofriendly (sort of), require almost no maintenance (sort of), and use no water. I'm oversimplifying significantly, but composting toilets are a lot like an indoor outhouse. Here is a brief overview of operation for one of the more popular units on the market.

A composting toilet unit can be installed in a RV bathroom in the same location as the original toilet by sealing and covering the original toilet's floor opening and installing the composting toilet in its place. The composting toilet has a 12-Volt DC fan and a vent hose, but nothing else really to worry about connecting.

Before using, and after each time that you empty a composting toilet, you must install a new collection bag, and add a few handfuls of pre-moistened peat moss. Then, simply close the composting toilet lid, and reattach the fan and vent.

To use, it is recommended that everyone "go" from the seated position. This is necessary as the urine is funneled out to a separate trap and this works more efficiently from a seated position. While I've not experienced it myself, I've read much on the subject and if you mix urine with the composting solids, you'll know in pretty quick order! Anyway, once the bag nears full, you open the unit, remove the bag, and dispose of it. You can either place the bag into a composting pile, bury the waste, or use any number of several other disposal methods. Some RV Parks we've visited actually had composting piles for use with these toilets in mind. A separate collection jug on the front of the unit collects the urine. When it nears full, you pull it out of the unit and dispose of the urine in a similar manner to disposing of the composted solids.

Composting toilets are not for everyone, that's for sure. But if your brand of camping involves at lot of boondocking, then you really owe it to yourself to give the composting toilet system a look.

As previously mentioned, using the RV sink and shower is just about like being at home, and the toilet is really simple once you've used it a few times. I find it funny but, after a weeklong camping trip, I find myself trying to flush our home toilet with my foot for a day or so once we return home. Remember, what's different from your home is that you've got gray and black water tank to deal with.

Referring back to our plumbing diagram, the sinks and shower in your RV drain into the gray tank. Everything from the RV toilet ends up in the black tank. The type of RVing that you're doing will determine how you deal with these tanks. What I mean is, if you're at an RV Park with complete sewer hook-ups, your tasks are greatly simplified. If you're at a campground without sewer hook-ups, you've got a little more work to do. If you're boondocking, you have yet more to deal with.

Gray and black tanks

Regardless of how or where you're camping, you're going to have to deal with emptying your gray and black tanks. The majority of RVs, from mini travel trailers to the largest Class As on the road, have some kind of electronic tank monitoring capability. This simply means that there are sensors attached to the tank walls that sense how full the tanks are and provide that information to a convenience panel inside the RV. Some sensors are attached on the outside wall of the tanks, and some are internal. Regardless, if the tanks are maintained properly, these sensors should provide you with fairly accurate information. Some RVs have a simple access door that you open and, by taking a look at the sidewall of the tanks, you can determine how full they are. It's a pretty foolproof method, just not a very convenient one.

Like so many things in this book, there are exceptions to the norms, and this area is no different. Normally, a RV has one sewer attachment point; recently, I have seen some very large RVs, motorhomes, and fifth wheel trailers that have two. This makes the tasks of dumping a little more complicated, but as with everything, there are trade-offs. We're going to focus on units with one sewer connection because the process is the same.

The sewer connection is the point where the black and gray tank drain pipes come together. The gray tank and black tank will each have their own waste gate, controlled by some type of valve (most commonly, a mechanical blade valve).

The sewer pipe has a connection on the end that allows a flexible sewer hose to be connected. This connection, or attachment point, is most often a bayonet connection. These are very secure and reliable and, as long as you're paying attention, are virtually impossible to connect incorrectly. The end of the sewer hose then mates to the RV Park or campground's

Figure 59 Typical flexible sewer hose with 90 degree elbow drain attachment.

dump connection. These points vary greatly in design from screw-in PVC pipe fittings to simple holes in the ground that require that the sewer pipe be weighted down to properly drain.

Once the flexible sewer pipe is connected, it's a great rule of thumb to open the gray water drain valve, slightly. Allow a slow flow of gray water to drain through the hose just to validate that you've got everything connected properly and that the hose is not damaged in anyway. It also validates that the drain actually drains. If you didn't use this method and immediately dumped your black tank, a loose fitting, failed connection, rip in the hose, or clogged drain would instantly become a nightmare scenario. Once you're convinced everything is operating correctly, you can open the valve completely.

Toilet paper, wipes, and other unmentionables

Yes, we're going there! What you put in to your black tank can create a whole lot of drama for you later, so pay attention now and save yourself the aggravation. Not all toilet paper (TP) is the same, just ask your bum! In recent years, people have gotten very used to freshening themselves up with all kinds of scented, triple-ply, quilted toilet papers and flushable wipes. You may ask yourself, why not? If they are good enough for a baby's bottom, they are certainly good enough for mine!

The problem is that whatever you put in to your black tank has to eventually (sooner than later), come out. It has to pass through a fairly small waste gate valve to drain into a sewer fixture, and that's where the problem can build up. Literally. Whatever you put in to your black tank must break down or dissolve quickly so that it does not interfere with the dumping operation. Make sure family and friends know not to put anything (**ANYTHING**) into the black tank that's not "naturally" produced, or some form of toilet paper (not gum, paper, wrappers, or any other unmentionables).

Sounds simple enough, so why am I still writing? Because I know inquiring minds want to know more! For purposes of an example, I'm going to perform and document a simple experiment using two types of toilet paper and one brand of wipes. The purpose of the experiment is to demonstrate just how long it actually takes for these items to break down.

To perform the test, we're going to use three identical containers (simulating black tanks), each filled with 1 cup of water. Each container will have a tablespoon of a popular RV black tank additive that is advertised to help break down everything in the tank for

218

problem-free dumping. For the demonstration, I'm going to use the following in one each of the simulated black tanks: Scott's one-ply RV toilet paper; Charmin two-ply quilted toilet paper; and Cottonelle, Safe Flush/Septic Safe wipes. I'll use five sheets each of the toilet paper and one wipe. I'll add each brand to its own container and swirl the mixture around for 15 seconds and then let them sit. (Figure 60) There is a misconception that TP and wipes breakdown immediately – not true...

TIME	Scott 1-Ply RV Paper	Charmin 2-Ply quilted toilet paper	Cottonelle Safe Flush/Septic Safe Wipes
15 minutes	Already beginning to dissolve	Appeared to begin dissolving	No change from original
30 minutes	Container was milky white and paper was 50% dissolved	Beginning to breakdown, but was clumpy	No change from original
1 hour	Toilet paper was mostly dissolved	Breaking down, but appears to be clumping instead of dissolving	No apparent change
2 hours	Almost 100% dissolved	Slowly dissolving, but still formed large paper clump	No apparent change
3 hour	Totally dissolved	Still a large paper clump, slowly dissolving	Water is beginning to turn a little milky white
6 hours		Maybe 25% dissolved; paper is large clump on bottom	No real change from 3-hour mark
24 hours		Little change from 6 hours; still a large clump of paper	Wipe is almost in its original condition

Figure 60 Comically unscientific test to observe degree to which toilet paper and septic safe wipes dissolved (or not) over various time periods.

So what's your bottoms line? If running the risk of clogging the drain or getting something trapped in the waste valve is an acceptable risk for you, then use whatever your bottom likes!

If you want to ensure success when dumping your black tank, I'd recommend you use a good-quality, single-ply toilet paper like Scott's RV paper (No, I don't know anyone who works for Scott, and I'm not a paid spokesperson.) I'm just someone who does not want to have to drop my black tank to fix a clogged line or fouled waste gate.

Dumping with full hookups

If you're staying at a RV Park with full hook-ups, you'll have a sewer connection at your site. Once you connect your RV to the sewer drain and test everything as described in the previous section, you're set up. I like to keep the gray tank valve open all the time. This way, I'm not worried at all about how much water we're using. I can take a long shower or do laundry without any concern of the tank filling up.

The black tank is another story. You need to keep the black tank valve closed. Keep an eye on the tank sensor and when it hits the halfway mark, close the gray tank. When the black tank reaches three-quarters full, open the black tank dump valve and drain the black tank. When the tank is finished draining, close the valve.

The reason for closing the gray tank earlier is that now you should have a good amount of soapy water to rinse the sewer hose. Open the gray tank dump valve again, and let the tank drain. Repeat this process as long as you're camping in this configuration.

Clear hose?

This is not as bad as it sounds and remember, seeing is believing! I recommend using a clear plastic 90-degree elbow on your sewer connection where it connects to the ground, or a clear plastic 6- to 12-inch-long straight piece where it connects to the sewer outlet of your RV. It is extremely helpful to "see" how your dumping process is going. It is even more beneficial when it comes time to clean your black tank. With this clear section, you can continue to rinse the black tank until the water runs clear. Without a clear section of hose, you're only guessing if the job is really done or not.

Tank flush

I just mentioned flushing the black tank and what a great help having a clear section of hose is to monitor how that job is going. Many RVs come with water inlets attached to the spray nozzles inside the black tank. Periodically, you connect a garden hose (**NOT your fresh water hose**) to the inlet and turn the water on. The spray nozzles will wash down the sides of the black tank and remove debris left inside the tank. This process can take several minutes to thoroughly rinse the tank.

For those RVs without these spray nozzles installed, no worries. Rigid and semi-flexible hoses are available that are specifically designed to help out. These require a little more effort, but the grief you save in the end will make it all worthwhile.

To use these hose systems, get a garden hose into the bathroom, either up the hall or in through a window. Attach the wand to the hose and open the ball vale of the toilet. Then, lower the wand down toward the black tank and turn on the water. High-pressure nozzles work the same way as the built-in ones. Again, this process takes time, so be patient and have someone watching the clear section of sewer hose so you know when you're finished.

Tank capacities

For purposes of example, I provide fresh-water, gray-water, and black tank specifications from four different models from the 2016 Forest River RV lineup: 1) a RPod RP171 (a small travel trailer); a Cedar Creek Silverback 331K (fifth wheel); a Forester 2861DS Class C motorhome; and a Berkshire 38A (diesel pusher). These examples and comparisons will help you align your needs with the tank capacities generally available in production units.

So, if you want to try boondocking, how long can you realistically plan for? How much water can I carry in my RV? Using our four example models, the capacities vary considerably.

RV Model	Fresh Water Capacity
RPod RP171 travel trailer	36 gal
Cedar Creek Silverback 331K (fifth wheel)	67 gal
Forester 2861 DS Class C	44 gal
Berkshire 38A (diesel pusher)	86 gal
RV Model	**Gray Water Capacity**
RPod RP171 travel trailer	35 gal
Cedar Creek Silverback 331K (fifth wheel)	80 gal
Forester 2861 DS Class C	39 gal
Berkshire 38A (diesel pusher)	66 gal

RV Model	Black Water Capacity
RPod RP171 travel trailer	35 gal
Cedar Creek Silverback 331K (fifth wheel)	40 gal
Forester 2861 DS Class C	39 gal
Berkshire 38A (diesel pusher)	42 gal

Winterization

Winterizing your RV takes many forms, but in this section, refers specifically to winterizing the plumbing system of your RV. For those not lucky enough to follow the sun in their RVs year-round, fall brings cold weather and, sadly, the end, for many of us, to the RV season.

To keep your RV investment protected from the damaging effects of a hard freeze, it is important to winterize your plumbing system. This section covers the basics and attempts to hit the points that will affect the majority of readers, taking into consideration that all RVs are not created equal.

Once the temperatures start routinely getting down near freezing, it's time to winterize your RV. The first step in the winterization process is to determine if your RV is set up for winterization from the factory, or if you are going to have to take matters into your own hands. I consider that a RV is setup for winterization if it includes two things: 1) the RV's plumbing is set up with a water heater bypass system; and 2) if the RV is set up to use the water pump to draw water from a stand-alone source. If the RV meets these two criterion, then winterization will be a quick and fairly straightforward process.

If you don't have one or either of these features, not to worry. Ready-made kits are available to help convert your RV for this process or, as previously mentioned, you can complete the job yourself with a little more leg work.

The most common process for winterization is to use RV-specific antifreeze. Other folks use a method using air. By connecting a compressor to a special hose adapter, you can force air through your plumbing lines which (at least in theory) will force all the water out of the lines. Folks who use this method, swear by it. I both have used it and have seen it demonstrated. My experience is that it is very difficult to get all the water out of the water lines by pushing air through them. The concern is that if you don't get all the water out, whatever water is left will eventually collect in a low point or valve, and then freeze and damage that component. You also have to be careful how much air you use, you must open the valves in the RV in the proper sequence to get the water out, and there are some additional considerations.

To ensure proper winterization and reduce the risk of damage, I believe that the far more foolproof method is to use RV antifreeze and, therefore, will discuss that process in detail. Our 38-ft motorhome and 43-ft fifth wheel used just about four gallons of antifreeze to completely winterize each.

To begin, drain all the tanks on your RV. Pay particular attention to the gray and black tanks, and ensure that sure they are thoroughly clean before putting the RV away for the winter. Drain the fresh-water tank by opening the low point drain. If you can use your RV jacks to tilt the RV to help ensure that the fresh tank drains completely, that's a plus.

Ensure that your water heater heating element or gas supply is turned off. Heating the tank with no water in it will cause the tank damage.

Drain your water heater (*CAUTION: DO NOT* drain your water heater until the water inside has had a chance to cool to ambient temperatures; **DO NOT** remove the drain plug while the tank is under pressure). Locate the pressure relief valve and open it to remove pressure from the tank, and remove the drain plug. On some brands of water heaters, the drain plug is also an anode rod. If this is true for your model, inspect the anode rod and replace if necessary. Don't skimp here. The anode rod protects your tank. It is normal to see debris (i.e., scale, small minerals, lime, and other materials) drain from your water heater. Once the water heater tank is drained, I recommend using a tank cleaning water wand to rinse the tank out and remove any remaining debris or deposits.

Evacuate all water in the water lines by opening both the hot and cold water valves.

Flush the toilets until there is no water left in those supply lines and don't forget to evacuate any water in hand sprayers, if so equipped.

Drain your outside showers and sinks if equipped.

Check your RV for what are called low point drains. On many RVs, there are drain values at the lowest part of the plumbing system (hot and cold sides). If your RV is so equipped, open those valves. After a few minutes, there should be no more water draining. At this point, close all the drains valves you opened and close all the faucets.

Water heater bypass setting or control valve

Check your water heater for a bypass setting or control valve. They are installed in a number of ways. Many RVs have a control valve in the utilities cabinet marked "hot water heater bypass valve." This option could not be simpler. You merely rotate to handle and the water system is in bypass mode. Many manufacturers still install

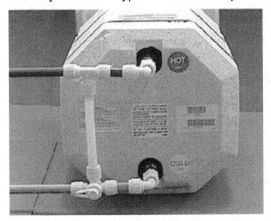

physical control valves on the rear of the water heater, and there can be single valve or multiple valve variants. (Figure 61 shows a single bypass valve version.) Simply rotate the valve to the 12 o'clock position and water bypasses the water heater.

Figure 61   The bypass valve is sometimes located on the back of the water heater tank.

Depending on the plumbing, there may be another valve on the hot side to turn. Hopefully, your RV owner's manual will detail what you have. If not, a short series of experiments will determine what setting the valve needs to be in to keep water from entering the water heater tank.

Previously, I mentioned that if your RV did not have a bypass kit, kits were available. Why would you want one? Pretty simple. At this stage of the

Figure 62 Common water heater bypass switch used in RVs.

226

winterization process, you're ready to start adding antifreeze to your unit. Without a water heater bypass, as you add antifreeze, it will want to fill the water heater tank first. If you have an 8-gallon water heater tank, you're essentially wasting 8 gallons of antifreeze. In simple terms, that's why a bypass is worth the effort to plumb in if you don't have one. I've read many stories and talked to several 'ole timers who disconnect the plumbing from the water heater and "cap" it temporarily while performing winterization. If you're going to the trouble of disconnecting and capping water lines, install a kit!

If your RV is equipped with water filters, remove the filters and discard them. Next season, install new water filters after flushing your system with a bleach water mixture.

Next, pump RV-specific antifreeze into your water lines. The preferred method of doing this would require that your RV's water system have a valve that uses the water pump to draw fluid from a stand-alone source. This can be in the form of an Anderson type water valve, or can be as simple as a valve at the water pump itself. Either way, the water pump will have a short length of hose that you can simply drop into an open RV-specific antifreeze jug.

Once the pump is turned on, the water system will start pumping the antifreeze. Over the years, I have found it easiest to fill up a 5-gallon plastic paint bucket with antifreeze and drop the hose into the bucket. This way, I don't require any help with someone outside swapping antifreeze jugs when they empty, nor do I have to run in and out.

What if your water pump isn't already set up to do this? No problem. This is very simple to solve. Purchase a pre-made kit, or plumb one in yourself. Simply tap the water line that comes from the fresh-water tank to the water pump. Insert a T-bypass-valve here, then select to draw water from the fresh water tank (normal position), or to draw from a stand-alone source (winterization method). I've done this mod for a few folks and it's as simple as it gets.

If you don't want to tap into your water lines, an even simpler method is to simply remove the hose from the suction side of the water pump, then temporarily replace that section of hose with a small section of hose that you can use to pump the antifreeze from the jug into your plumbing.

Having the ability to draw your antifreeze directly into the pump is fairly important. I have talked to some folks who pump antifreeze into the fresh tank and draw from there. Please don't do that. While it may not be dangerous, there's no reason to do it that way. If you don't feel comfortable adding the valve, use that handy tool in your wallet again and pay to have one professionally installed. I've talked to several Mobile RV Repair guys who will install the units for parts plus 30 minutes of labor. Remember, you can temporarily add a hose to the pump and then remove it when winterization is complete. The beauty of having this bypass is that now, when you're preparing your RV for a new camping season, you can use a mixture of water and bleach to sanitize the water system.

Next, pump RV-specific antifreeze into the system. Turn the water pump on, ensuring that the water pump hose is inside a full antifreeze jug or bucket of antifreeze. Starting at the closest valves to the water pump, open the hot and cold valves. Run the cold and hot valves separately until nothing but antifreeze is flowing from both. Run enough additional antifreeze to fill the drain trap with antifreeze. Close the hot and cold valves and move the next water valve. Repeat the process at each water valve until you have completed them all.

Run the toilet and spray wands until pure antifreeze is present. Run the showers, inside and outside. If you have a dishwasher and/or clothes washing machine, look in the owner's manual for specific instructions. Likely, the process will be to run a short cycle which will ensure the lines and pumps for the appliances will be adequately protected.

Residential refrigerators

This discussion point gets a lot of debate. I have a residential refrigerator in our unit, and I do not run RV antifreeze into the system. For winterization, I close the water valve source and, using the water dispenser, I run it until the system is purged. I just don't want to have to sanitize the system. Some folks disagree and that's OK. You decide what you're comfortable doing, the process is the same as described.

Once all the valves have antifreeze flowing, your water line winterization is complete. The amount and combination of water and antifreeze that has been dumped into both the gray and black tanks will ensure that the waste gate valve is protected.

To ready your RV for next camping season, simply reverse this process. Use a mixture of ¼ cup bleach to every 15 gallons of fresh water to sanitize the system. Use the water pump in the same method as you did to add antifreeze to the system. Open and run all the taps, including faucets, shower, dishwasher, and clothes washing machine. Run the water until you can smell a faint odor of bleach coming from each faucet. Also add some of the water and bleach mixture to the fresh-water tank to sanitize the fresh water tank. I personally like to add about 10 gallons of the bleach mixture to the fresh tank, drive around for a few miles to splash the mixture all over the tank, and then drain it. The more thorough your sanitization process, the safer your water supply for your upcoming camping season will be.

Water filters

Inline filters

Not all RVs are installed with water filters. Many require that you use an external, in-line water filter attached to your fresh-water hose. These systems are fine, work well, and are easy to maintain; however, some restrict the supply of fresh

Figure 63 Typical inline water filter connects between the RV and the water

water to the RV. When selecting an external filter system, pay attention to the water flow and micron rating of the filter. The smaller the micron rating, the tighter the filter is and, usually, the more restrictive the filter will be.

Cartridge filters

Many RVs have cartridge water filter systems installed with the cartridge filters located in the basement area of the RV or in the water distribution center. These cartridge systems are different in that they use a disposable cartridge that, when it needs replacing, you simply unscrew the cartridge and replace the filter cartridge. Again, these systems can be restrictive, so pay attention to the filter type you are selecting and the specific ratings of

the filter.

Filter types

Figure 64   Canister systems have removable canister that houses a replacement cartridge (usually located in basement area of RV).

If you have a cartridge-based water filtration system, you need to be aware that there are several types of filters that will fit into your cartridge. Most common of these include carbon, sediment, and combination cartridges. The carbon cartridges do a great job if your water tastes or smells bad. Sediment cartridges are good at removing small debris. Some people use a sediment cartridge in line before a carbon cartridge. Some dual filter systems come set up this way. There are also specialty cartridges produced specifically to remove certain kinds of metals in the water.

FUN FACTS

RV

There are more than 16,000 public and privately owned campgrounds nationwide (Source: RVIA.Com)

Chapter Twelve

RV Electrical

Electrical systems in RVs can be fairly complex to understand. This chapter provides an overview to help you get acquainted with the basics of RV electrical systems. Unlike other systems in your RV, the electrical system can pose quite a safety risk. For that reason, you must be extremely cautious when dealing with the electrical system, and use good judgement when making any connections or changes to your electrical system.

This specific chapter is one of the primary reasons I decided to write this book. Many times when researching issues, information on RVs was limited to the 120-Volt AC side of the system. I find that unfortunate as the electrical system in most RVs is much more complex than that.

Most RVs have a combined system of 12-Volt DC and 120-Volt AC power sources that makes everything electrical in your RV actually function. Many folks enjoying their RVs often do not know which side of the combined system actually helps to operate an electrical device in their RV. We'll attempt to clarify much of that confusion in this chapter.

I will address the 120-Volt AC and 12-Volt DC sides of the electrical system individually. If you're researching a rig, it will help determine your needs. If you already own a rig, it will help you understand how your electric system is configured.

The electricity in your RV can be supplied in a number of ways. The 120-Volt AC can be provided from the RV Park power pedestal, by a generator, or by on-board batteries through an inverter. The 12-Volt DC power is provided by converting 120-Volt AC power to 12-Volt DC power, or is provided directly from the battery. Today's RVs offer all of these configurations.

Alternating current, AC power

Let's begin with 120-Volt AC (commonly referred to as standard household current). Virtually all RVs use some form of AC power. The 120-Volt AC power can be generated by either an on-board or a portable generator system (see chapter 13), by connecting directly to a 120-Volt AC power source or by inverting 12-Volt DC. Most RV Parks have 120-Volt AC power pedestals.

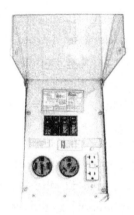

Figure 65 Typical power pedestal hookup panel found in most RV parks.

These power points normally have connections that support the range of RV power requirements, from standard 15 amp all the way to 50 amp service. Normally, each type of outlet has its own dedicated circuit breaker; 50-amp service should have two circuit breakers (more on that in a bit). Your RV will have a power inlet specific to the electrical capacity of your RV. This inlet may be located on the side of your RV under a spring-loaded cover, or it may be located in a storage bay in your RV's basement.

You will also have a power cord. To power your RV, simply plug one end of the power cord into the RV power inlet, and plug the other end into the electrical power source. If you are plugging into a RV

Park power pedestal, ensure that **ALL** circuits are in the **OFF** position. Inspect the pedestal for signs of damage or indications of burn or scorch marks. If you detect any signs of damage on the pedestal, I highly recommend asking a park attendant to verify that the pedestal is functioning properly. This is **NOT** something you should do yourself unless you specifically understand electrical circuitry and the proper use of voltage meters. Remember, these pedestals carry enough electrical current to cause significant injury or death. If the pedestal appears in good condition, plug your cord in and switch on the appropriate circuit breaker.

How much power does your RV need?

RVs come in all shapes and sizes, and with various electrical configurations. Recall, *wattage = amperage x volts*.

All RVs are designed with a specific electrical system engineered specifically for that unit. Manufacturers exercise some care to try to match the installed electrical system with the intended use of the RV and its potential target audience (this is not to say they always get it right!). We know lots of folks with 30-amp systems that wish they had paid a little more attention on the front end—that they well may have upgraded to a RV unit with 50-amp service.

What really is the difference between 30-amp and 50-amp electrical service units? As indicated on Figure 66, the difference is significant: the 30-amp system provides 3,600 watts of power as compared to the 50-amp system, which provides 12,000 watts of power. A major difference is that, with 30-amp service units, you have to pay close attention to what electrical devices you're using; the cumulative use of these electrical items can lead to a blown circuit. With a 30-amp service unit, you are limited to using a total of 30 amps (or 3,600 watts of power) at one time.

Some mini towables and van-style RVs have a single 15-amp or 20-amp electrical connection (20-amp service provides 2,400 watts of power). This is often used to power a battery charger, small air conditioner, or small microwave. These electrical plugs are the same that you would have in your home.	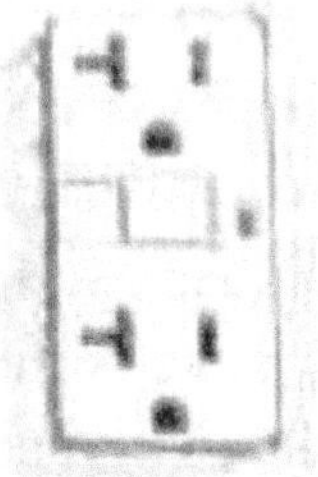
Mid-sized RVs (like travel trailers, fifth wheels, and many motorhomes) have 30-amp service (30-amp service provides 3,600 watts of power). This plug and its cord are significantly more substantial than 15-amp or 20-amp connections. 30-amp service has a single, 120-Volt hot leg.	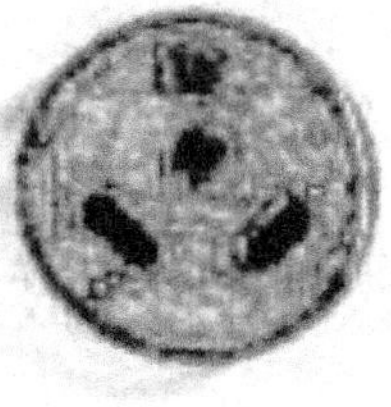
Larger RVs often are equipped with 50-amp service connections due to the number of larger appliances and air conditioning units (50-amp service provides 12,000 watts of power). 50-amp service is wired and configured differently from 30-amp service. 50-amp service has two, 120-Volt hot legs; (50 amp x (2 x120-Volt legs). Although 50-amp service is often mistakenly called a 240-Volt connection, it is important to understand that it is not; it is dual 120-Volt hot legs. That is why 50-amp service has two circuit breakers on 50-amp service.	

Figure 66 Power connection and comparison chart.

Figuring out how much electrical power that each device you use will require to operate takes a little work and a bit of math, but it can be eye opening. Figure 67 provides information about the required wattage and amps to operate some common RV appliances and electronics. To determine how much power you will use at any given time, make a list of the electrical devices that you use routinely. By totaling the wattages of **ALL** the devices that you may use at one time, the highest total represents your worst-case power demand requirement.

APPLIANCE	WATTAGE	AMPS
Air Conditioner, 13.5k	1,700	14
Air Conditioner, 15k	1,950	16
Ceiling Fan	25	0.2
Cell Phone Charger (in use)	5	0.05
Clock Radio	2	0.02
Coffee Maker	900	7.5
Converter, 40-amp	650	5.5
Electric Blanket	100	0.8
Electric Space Heater	1,500	12.5
Electric Water Heater	1,200	10
Fan, Medium, tabletop style	55	0.45
Hair Dryer	1,200	10
Laptop Computer	120	1
Microwave	1,300	10.5
Refrigerator (residential style)	600	5
Suburban 12,000-Btu furnace fan	DC	2
Television, 20" flat-screen LCD	60	0.5
Television Satellite Receiver	170	1.5
Toaster Oven	960	8
Washer/Dryer RV Combo	1,900	16
Vacuum Cleaner	840	7

Figure 67 Chart showing common appliances and their respective wattage and amperage requirements.

Common appliance and electronics electrical requirements

To identify what you and your family are likely doing, devices you are using, and the power draw created by using those devices, I find it best to break the table in Figure 67 into four-hour blocks for an entire 24-hour period.

Let's start our example power utilization evaluation at midnight just for ease of creating the example list.

Midnight to 4 am. We're sleeping. Maybe the Suburban furnace is running, depending on time of year. The furnace operates using liquid propane, and the control board and blower fan each run on 12-Volt DC. So, our only real electric draw is the RV converter, clock radio, and cell phone charger.

APPLIANCE	WATTAGE	AMPS
Cell Phone Charger	5	0.05
Clock Radio	2	0.02
Converter	650	5.5
TOTALS	**657**	**Under 6**

4 am to 8 am. We're waking up and moving around, working on that first cup of coffee, cooking breakfast, and showering.

APPLIANCE	WATTAGE	AMPS
Cell Phone Charger	5	0.05
Clock Radio	2	0.02
Converter	650	5.5
Coffee Maker	900	7.5
Hair Dryer	1,200	10
Microwave	1,300	10.5
TOTALS	**4,057**	**Under 44**

8 am to Noon. Our day is underway. We're in and out of the RV, getting warm as the sunshine starts covering the travel trailer, and maybe checking out a little television to keep up on world events.

APPLIANCE	WATTAGE	AMPS
Air Conditioner	1,700	14
Cell Phone Charger	5	0.05
Clock Radio	2	0.02
Converter	650	5.5
Microwave	1,300	10.5
Television, 20" flat-screen LCD	60	0.5
TOTALS	**3,717**	**Under 31**

Noon to 4 pm. Same as before, minus the microwave. The day is in full swing!

APPLIANCE	WATTAGE	AMPS
Air Conditioner	1,700	14
Cell Phone Charger	5	0.05
Clock Radio	2	0.02
Converter	650	5.5
Television, 20" flat-screen LCD	60	0.5
TOTALS	2,417	Under 21

4 pm to 8 pm. Still warm from the daytime sun. Steaks are on the grill, and curly fries are in the microwave. Caught up on emails with the laptop, and the big game is on the television. Need to do a little cleaning after all the dirt we dragged in, so the vacuum comes in handy, as does the washing machine.

APPLIANCE	WATTAGE	AMPS
Air Conditioner	1,700	14
Cell Phone Charger	5	0.05
Clock Radio	2	0.02
Converter	650	5.5
Laptop Computer	120	1
Microwave	1,300	10.5
Television, 20" flat-screen LCD	60	0.5
Washer/Dryer RV Combo	1,900	16
Vacuum Cleaner	840	7
TOTALS	6,577	Under 55

8 pm to Midnight. Worn out! Time to unwind and watch news on the television as just the fan keeps the trailer plenty cool.

APPLIANCE	WATTAGE	AMPS
Cell Phone Charger	5	0.05
Clock Radio	2	0.02
Converter	650	5.5
Fan, Medium, table-top-style	55	0.45
Television, 20" flat-screen LCD	60	0.5
TOTALS	**772**	**Under 7**

Creating this list makes it easy to see how the items you're using can quickly create a strain on your electrical service. In our example 24-hour period above, we used the air conditioner for limited periods during the day, the microwave, and the television to watch the big game. A LP gas water heater and refrigerator is a great relief to the electrical load. Even so, it's clear that, during several portions of the day, we're using a lot of electricity, and using the majority of electricity between 4 and 8 pm.

Now, before you get too worried, these example 4-hour blocks each represent a worst-case snapshot. These examples would require everything for that 4 hour period to be in use at the same time. The good news is it is unlikely you'd be using all these appliances simultaneously. For example, in the 4 am to 8 am block, we have the coffee maker, hair dryer, and microwave all listed, but would you really be cooking in the microwave and drying your hair at the same time? I hope not! The point is, while the microwave draws

1,300 watts, the microwave is normally only used for a few minutes at any given time. The hair dryer draws 1,200 watts, but you're not drying your hair all morning long. Your electrical system has power limitations, but as long as you're aware of the power draw of the devices you're using and plan to space out their usage, you can manage very efficiently.

Many have told me that after a short learning curve, they have gotten to the point where it's no longer something they worry about. Subconsciously, they just know their system limitations and work within them.

Adapters, pigtails, dog bones (a.k.a. electrical adapters)

A specific power cord will be required to attach your RV to a power source. What happens when you need to use a different electrical connection?

Say you've got a 50-amp motorhome, but you've arrived at a RV Park that only has 30-amp sites available. No problem. You can connect your 50-amp cable to the 30-amp pedestal connection with something called a dog bone adapter—specifically a 50-amp-to-30-amp dog bone.

Figure 68 Typical 30-amp to 50-amp dog bone.

These adapters come in a wide variety of configurations, allowing almost any conceivable connection. Some examples include 50 amp to 30 amp; 50 amp to 15 amp; 30 amp to 15 amp; and other configurations.

Figure 69 Typical 30-amp-to-20-amp connector.

These adapters do require some attention, meaning that if you need to use one, be aware what has changed. As in our example above, our 50-amp rig can connect to 30-amp service in a pinch, but that's all the power you're going to have. It means you're going to have to pay attention to what power you're consuming at any given time. What if you want to put your 50-amp rig in storage, but you want to keep the batteries charged and the storage facility only has a 20-amp plug nearby? Again, no problem. You could use your 50-amp-to-30-amp dog bone coupled with a 30-amp-to-20amp adapter.

As mentioned before, adapters are available for just about every requirement. If you need to use one, read the safety instructions included with the adapter, and follow the instructions to the letter to ensure you don't damage anything in your RV—or worse, yourself.

Surge protection

I find it interesting that folks will invest in a surge protector at home for their computer or new big screen television, but never consider this critical appliance for their RV. RV Parks do a great job, in my estimation, with keeping up with the infrastructure that is required to keep a quality park running smoothly. That said, there are just too many variables when it comes to electricity (i.e., high voltage, low voltage, shorted-out power pedestals, among other electrical misfortunes).

Because one shorted out wire in a power pedestal could cause significant damage to a RV, I think that a surge protection device is one of the most important accessories you can purchase for a RV. Surge protection devices are available in 30-amp and 50-amp versions; permanent, hard-wired installations; and portable units that plug into the power pedestal in line with your RV's power cord.

While I'm not an electrician, I can speak about my personal experiences. Our motorhome was spared potential significant damage at a RV Park when we plugged into a misconfigured pedestal. We had permanently installed a Progressive Industries 50-amp unit that took the brunt of the rogue pedestal. The electrician that we asked the RV Park to send out checked the issue and confirmed that the 50-amp plug was completely miswired. The control board inside our unit had to be replaced, something that was accomplished in just days by the wonderful folks at Progressive Industries. SurgeGuard® is a competing brand that also provides an excellent product. You're very perceptive if you detect that I'm convinced this is absolutely something you must have. Enough said.

Direct current, DC power

Direct current is normally provided by your RV's batteries, but is also provided in many RVs by using a "converter" to transform 120-Volt AC to 12-Volt DC power. A converter is an incredibly handy device, as so many RVs now use 12-Volt lighting systems, multi-power refrigerators, 12-Volt ceiling/exhaust fans, etc. Converters normally charge the batteries in RVs, so they are a very important appliance in your rig.

If you are not plugged into shore power (a power pedestal), then what is the source of power for devices you wish to use in your RV?

If you don't have a generator, then on-board batteries and solar are the only real remaining sources of power available for use. RV batteries (referred to as "house batteries") can provide a significant amount of power, depending on how many batteries you have and in what configuration they are connected.

Batteries also can supply some amount of AC power using a device called an "inverter," which uses DC power from the batteries to create AC power. One disadvantage of using an inverter is that is takes an incredible amount of DC power to produce AC power. No need to make this a math class, but some background is useful for understanding.

While AC and DC both can provide power to appliances, motors, and electronics, they accomplish it in very different ways. I'm going to provide a very high-level description of the two. (Some additional reading on AC and DC power systems may well provide more worthwhile information as you become more familiar with each.)

AC is alternating current, meaning that it moves across an electrical wire, changing direction back and forth. DC is direct current, and means just that: current flows only in one direction, always. Interestingly, DC was once standard in the United States, but was eventually replaced by AC because of its robustness, reliability, and efficiency of moving power over long distances.

Electric current in AC wiring is rated at 120 Volts. Electric current in DC wiring is rated at 12 Volts. This demonstrates that AC current travels through wiring at a rate 10 times more than DC.

If you're thinking so what? Here's the same statement made in a more useful way. If an appliance that you use in your RV everyday requires 10 amps of AC power to function, using that same appliance using DC power would require 100 amps of DC to operate.[27] Batteries can indeed power just about anything and everything in your RV, including televisions, lighting, and even your microwave. Only a few items associated with your RV cannot be tacked by batteries. High-demand motors and compressors (for example, used in air conditioning units), would deplete your house batteries in short order.

Batteries

Batteries are a source for powering items and systems in your RV. Battery configurations in a RV run the entire spectrum, from single, 12-Volt rechargeable units, to entire battery banks that can potentially occupy an entire RV basement storage area. These battery banks can be very complex, requiring automated monitoring and charging systems just to keep the battery systems in optimal operating condition. For our purposes, we'll discuss installations that are more commonly used. If you have or need something more unique, it's likely that you've already researched this area at length.

To understand the many options and considerations when discussing RV batteries, you first need to gain a more in-depth understanding of batteries. RV batteries are more than traditional car batteries, which are designed to provide the surge of power necessary to start your car in the worst of conditions. Car batteries are usually rated by their cold-cranking amps, CCA.

The battery market includes other types of batteries as well; however, for the rigors of RV use, a deep-cycle battery is considered the most appropriate. Deep-cycle batteries are specifically designed to be charged, discharged, and recharged, potentially hundreds of times.

Deep-cycle batteries come in a few variants which include Flooded, Sealed Gel, and Absorbed Glass Mat (AGM). Flooded batteries come in "fillable" and maintenance free models. The maintenance-free versions of Flooded, Sealed Gel, and AGM batteries are just that—maintenance-free and, therefore, offer no filler caps for adding water. Battery technology has come a long way; batteries are more robust and reliable than ever. That said, many folks still prefer to "maintain" their batteries by continually checking them and managing the water level inside the battery. Flooded cell batteries are less expensive (sometimes significantly so, depending on the brand) than Sealed Gel and AGM batteries.

RV batteries, regardless of type, are rated by their capacity to deliver AmpHours. A standard formula for calculating AmpHours is to measure the electrical current that a battery delivers over a fixed, 20-hour period. For example, a battery that can provide 10 amps for 20 hours is a 200 AmpHour battery (*10amps x 20 hours = 200 AmpHours*).

Also note that batteries are often rated in groups (e.g., Group 24, Group 27, Group 31, etc.). This group rating, determined by the Battery Council International (BCI)[28], is specific to the physical size of the battery, not the capacity of the battery. Larger batteries do, however, normally have higher AmpHour ratings.

Here are some examples of various battery groups and associated AmpHours.

Battery Type	AmpHours	Voltage
Group 24	70 to 85	12
Group 27	85 to 110	12
Group 31	95 to 125	12
T105 (Golf Cart)	180 to 230	6

Figure 70 Battery AmpHour by Battery Type.

Battery life span is always a challenging topic, and is highly dependent on how you exercise and charge your batteries. Batteries have a finite number of charging cycles. When looking at battery specifications, this is one of the technical details provided.

Many batteries have a 50-charge/discharge life span. In simple terms, this means that once a battery has been charged, drained, recharged 50 times, the battery has reached its end of life. While that seems straightforward, unfortunately it's not. There is actually a curve associated with battery life span relative to charging. For example, if you only discharge this same battery to 50% before recharging each time, you may increase the life span to 200 charging cycles. Only using 25% of the battery between charges may increase the life span to 1,200 charging cycles.

WARNING: Batteries produce explosive gases and can explode. Keep all batteries away from flames, cigarettes, and sparks. Be sure your battery compartment is properly vented. Keep vent caps tight and level. Check your battery monthly.

Replace swollen batteries immediately. Use extreme care when handling batteries.

Battery charging

Before using your batteries, ensure that they are charged. Charging batteries can be a complex process that involves a number of components and technologies, but the bottom line remains the same: you've got to replace the amps you've used.

Converters

A RV Converter is perhaps the most basic system used to recharge a RV battery. In general terms, a converter uses 120-Volt AC power and converts it to 12-Volt DC power. This is common as many RVs have numerous 12-Volt powered components, such as

Figure 70 Common power converter by IOTA.

lights, fans, refrigerator controls, heater controls, and blower motors, etc. These converters often provide 50 or more amps for those 12-Volt components in your rig, and provide a means of charging your batteries. The drawback to charging batteries with a simple converter is that there is no intelligent circuitry for the charging system. In some cases, converters provide more of a float charge which, over time, will decrease the life span of a battery.

Multi-stage converter charger

Ideally, a multi-stage converter charger will provide the necessary logic to ensure not only that your RV batteries are properly charged but, more importantly, will keep them efficiently charged to their full capacity by managing the type of effective charge rate. These smart systems usually may include bulk charging, which applies maximum current until the batteries reach a predefined charge state. Absorb charging then provides the batteries with sufficient current to continue charging to the extent possible without overcharging, and keep the batteries at their maximum charge for a predetermined time period before moving to a "float" state. In a float state, sufficient current is applied to keep the batteries topped off. While this newer generation of smart chargers works similarly, different brands incorporate their charging methodologies slightly differently. The algorithms for these devices are very complex, but with the price of replacement batteries, believe me, it is money well spent.

Inverter charger

An inverter is the opposite of a converter. An inverter creates 120-Volt AC power by using the 12-Volt DC power provided by the RV battery bank. The inverter is wired into the electrical circuit(s) in the RV to power certain AC devices while the RV is not connected to shore power. Additionally, some AC receptacles may be powered only through the inverter.

Simple inverters do not usually have charging circuits; however, more robust inverters (like those found in motorhomes or RVs with larger battery banks) do include smart charging technology similar to the technology used in multi-stage converters. In RVs where there is an inverter charger, there may not need to be a stand-alone converter.

Equalization

As previously discussed, batteries are complex devices that require you to pay attention to their state of health. As batteries are continually used and recharged, it is common for a small amount of sulfate to attach to the battery plate. As this happens, the battery loses some of its potential capacity. Periodically, it is beneficial for the health and longevity of the battery to utilize a process called equalization.

Many converters and inverter chargers have this capability. During equalization, the batteries are charged using more voltage than a normal charge cycle. This added voltage causes the electrolytes in the battery to boil. As the electrolytes boil, most of the sulfate that has attached to the battery plates is removed and added back into the battery electrolytes. This process restores the health of the battery if done properly and regularly. This process is time-consuming and requires a substantial amount of power from the converter or inverter charger.

I've provided only a generic overview to the process. Review the user's manual for your charger or inverter charger for specific directions on using the equalization option, and follow the instructions very carefully.

Solar charging and use

Solar charging is another quickly growing segment of the RV industry. Solar is very popular, especially for those who like to camp off-the-grid. Many RVs are now pre-installed with solar panel connections. Some units come completely ready to go, and include solar panels and charge controllers.

To highlight some of the issues surrounding solar, let's assume you've got a mid-sized travel trailer and you are thinking adding solar to your rig will enhance your RV experience. Well, it might, and it might not. Solar is not the dilithium crystal of the RV industry. Before you jump into solar, you need to weigh the cost and benefit.

Here are some considerations when determining if solar fits into your RV lifestyle. First and foremost, getting a complete solar system setup will likely require a significant up-front expenditure. I'm not sure that, for the majority of solar users, the goal of a quick return on investment is realistic. For some, they will never realize a profitable return on their investment, but that may not be the point. Solar is a way to benefit our environment, and is the ultimate in clean energy.

Using solar in your RV requires planning, wiring, potential changes to your on-board battery layout and, for permanent solar installations, a significant amount of rooftop real-estate. If you're limited to a single on-board battery, using much more than a small solar panel to keep your battery "topped-off" might not make sense.

If your RV has no workable space on the roof, or the roof itself is not constructed in such a manner to support solar panels, a portable ground installation may be your only option. Portable solar panels certainly are available, but you've added yet another layer of complexity to something that was supposed to make RV life easier.

Before considering a solar installation on your RV, determine how and where you would use it. In what conditions do you find yourself camping most often? If your idea of camping is a full-featured RV Park with complete hook-ups and that's not going to change, going solar makes little, if any, sense. If your camping seasons or choice of locations frequently finds you in areas where there is little direct sunlight, again, solar simply does not make much sense.

Now, if you find that your rig has rooftop real estate; you have (or can add) an adequate battery bank; and your goal is to be able to be self-sufficient as much as practical, then some type of solar panel installation probably does make sense.

More and more RV Parks are beginning to charge for electricity using individually metered spaces. Solar can absolutely help reduce your electric bill at an RV Park.

Some RVs out there have extreme solar installations. Those owners will proudly tell you that, depending on the time of year and need to run air conditioning, they do not use any Park electricity at all. While that may be absolutely true, it is not the norm.   My focus of this section on solar is for those who can potentially add a few panels and a smart charge controller to supplement their power requirements.

What makes up a solar system? In fairly basic terms, a complete solar installation for our mid-sized travel trailer example would include solar panels, mounting hardware, a specific charge controller, cables, and connectors. If your RV does not have an inverter and you wish to operate 120-Volt AC appliances or electronics, you'll need an inverter as well.

Solar panels come in many sizes, configurations, and power output ranges. Battery maintenance panels that are intended to keep your

RV batteries just topped off while in storage put out only a handful of watts.

A common size of solar panel that I see advertised often is for a 100-watt panel, with the extremes up over 150 watts per panel. What do these figures really mean? That's a great question and part of what makes right sizing solar installations a bit of a challenge.

Let's use the 100-watt solar panel mentioned above as an example. In the best of conditions (meaning a bright sunny day with the sun at, or near, its peak elevation relative to your RV), the solar panel might indeed produce 100 watts per hour. That's pretty significant, but that's also the ideal condition—only really available in optimal conditions. Add a little cloud cover and charging is reduced. Add complete cloud cover or a storm, and charging is all but stopped. Although 100 watts per hour is what you might expect the panel to produce when the sun is virtually directly overhead, remember that the amount of charging decreases as the position of the direct sunlight decreases. It only makes sense.

For sake of this example (and simple math), let's assume you have good weather and 10 hours of sun per day. Let's further assume that the panel is 50% effective for those 10 hours. That means that a 100-watts-per-hour solar panel could replace 500 watt hours of power, two panels could replace 1,000 watt hours of power, etc.

Businesses that specialize in RV solar equipment and installations are located all over the country. Big RV box stores (like Camping World) now carry a complete line of solar panels and accessories. This is the point where some research and calculations on your end become important to right sizing your solar installation.

Earlier in this chapter, we discussed the amount of power required to operate commonly used items in your RV. You can refer to that chart, for various periods throughout a day, to determine the approximate amount of watt hours you're using. Understanding this usage rate will help determine the appropriate size solar installation you need. Remember, a watt hour is the amount of electricity it takes to run a 1-watt device for one hour. Using your 20" flat-screen LCD television (60 watts) for three hours per day would consume 180 watt hours. Using your microwave (1,300 watts) for a total of 30 minutes per day would consume 650 watt hours. These two examples show how quickly your usage adds up.

Back to our mid-sized travel trailer example. Let's assume that we, as fairly moderate electricity users, consume 1,500 watt hours per day. If we invested in a couple of 100-watt panels and the necessary batteries and associated solar charging equipment, on any given day with good, clear weather and no need to use the rooftop air conditioner, our actual electricity usage would be fairly minimal.

Like converters and inverter chargers, solar installations include a charge controller. These smart devices control the charge rate to the batteries to be the most efficient based on conditions. The controller must be sized properly to not only the number and capacity of the panels, but also the battery bank.

As stated before, although solar installation requires some thought and effort, it may be a worthwhile investment for you.

Battery state

Knowing what level of charge your batteries have at any given time will help you extend the life of your batteries. Remember, allowing batteries to completely drain is extremely hard on them and will greatly shorten their life span.

The following chart shows the "charge state" of your batteries. It is generally accepted that you should not allow your batteries to fall below 40% charge. Once a battery falls below 40%, its life span is diminished.

Voltage	% of Charge	Operating Range
12.6 +	100	
12.5	90	
12.42	80	Safe
12.32	70	Operating
12.20	60	Range
12.06	50	
11.9	40	
11.75	30	Too Low - Charge
11.58	20	
11.31	10	Damaging Low - Charge
10.5 -	0	

Figure 71 Percentage of battery charge based on battery voltage.

Battery configuration

Battery configuration in your RV is dependent on your RV's available real estate. If you only have space to accommodate one battery, you'll want to invest in the best 12-Volt deep-cycle battery you can find.

If you have room for two batteries, it's time to consider installing two, 6-Volt, deep-cycle golf cart batteries, which have tremendous AmpHour ratings. If you have space to accommodate four batteries, an array of golf cart batteries will provide you some serious time off the grid!

Battery wiring

As previously mentioned, if you only have space to accommodate one battery, you'll want to invest in the best 12-Volt deep-cycle battery you can find. However, if you find that you have a little room with which to work, you can really add capacity to your RV by creating a battery bank—two or more batteries connected to serve a specific application (in this case, your RV). You can wire the batteries in your battery bank in series, in parallel, or in a hybrid of both; the way you choose is dependent on your end goal.

Series wiring

Series wiring combines the voltage of the batteries while keeping the AmpHours of the individual batteries the same. For example, two, 6-Volt batteries rated at 200 AmpHours each, when combined in series, would provide a 12-Volt, 200-AmpHour battery bank.

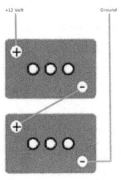

Figure 72 Batteries wired in series.

To connect batteries in series, place a jumper wire from the negative terminal of battery one to the positive terminal of battery two. Connect the open positive and negative terminals to the RV. It is important that both batteries in the series have the same voltage and capacity to prevent issues with charging and premature failure.

 Italian physicist Alessandro Volta is credited with producing the first battery, the "voltaic pile", in 1798. (Source: The Battery House)

Parallel wiring

Parallel wiring keeps the voltage the same, but increases the total AmpHour rating. For example, two, 6-Volt batteries rated at 200 AmpHours combined in parallel would provide a 6-Volt, 400-AmpHour battery bank.

To connect batteries in parallel, place a jumper positive to positive, and a jumper negative to negative. Connect the RV to one battery (but the batteries are used equally).

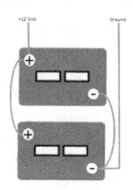

Figure 73 Batteries wired in parallel.

257

A battery bank actually exists that uses both series and parallel connections. If you have a larger RV with space to accommodate four batteries, you could connect four golf-cart batteries to create an incredibly powerful battery bank. To create 12 Volts as the end voltage, connect two sets of 6-Volt batteries in parallel. Then, connect the two separate parallel banks together using a single jumper wire from a positive terminal from one battery bank to the negative terminal on the other battery bank.

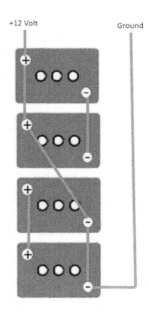

+12 Volt   Ground

Figure 74 Hybrid battery connection using series and parallel connections.

In the series and parallel wiring examples provided above, we used 6-Volt, 200-AmpHour batteries. We'll use those same style batteries in this example to highlight the difference. For example, you have two battery banks of 6 Volt batteries, each connected in parallel. The result is two banks of batteries (each now 6 Volts, 400 AmpHours). Now, by connecting the battery banks together in series, we get an end result of a four-battery bank that provides 12 Volts, 400 AmpHours.

The take-away here is that there are untold options available to you when it comes to batteries and how to configure them to support your desired lifestyle. Certainly there are limitations, but batteries offer the ability to use most things in your RV while you're on the go.

Lithium batteries

Lithium batteries may be relative newcomers to the RV industry, but are not to any product manufacturer whose product requires battery power. Lithium batteries are incredibly popular and have many significant benefits over normal, more traditional batteries.

With few exceptions, lithium batteries require almost no maintenance. They contain no water to manage or check, and they offer significantly longer shelf lives and hold their charges longer when not in use. Lithium batteries don't deteriorate like lead acid batteries.

Many lithium batteries also include smart electronic technology within the battery itself. This technology can monitor a battery and turn it off if it gets too hot; or stop charging cycles if it "senses" a battery anomaly.

Speaking of charging, lithium batteries can essentially be charged to 100% of their capacity each and every time, where charging lead acid batteries can be a little tricky, especially if you don't have a smart multi-stage charger.

Lastly, for those concerned about the environment, lithium batteries have demonstrated incredible life spans—often 10 times the life of a traditional battery. While it seems clear to me that there are amazing advantages to the use of lithium batteries in RVs, my research to this point leaves me a little on the fence about how to discuss them and offer suggestions about converting to their use. For now, I'm letting you know available options beyond use of traditional batteries. Perhaps a subsequent edition of this book will include lithium batteries as one of the standards in the industry.

Chapter Thirteen

Generators

Generators provide RV owners with some additional capabilities and travel options that are not available to RV users that don't have a generator. Generators come in a wide variety of sizes and fueling options. The decision to get and use a generator depends on how you want to use your RV. Generators are a critical component of the RV experience for many folks.

Generators can be small, portable, stand-alone units that can be carried and set up at your campsite, or can be large, built-in units whose operation can use the RV's fuel source. The type of generator you have installed (or need to have) really depends on the type of RV and your camping needs.

Most RVs purchased do not include a generator. The majority of travel trailers and fifth-wheel trailers do not have a built-in generator. Exceptions are larger fifth-wheels that are designed more for year-round use, and many fifth wheel toy haulers, both of which are often delivered with built-in generators. Generators have become more common in motorhomes, and are almost the norm in diesel pushers, and standard in many gassers.

Why you may need a generator depends on a couple of factors. If your style of camping involves a lot of boondocking, then a generator is incredibly handy since you're off the grid! While you may predominately use the on-board batteries for your power needs, the batteries still need to be charged. This is where a generator really earns its keep. Also, if you plan to use an air conditioner, chances are, you'll need a generator.

For some larger RVs that may have residential appliances like refrigerators and multiple air conditioning units, the need for a generator increases. During the summer months, lots of motorhome owners we've met over the years run their on-board generator while traveling down the road so they can keep the roof-top air conditioner running to keep the entire coach cool. The bottom-line in determining your need for a generator is how you plan to use your RV.

If you travel from RV Park to RV Park, never boondock, and your RV has typical RV appliances with multi-power modes, you likely never would use a generator. Weigh the cost versus the benefit of buying and maintaining a generator.

Generators generally come in a couple of form factors: built-in or some form of portable. Built-in units normally take advantage of initial design engineering from the RV manufacturer (meaning a predetermined mounting location, pre-wiring, and access to a fuel source). For purposes of this book, if you have a built-in unit, there's little in this section you need to concern yourself with beyond your daily power requirements, which concern all generator users.

Clearly, the purpose of having a generator is to provide standard 120-Volt AC electricity. Generators create electricity in different ways, depending on the type of generator you have. All generators use a motor to create power. This power is then converted to electricity; this is where generators differ. More on that shortly.

Portable Generators

Traditional generators use a motor to turn a shaft that drives an alternator, which is then connected directly to the load. These generators run at a set speed (about 3,600 rpm). This constant speed is what produces the set 120 Volts AC at 60 hertz. Traditional generators are popular because of their ruggedness and simplicity of design. They have no special electronics, inverter, or control boards to fail. A drawback to these units is that simplicity. Because they run at a set rate, they use more fuel than their inverter generator brethren and, as a general rule, they are loud—very loud in some cases.

Portable generators are incredibly popular and offer capabilities that you don't get with embedded units. You can take a portable generator with you for a special event, or use it at your permanent home in the event of a power outage. You can't do those things with a built-in unit. Portable units, by definition, should be just that—portable.

Figure 75 Typical portable generator with wheel kit.

If your generator weighs so much you can't move it from one location to another, then it's not really portable. Portable generators vary widely in size and load capacity. For example, the very popular Honda generators range from 1,000 watts (weighing under 30 lbs) to 10,000 watts (tipping the scales at over 400 pounds). While the large generators have wheel kits to move them around, 400 pounds is hardly portable.

Depending on your specific needs, portable generators are available in gas, liquid propane, and in dual fuel (gas and liquid propane) models.

Figure 76 Inverter generators are lightweight and fuel misers.

Inverter generator units are considered newer but, in reality, have been around for a number of years. Inverter generators use a motor to create power (just like traditional generators), but that power is converted to Direct Current (DC) and then passed to an inverter, which creates very clean, reliable, 120-Volt AC. These units have more electronics and technology, so they are generally more expensive. However, unlike traditional generators that run at a set speed, these units react to the demand being placed on them, so they are usually more fuel efficient and most always more quiet.

Built-in Generators

Built-in generators are incredibly convenient. The electrical systems of RVs with built-in generators are slightly different than RVs without. Built-in generators require a transfer switch, which detects power from the generator and switches the internal

Figure 77 Slide out door in front of diesel pusher houses large built-in diesel generator.

circuitry from external to internal. In model literature, this is often referred to as generator prep or generator capable. If installed, a simple press of a start button from inside the RV, and your generator is running and providing power to your RV within a minute. Built-in units are available from a number of sources; Cummins-Onan and Generac own most of the market share of built-in generators.

Built-in generators do have some options to consider to ensure that you're getting the most out of your investment. In motorhomes, generators most often use the fuel source of the chassis (gas or diesel), depending on the make of the chassis. As always, there are exceptions to every rule!

Some motorhomes use generators that are fueled by the liquid propane tanks. Common installation for generators in diesel pushers is right up front, between the driver and passenger seats, concealed on a slide-out tray. In Class B and C units, generators are often located in an underneath bay, near the rear of the unit, closer to the fuel source.

In travel trailers and fifth wheels, generators are often fueled by internal liquid propane tanks. Many toy hauler units are a notable exception to this, many of which include a gasoline

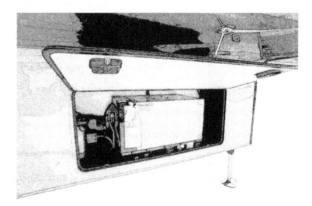

Figure 78 Storage area in front of fifth wheel has generator bay complete with electrical connections and fuel lines.

fuel tank for all of those toys that they're designed to carry. Generators in those models are often plumbed to the gasoline fuel tank. In fifth-wheel installations, the most common location for a generator is in the storage bay underneath the front cap, just behind the fifth-wheel hitch.

Just like their portable generator brethren, built-in units come in a wide variety of sizes. The popular Cummins-Onan generator units come in models ranging from 2,500 watts to 12,500 watts, with gasoline, diesel or liquid propane fuel options.

What generator is best for you?

What do you need to be concerned with when deciding what type generator will best suit your needs? Many factors are worth consideration, with a few that stand out (like fuel consumption, noise, and weight).

Fuel consumption

The type of fuel that your generator uses is not only a convenience factor, but also a significant efficiency variable. According to the Energy Information Administration, the type of fuel you use impacts how efficiently your generator produces power. For example, one gallon of liquid propane produces about 91,000 BTUs of energy. One gallon of unleaded gasoline produces about 120,000 BTUs of energy. Diesel fuel is the most efficient of the three generator fuel types, producing almost 139,000 BTUs of energy for every one gallon of fuel.[29]

What does this all mean? It means that liquid propane is only 76% as efficient as gasoline, and only 65% as efficient as diesel. Also, it demonstrates that gasoline is only 86% as efficient as diesel. This is important because it has an impact on your wallet, depending on how much you need to use your generator. Many sources are available that discuss generator efficiency. The point here is to illustrate the difference in efficiency.

Now, armed with this information, don't run off to Wikipedia and download BTU to kilowatt conversion tables; it's not that simple! Here are some "non-scientific" stats I've compiled over the last few years while chatting up RV owners, attending RV shows and demonstrations, and having lots of discussions with fellow RVers on manufacturer forums. Again, this is in no way a 'scientific" analysis, but a means to illustrate the differences in generators.

At a RV Trade Show a couple of years ago, I watched an incredibly useful demonstration by the Onan generator folks that was intended to detail the differences between gas and diesel generators. For their demonstration, the Onan representative had a diesel pusher (a 2014 Thor Palazzo) and a gasoline-powered Class C (a 2014 Thor Chateau, as I recall). Both units were equipped with similar generators—an EFI 5500 in the Chateau, and a Quiet Diesel 6000 in the Palazzo. While not identical, both generators are very close, except for fuel type.

A flow meter was connected to the fuel lines, and the representative started both units. After a few minutes, the roof-top air conditioners, televisions, and other like appliances were powered on, the purpose of which was to generate a similar electric load for each coach (which as I recall was about 2,500 watts—less than half the power rating for each unit).

The gasoline Onan 5500 consumed one gallon of fuel at 1 hour, 35 minutes, while the diesel QD6000 was still running at 2 hours, and had not yet burned one gallon of fuel.

Similar data are available directly from Onan, specific to fuel consumption for all of their generator models. The Onan literature shows that the Diesel Q6000 consumed 0.4 gallons an hour at half-load, while the gasoline EFI 5500 consumed about 0.6 gallons an hour at half-load. [30] This demonstration served to reinforce the efficiency of the type of fuel used.

Another way to illustrate the point is that, to produce 1 kilowatt hour of power consumes approximately 0.25 gallon of liquid propane; 0.2 gallon of gasoline; and 0.15 gallon of diesel. To find specific performance information on any generator, refer to the manufacturer's web site or individual product manuals.

Noise

Noise is always an issue in RVing, and definitely should be a concern when selecting a generator. You don't want to use a generator that makes it impossible to carry on a conversation or violates noise rules at RV Parks. The National Park System has published a mandate that generators be less than 60db(A) at 50 feet[31]. Most built-in RV generators fit within this requirement, as do many of the portable generator inverter units. Beware, however, that use of many traditional luggable standard generators would not meet the National Park requirements. Also, many RV Parks have quiet hours where generators are not allowed, regardless of type.

Weight

Weight is an important factor when considering generators. Portable generators should be just that—humanly portable. Just because a generator has a wheel kit does not make it truly portable. Likewise, the weight of permanently installed generators is also important as that weight must be added when calculating your RV's gross weight. Portable units weigh as little as 29 lbs, where some larger diesel models used in high-end coaches can tip the scales at almost 800 lbs.

Quality of power output

Conventional units connect their AC alternators directly to the load without any type of processing. Inverter generators convert their AC output to DC, then transform that power back to AC using an inverter. The benefit of this is that you get very clean, high-quality power, which is actually very important in this day and age as so many of the items we take for granted day-to-day have micro-processors (or mini computers) inside. The cleaner power from inverter generators is certainly a benefit.

Right sizing

So what size generator do I really need? That question has to be one of the most debated topics on several of the RV forums that I frequent. I think that the answer is fairly easy to determine, but it does take some thought!

If your unit has a generator installed from the factory, it was installed based on calculations made by the design team and you can relax. You're done! If your unit is "generator prepped" or "generator ready," you need to consult with your RV's manufacturer as they have probably identified a specific unit to be dropped in.

Our Heartland Landmark came generator prepped. That means that the bay for the generator was sealed so that noxious fumes could not enter the coach. It was also pre-wired with the appropriate plugs and switches to allow for a quick installation. Heartland spec'd the Cummins Onan 5500LP unit and, indeed, it would require very little effort on our part to add the generator.

If your RV was not equipped with a generator (or it's not generator prepped), a little legwork will be necessary to ensure that you get what you really need. For starters, what is the electrical system in your RV? Some micro-trailers or van-type RVs have a single, 15- or 20-amp circuit. Many trailers and motorhomes have 30-amp service, and some larger RVs have 50-amp service. What capacity service you have is important to understand as a baseline. Remember:

AMPERAGE x VOLTAGE = WATTS

A RV that has 15-amp service means that the RV can support 1,800 watts (*15 amps x 120 Volts = 1,800 watts*).

A RV that has 20-amp service means that the RV can support 2,400 watts (*20 amps x 120 Volts = 2,400 watts*).

A RV that has 30-amp service means that the RV can support 3,600 watts (*30 amps x 120 Volts = 3,600 watts*).

It, therefore, seems pretty straightforward that a RV with 50-amp service should be able to support 6,000 watts. As we discovered previously in chapter 12 when learning about the variety of options for electrical service for various RVs, 50-amp service actually supports up to 12,000 watts! (Recall that, in short, 50-amp service has two 120-Volt power wires, not just one like 30-amp and 20-amp services).

So, to calculate 50 amp, you have to double the 120-Volt service. This does NOT mean that you're getting 240 Volts; it means you're getting two hot feeds of 120 Volts each (*50 amp x (2 x 120 Volts) = 12,000 watts*). This is why so many of the larger RVs with 50-amp service come with large generators pre-installed. By far, the majority of "add-on" generators in use are 30-amp configurations.

To determine what you really need, answering a few questions is in order:

- Will this generator be needed so you can boondock?
- How long will you need it to run?
- What fuel source do you want to use?
- What's your power requirement?

Generators normally have a maximum wattage rating and a running wattage rating. As an example, a portable 3,000-watt generator may have a maximum rating of 3,000 watts, but may normally provide power at only 2,600 watts. The generator has the capability to "surge" up to 3,000 watts to help when appliances start up, but then will slowly reduce back down to 2,600 watts of continuous output. This is an important factor when sizing a generator. If you really need 3,000 watts, then you to make sure the generator is rated at 3,000 watts of continuous power.

Let's assume you have a 30-amp travel trailer and you want the generator to use for an occasional boondocking, or for an emergency, like if your RV Park loses power. You want the generator to run for a long weekend, and you think it best if you use liquid propane for a fuel source since you already have liquid propane tanks in the RV. How much power do you need?

To determine that, you need to build a list of all the items, appliances, devices, and accessories that you plan to use during the day. Indicate the wattage of each of the items, and try to list them by the times of the day that they might be in use. It is this step that best qualifies the size generator you need. By totaling the wattages of **ALL** of the items you may use at any given time, the highest total represents your worst-case power requirement. In our example, we're again using the information and calculations that we used in chapter 12 when learning about RV electrical systems.

APPLIANCE	WATTAGE	AMPS
Air Conditioner, 13.5k	1,700	14
Air Conditioner, 15k	1,950	16
Ceiling Fan	25	0.2
Cell Phone Charger (in use)	5	0.05
Clock Radio	2	0.02
Coffee Maker	900	7.5
Converter, 40-amp	650	5.5
Electric Blanket	100	0.8
Electric Space Heater	1,500	12.5
Electric Water Heater	1,200	10
Fan, Medium, tabletop style	55	0.45
Hair Dryer	1,200	10
Laptop Computer	120	1
Microwave	1,300	10.5
Refrigerator (residential style)	600	5

Suburban 12,000-Btu furnace fan	DC	2
Television, 20" flat-screen LCD	60	0.5
Television Satellite Receiver	170	1.5
Toaster Oven	960	8
Washer/Dryer RV Combo	1,900	16
Vacuum Cleaner	840	7

Midnight to 4 am. We're sleeping. Maybe the Suburban furnace is running, depending on time of year. The furnace operates using liquid propane, and the control board and blower fan each run on 12-Volt DC. So, our only real electric draw is the RV converter, clock radio, and cell phone charger.

APPLIANCE	WATTAGE	AMPS
Cell Phone Charger	5	0.05
Clock Radio	2	0.02
Converter	650	5.5
TOTALS	**657**	**Under 6**

4 am to 8 am. We're waking up and moving around, working on that first cup of coffee, cooking breakfast, and showering.

APPLIANCE	WATTAGE	AMPS
Cell Phone Charger	5	0.05
Clock Radio	2	0.02
Converter	650	5.5
Coffee Maker	900	7.5
Hair Dryer	1,200	10
Microwave	1,300	10.5
TOTALS	**4,057**	**Under 44**

8 am to Noon. Our day is underway. We're in and out of the RV, getting warm as the sunshine starts covering the travel trailer, and maybe checking out a little television to keep up on world events.

APPLIANCE	WATTAGE	AMPS
Air Conditioner	1,700	14
Cell Phone Charger	5	0.05
Clock Radio	2	0.02
Converter	650	5.5
Microwave	1,300	10.5
Television, 20" flat-screen LCD	60	0.5
TOTALS	**3,717**	**Under 31**

Noon to 4 pm. Same as before, minus the microwave. The day is in full swing!

APPLIANCE	WATTAGE	AMPS
Air Conditioner	1,700	14
Cell Phone Charger	5	0.05
Clock Radio	2	0.02
Converter	650	5.5
Television, 20" flat-screen LCD	60	0.5
TOTALS	**2,417**	**Under 21**

4 pm to 8 pm. Still warm from the daytime sun. Steaks are on the grill, and curly fries are in the microwave. Catching up on emails with the laptop, and the big game is on the television. Need to do a little cleaning after all the dirt we dragged in, so the vacuum comes in handy, as does the washing machine.

APPLIANCE	WATTAGE	AMPS
Air Conditioner	1,700	14
Cell Phone Charger	5	0.05
Clock Radio	2	0.02
Converter	650	5.5
Laptop Computer	120	1
Microwave	1,300	10.5
Television, 20" flat-screen LCD	60	0.5
Washer/Dryer RV Combo	1,900	16
Vacuum Cleaner	840	7
TOTALS	**6,577**	**Under 55**

8 pm to Midnight. Worn out! Time to unwind and watch news on the television as just the fan keeps the trailer plenty cool.

APPLIANCE	WATTAGE	AMPS
Cell Phone Charger	5	0.05
Clock Radio	2	0.02
Converter	650	5.5
Fan, Medium, table-top-style	55	0.45
Television, 20" flat-screen LCD	60	0.5
TOTALS	**772**	**Under 7**

For our example, remember, we're wanting to power a travel trailer for a long weekend of boondocking. We'll need the air conditioner for limited periods during the day; and will use the microwave and the television periodically during the day. Since our travel trailer has a dual-power refrigerator, it will cool using LP gas and 12-Volt DC; the same with the gas water heater.

Using the power matrix, it seems clear we'll use the most power during the 4-to-8 pm block, but other blocks of the day are fairly heavy power draws as well. This is where you have to drill down into the weeds a little. Your travel trailer is 30-amp service, so the reality is, even with your RV is hooked up to shore power, you would have exceeded your travel trailer's maximum service.

There are a couple of factors at play here. First, many of these electrical appliances draw a lot of power to start, but not as much while they are running. Air conditioners are a great example. A 15k unit may peak at 3,300 to 3,500 watts to start, but only 1,300 to 1,800 watts while running.[32] The other factor (the one really controlled by you) is what is actually draw is at one specific time. In the 4 am to 8 am block, the coffee maker, hair dryer, and microwave are all listed, but it is unlikely that you would be using them all at exactly the same time; that's the key. While the microwave draws 1,300 watts, the microwave is normally only used for a few minutes at any given time. The hair dryer draws 1,200 watts, but you're using it for a very limited period of time.

Your travel trailer has power limitations just as any generator will. Being aware of the power draw of the devices you're using and spacing out their use is something that you can get accustomed to doing without really even thinking about it.

For our example, we wanted a portable, inverter-style generator that needs to be about 3,500 watts and use liquid propane. A quick internet search reveals some immediate options, one of which is the Champion Dual-Fuel 3400/3060 inverter generator. While other options are available, this unit supports liquid propane right out of the box and, in a pinch can use unleaded fuel as well.

While we spent a lot of time creating the power matrix to understand our power requirements, in a travel trailer with 30-amp/3,600-watt service, it serves no purpose to supply a 5,000-watt generator. However, if you need 3,600 watts and only purchase a 1,000-watt portable generator, you'll be camping in a rig with no air conditioner, microwave, hair dryer—you get the point.

Figure 79 Champion's dual-fuel inverter generator runs on unleaded gasoline and LP fuel.

Chapter Fourteen

Hitches

Hitches are an integral, but sometimes overlooked, component of the RV experience. Many options and choices are available, and making the proper selection is key to getting the most out of your RV experience. Since trailers represent the majority of RV sales, properly equipped tow vehicles ensure their safe operation.

Outfitting your tow vehicle with a hitch (especially the proper hitch) can be a challenge, to say the least. Hitches fall into a series of categories. For RV use, however, the most common hitches are receiver hitches and fifth-wheel hitches.

NEVER EXCEED THE CAPACITY OF THE LOWEST-RATED COMPONENT.

Bumper Ball Mount

Many trucks and sport utility vehicle (SUV)-type vehicles come equipped from the manufacturer with bumpers that include standard trailer ball mounting holes. This is the extreme low end of capacity and capability for towing; however, if you have a small, very lightweight RV, this may be sufficient for your needs. Generally, these configurations

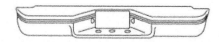

Figure 80 Typical truck step bumper with ball hitch mounting positions.

are limited to trailers that weigh less than 1,000 pounds and have less than 100 pounds of tongue weight.

Bumper receiver mount

Some hitch manufacturers market a hitch that includes a receiver and bolts to your vehicle bumper. While these offer some flexibility over the bumper ball mount, they do not change the towing capacity at all. A

Figure 81 Typical bumper receiver mount hitch.

bumper receiver mount does not use the frame to support the trailer weight, so the maximum capacity is the same as that for which the bumper is certified. A bumper received mount should not be mistaken for an actual Class I or above receiver hitch.

Receiver hitch

Receiver hitches, perhaps the most common hitch used for trailer towing, are specifically designed to attach to the tow vehicles frame. This design makes them substantially more suited for towing than simple bumper ball mounts.

The receiver hitch incorporates a tube (ranging from 1.25 to 2.5 inches), into which slides a steel shank; the hitch ball is then fastened to the steel shank. This feature makes these hitches very capable and allows for different ball mounts to be changed with ease.

Receiver hitches are divided into five classes, each with a specific weight rating and capability. It is important to note, the original equipment manufacturer (OEM) tow rating limits take precedence over the weight rating a specific hitch. No hitch increases the tow rating of a tow vehicle. Simply put, if your new SUV has a towing weight limit of 5,000 lbs, putting a hitch capable of towing 8,000 lbs does not increase your SUV's towing capability (it is still 5,000 lbs). A small SUV may come with a Class I hitch, but have limited tow ratings of 1,000 lbs and a 100-lb tongue weight.

You **MUST** consult the owner's manual of your tow vehicle to ensure that you do not exceed the manufacturer's designed towing limits.

Class I receivers

Class I receivers, light-duty receivers that are engineered most often for passenger cars and smaller SUVs, are widely available from various manufacturers. Class I receivers use a 1.25-inch receiver and are generally rated to tow up to 2,000 lbs and handle a 200-lb tongue weight.

Class II receivers

Class II receivers use the same 1.25-inch receiver as the Class I hitch, but can support trailer weights up to 3,500 lbs and a 350-lb tongue weight.

Figure 82 Typical frame-mounted Class I and Class II receivers.

Class III receivers

Class III receivers, the most commonly used, are often installed by the OEM as part of its tow package equipment. Class III hitches use a 2-inch receiver

Figure 83 Frame-mounted Class III receiver.

tube that is capable of towing up to 8,000 lbs and have an 800-lb tongue weight.

Class IV receivers

Class IV receivers, available for a smaller range of vehicles, consist of a more robust box design and maintain the 2-inch receiver size. Class IV receiver hitches can tow up to 10,000 lbs and have a 1,000-pound tongue weight.

Figure 84 Frame-mounted Class IV receiver.

Class V receivers

Class V receivers, the high-end capacity for receiver hitches, are capable of towing to 12,000 lbs, and have a 1,200 pound tongue weight. Class V receivers most often incorporate a 2.5 inch receiver tube, and are found on one-ton pickups and larger truck chassis.

Weight-distributing hitches

Weight-distributing hitches, used in conjunction with most any Class III, IV, and V hitch, provide enhanced load distribution, thus increasing the tow vehicle's stability and stance. By design, weight-distributing hitches use spring bars, rods, and chains to distribute the trailer's tongue weight across both the tow vehicle and trailer chassis.

How does it work? Essentially, a weight-distributing hitch redistributes the hitch weight forward across the tow vehicle's axles and backwards across to the trailer axles. Spring bars attached to the weight distributing hitch apply force downward on the rear of the trailer tongue, thereby transferring weight to the trailer axles. In turn, the springs apply upward pressure on the hitch, transferring weight from the hitch across the tow vehicle's front axle. The result is that the weight is distributed more evenly among all the axles of the tow and trailer, resulting in a more stable and comfortable towing experience.

Figure 86 Illustration of tow vehicle and trailer equipped with weight-distributing hitch.

Figure 85 Illustration of tow vehicle and trailer not equipped with weight-distributing hitch.

Without a weight-distributing hitch, the entire tongue weight of the trailer is basically applied against the rear suspension of the tow vehicle. With heavier trailers, this often results in the tow vehicle sagging in the rear, which is amplified as the tow vehicle and trailer hit bumps and dips in the roadway.

Weight-distributing hitches have many options and are highly configurable. Their height can be adjusted to align with most any pulled trailer. Sway control apparatus can also be installed on several models, further enhancing the resulting ride.

References on some internet forums equate weight-distributing hitches to weight-carrying hitches; this is confusing and certainly inaccurate. Class I thru V hitches with a shank and a ball mount installed would, by definition, be a weight-carrying hitch. The tongue weight of the trailer is applied to the ball, which is mounted to the shank installed in the hitch receiver. This direct tongue weight is only distributed with a weight-distributing hitch.

Weight-distributing hitches can, in some cases, increase the towing capacity of a specified hitch. Some hitch manufacturers have dual ratings for the receiver hitches. Based on the specific hitch and the appropriate tow vehicle, a weight-distributing hitch may increase the towing capacity and tongue weight.

For example, a Class III hitch with the proper weight-distributing hitch could increase the towing capacity from 8,000 to 12,000 lbs. A Class IV hitch could be capable of towing up to 14,000 lbs from the original 10,000 lbs. Again, it is important to understand that this is not the standard, but is an option afforded by some weight-distributing hitches. As always, you must read and follow the directions of your hitch to the letter.

WARNING: As previously stated, but worth repeating: NO hitch attachment or enhancement can increase a tow vehicle's towing limits. Those design limits are set and determined by the tow vehicle manufacturer.

Do you need a weight-distributing hitch?

If your RV trailer is much more than a teardrop style, then chances are you might! Like many other topics in the RV world, this topic gets a lot of folks fired up, and opinions in this realm abound. I'm going to provide a few facts and restate some interesting information from a few major vehicle manufactures and then move on.

Figure 87 Typical weight distributing hitch - distributes trailer tongue weight across all axles of the tow vehicle and trailer.

Several RV safety sites and organizations state that a weight-distributing hitch should be used whenever a trailer weighs more than 50% of the tow vehicle's weight. That's simple enough, but not very direct. So, let's just take a quick look at the most popular RV tow vehicle segment (the pickup truck market), and review statements from the four major truck manufacturers.

Tow vehicle manufacturer statements

2016 Dodge Ram 1500/2500/3500 pickup truck

The Dodge RAM 1500/2500/3500 pickup truck owner's manual includes the following warning box:

"WARNING: If the gross trailer weight is 5,000 lbs (2,267 kg) or more, it is mandatory to use a weight-distributing hitch to ensure stable handling of your vehicle. If you use a standard

weight-carrying hitch, you could lose control of your vehicle and cause a collision."[33]

2016 Chevrolet Silverado pickup truck

The 2016 Chevrolet Silverado pickup truck owner's manual states:

"Weight distribution hitch required for trailers over 7,000 pounds."[34]

2016 Ford F Series pickup truck

The Ford RV and Trailer Towing Guide states:

"Most applications require a conventional weight-distributing hitch." The guide further mentions that the owner is responsible for obtaining the proper weight-distributing equipment, specifically to include sway control.

The included towing data spreadsheet shows that a weight-distribution hitch is required on F-150 for trailers weighing more than 5,000 lbs, or with a 500-lb tongue weight.[35]

2016 Toyota Tundra pickup truck

The Tundra owner's manual states:

"If the gross trailer weight is over 2,000 lbs (907 kg), a sway control device with sufficient capacity is required. If the gross trailer weight is over 5,000 lbs (2,268 kg), a weight-distributing hitch with sufficient capacity is required."[36]

Fifth-wheel hitches

Fifth-wheel hitches are in the same family as hitches used by commercial tractor trailer rigs across the country. Fifth-wheel hitches are necessary for heavier trailers, and work by allowing the weight of the trailer to be carried and

Figure 88 Typical rail mounted fifth-wheel hitch assembly.

spread across the rear axle of the tow vehicle. Fifth-wheel hitches have capacities up to 30,000 lbs with a 5,000-lb trailer pin weight.

Manufacturers offer many types of fifth-wheel hitches. Many newer pickup truck models offer pucks in the pickup bed into which a fifth-wheel hitch can be dropped and locked into place, thereby avoiding the necessity for traditional bedrail installations. Fifth-wheel hitches are popular for their large weight ratings and ease of hookup, stability, and ease of maneuvering. Most drivers find that backing up a fifth-wheel is easier than backing up with a traditional bumper pull.

FUN FACTS

RV

Otto Neumann and August Fruehauf invented the semi-trailer, incorporating a fifth wheel hitch plate and trailer king-pin in 1914. (Source: Fruehauf Historical)

Hitching your travel trailer

	Ensure trailer is chocked.
	Using tongue jack, raise trailer sufficiently to clear tow vehicle's hitch ball.
	Preferably with a spotter, back tow vehicle hitch ball under trailer ball socket.
	Open trailer ball socket locking latch, greasing inside slightly, if needed.
	Slowly lower trailer, nudging trailer as necessary to align with ball socket.
	Once trailer ball socket is correctly seated on hitch ball, close and lock coupler latch.
	Pull sufficiently on trailer tongue to ensure that trailer is connected to hitch ball.
	Remove trailer chocks.
	Retract the tongue jack, stow in lock position (for articulating tongue jacks)
	Pull the tow vehicle forward slightly if you are connected at an angle.
	Connect appropriate spring bars or rods of weight-distributing hitch and adjust to appropriate settings per hitch manual.
	Check tow vehicle and trailer for proper alignment; adjust as necessary.
	Check trailer safety chains for damage. If in serviceable condition, attach them by crisscrossing them under trailer tongue and attach them to frame of tow vehicle or hitch chain attachment loops. Ensure chains are long enough to allow for tight turns with little slack beyond that. If quick links or couplers were used, ensure they are closed tightly.
	Connect trailer breakaway lanyard.

	Connect trailer wiring harness.
	Perform light and brake checks.
	Pull forward a few feet and stop. Check hitch attachment again to ensure it is properly mated.

Unhitching your travel trailer

	Place tow vehicle in park and set emergency brake.
	Chock trailer tires.
	Disconnect breakaway and power umbilical.
	Extend trailer tongue jack to take weight off of tow vehicle.
	Verify that coupler ball and trailer coupler do not have pressure applied to them.
	Remove safety chains.
	Remove safety locking device from hitch ball coupler and, using release handle, unlock hitch ball coupler.
	Once released, continue raising trailer using tongue jack until trailer ball coupler and tow vehicle tow ball are completely separated and there is appropriate clearance to pull away tow vehicle from trailer.
	Release tow vehicle parking brake and pull forward, providing safe space between tow vehicle and trailer to setup.
	Level travel trailer using appropriate process.
	Lock travel trailer ball coupler with suitable locking device.
	Verify that chocks are firmly in place.

Hitching your fifth wheel trailer

	Ensure trailer is chocked.
	Using the front trailer jack stands, raise trailer to sufficient height to allow for backing tow vehicle underneath.
	Lower tailgate for pickups not equipped with V-shaped tow gates.
	Lock fifth-wheel jaws in coupling (open) position.
	Preferably with a spotter, back tow vehicle under front nose of fifth wheel, stopping short of attaching fifth wheel.
	Perform final height adjustments on trailer. Trailer kingpin box should be slightly lower than trailing, sloped edge of fifth-wheel plate. This will ensure that, when backing, tow vehicle slightly lifts trailer, ensuring kingpin and fifth-wheel locking jaws properly mate.
	Slowly back under trailer kingpin box, ensuring that kingpin is lined up with open jaws of fifth-wheel plate.
	As kingpin enters jaws of fifth-wheel plate, be prepared to stop once you hear fifth-wheel jaws slam closed and latch.
	Stop truck and allow truck to rock forward slightly to ensure the kingpin/locking jaws are not under pressure. Set emergency brake.
	Visually inspect fifth-wheel jaws to ensure that they are properly locked and that kingpin is properly seated.
	Once you have confirmed that jaws are engaged, lock fifth-wheel release with appropriate latch and safety lock.
	Connect fifth-wheel power umbilical.
	Connect trailer breakaway lanyard to fifth-wheel hitch base.
	Raise front trailer jack stands slightly off ground.

	Remove chocks.
	With full weight of trailer on tow vehicle, put tow vehicle in drive and pull forward slightly while applying trailer brakes. This pull test will ensure that you properly connected trailer kingpin to fifth-wheel hitch.
	Fully raise front jack stands.
	Perform full light and brake check.
	Close tailgate and secure all items before moving forward.

Uncoupling your fifth wheel trailer

	Place tow vehicle in park and set emergency brake.
	Chock trailer tires.
	Disconnect breakaway and power umbilical.
	Lower pickup truck tailgate.
	Extend trailer front jacks to take weight off of tow vehicle.
	Verify that kingpin and fifth-wheel locking jaws are not bound.
	Remove safety locking device from fifth-wheel plate and, using release handle, unlock jaws.
	Visually **VERIFY** that locking jaws are uncoupled.
	Release tow vehicle parking brake and pull forward slowly.
	Once verified that tow vehicle and trailer are disconnected, pull tow vehicle completely away from fifth wheel.
	Level fifth wheel using appropriate process.
	Lock fifth wheel kingpin with suitable locking device.
	Verify chocks are firmly in place.

Chapter Fifteen

Tires

Tires are an aspect of purchasing a RV that is often overlooked. Interestingly, many don't understand how critical RV tires are to ensuring that your safety and your trip are not ruined by a catastrophic tire failure.

Owning an RV should be an awesome experience! You should be enjoying exotic destinations; savoring new foods; and relaxing in the comfort of your home-away-from-home. To ensure that these things happen, you have to get there, and you can't get there safely without good quality tires that are properly maintained.

As previously discussed in other chapters of this book, tires can be a source of great consternation when discussing the topic with other RV owners. Because of a tire purchase's significant investment, many RV owners are totally invested in the topic, and are usually quite happy to share their opinions and experiences.

As with everything, accept that "your mileage may vary." What has worked well for one RVer may not work out at all for you. Just because one RV owner has driven their RV for 10 years on the same set of rubber and never had any problems does not constitute acceptance that your tires will last for 10 years. Conversely, RV owners have had tire failures upon leaving the dealership after purchasing their new rigs!

Some basic tire information is provided in this chapter, like differences between tire types, condition issues of which to be aware, and various manufacturer information and recommendations.

Armed with this information, you'll be ready to make an informed decision on your own.

Types of tires and tire markings

To begin, it's important to understand that, while tires may all appear to be very similar, all tires are not alike. In fact, tires are actually manufactured for a wide variety of specific purposes. A wealth of information can be gained by examining a tire's sidewall. In the following sections, we'll look at some of the important information that is molded into a tire's sidewall, and explain what some of the various codes and numbers mean. This list is not all-inclusive, but it does cover the basic information that you'll need to understand to ensure your tires are what are really required by your specific type of RV.

The illustrations that I've included here include white-lettered tires. I'm guessing that the majority of truck and trailer tires are probably traditional black, not raised white-letter. Also, my illustrations are not in proportion. Some of the data you'll need to find may be fairly small and close to the sidewall bead. Regardless, take the time necessary to locate this information on your tires.

A tire will most likely include the tire manufacturer's name and a model name. For example, a truck tire may include the tire manufacturer GOODYEAR, and the tire type WRANGLER. On a

Figure 89 Tire Manufacturer identified on tire's sidewall.

trailer tire, you may see CARLISLE as the manufacturer, and RADIAL TRAIL as the type.

One of the most important pieces of information molded on the tire is the tire type, size, and load range. The representation I've shown here is fairly standard, but again, the information on your tire could be shown differently. The identified numerical codes all mean something very specific. Let's break the information down by section.

Figure 90 Tire size and load range information on sidewall.

On Figure 91, for example, the tire is marked LT, which indicates use for Light Truck. Here are some other common tire codes:

P	Passenger tires (designed for use on passenger vehicles, like cars, mini vans, small SUVs, and some trucks)
LT	Light Truck tires (designed for use on trucks, large SUVs, or vans; designed to carry fairly heavy loads or to pull trailers)
ST	Special Trailer tires (designed for use on trailers and specifically designed for specific demands of trailers)

Tires for motorhomes, which require large tires, are often not marked with one of the identifiers above, if at all. These larger tires are often marked proprietarily based on the manufacturer, but will still indicate tire size and other information, which we'll cover in later on in subsequent sections of this chapter.

Large motorhome tires (more like commercial truck tires) require a little more research. When purchasing these large tires, you may see references to "steer axle" or "all position" use. On these larger tires, many manufacturers design and build different tires for the steering axle (front wheels) and the drive axles (rear tires). Steer axle tires can only be used on the front tires, where all position tires can be mounted in any position.

Next to the LT on the tire illustrated in Figure 91, the numbers "235" refer to the cross-sectional width of the tire in millimeters. This measurement is taken at the widest point of the inner and outer sidewalls. This measurement can be converted to inches by dividing by 25.4. In our example, *235/25.4 = 9.25 inches.*

After the "235/" are the numbers "85," which refer to the aspect ratio of the tire, which is the distance from the wheel to the outside of the tire tread. The smaller the aspect ratio, the shorter the sidewall. In this example, it is 85% of the width. We already determined from our conversion calculation above that our "235" tire is 9.25 inches wide. With an aspect ratio of 85%, we can determine the sidewall using the following calculation: *9.25 x .85 = 7.86 inches.*

Next to the numbers "85" is the letter "R," which refers to the tire's construction. In this example, the R stands for Radial, which is the most common type of tire construction, representing well over 95%

of all tires manufactured today. Other tire types include "D" for Bia-Ply construction, and "B" for internal belt design.

The numbers "16" after the letter "R" refer to the wheel size. In this example, the wheel is 16 inches. Some small, pop-up-style trailers have wheels in the 10-inch range, while large Class A motorhomes have wheels in the 25-inch range.

The letter "D" after the numbers "16" on our illustration (Figure 91) refers to the load range. Load range markings differ depending on the type of tire you're looking at.

Passenger tires (P) typically include the following markings:

LL	Light Load (usually 36 psi or less; designed for vehicles of relatively small vehicle weight and very limited cargo capacity)
SL	Standard Load (usually 36 psi or less; most passenger car tires are manufactured in this range)
blank	Standard Load (passenger [P] tires with no load rating are normally in the Standard Load range)
XL	Extra Load (usually 42 psi or less; designed for use on larger vehicles and those designed for carrying additional cargo)

Figure 91 Passenger tire load range codes.

Light Truck tires (LT) and Special Trailer tires (ST) typically include the following markings:

B	4-ply	35psi
C	6-ply	50psi
D	8-ply	65psi
E	10-ply	80psi
F	12-ply	95psi
G	14-ply	115psi
H	16-ply	125psi
J	18-ply	130psi

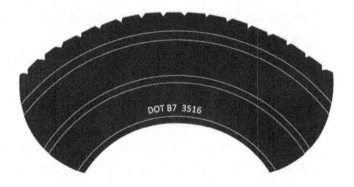

Figure 92 DOT marking reveals that DOT has approved this tire manufacturer (identified by code next to DOT marking). Date code is provided on the sidewall.

The Department of Transportation (DOT) symbol and code immediately tells you that the tire has been manufactured in full compliance with DOT tire safety guidelines. Is that important?

Absolutely it is. Tires are manufactured all over the world to a wide range of quality standards. Many "American" tires are not made in America at all—a fact which has caused great debate and stress for many, but nonetheless is a fact of free enterprise.

The DOT code provides a great deal of information about your tires. The DOT code is a collection of up to 12 letters and numbers, with the last four digits specifically reserved for four numbers. The DOT code provides the tire manufacturer, production facility, and date the tire was produced.

The example illustrated in Figure 93 shows a basic DOT code. The "B7" refers to the manufacturer of the tire (in this case, Michelin North America in Dothan Alabama). A great resource for researching a complete set of available DOT codes is the Tire Safety Group's website,[37] which provides a wealth of information, including manufacture data, recalls, service bulletins, and other valuable information.

The next four digits in our DOT code example (Figure 93) indicate the tire "born-on date." The first two numbers indicate the week, while the second two numbers represent the year. Our example tire was produced in the Michelin plant in Dothan, Alabama, during the 35th week of the year 2016.

This date information is very important because, unlike what some will tell you, a tire is NOT good or safe just because the tire still has usable tread left. A five-year-old tire that has never been installed on a vehicle is still an old tire. This topic is one that gets a lot of RVers fired up, and the fact that the wrong information continues to flourish is a major source of my concern. There are those folks who will stand tall and proffer that the only reason tire manufacturers claim that tires should be regularly replaced is because it forces you back to their stores. Just not so.

Tire life is based on many factors, including tire type, use, care, and age. Major tire manufacturers are pretty consistent on tire life. Michelin states that, after 5 years, you should inspect your tires very critically, and that 10 years should be the maximum age of any tire, regardless of what its condition appears to be. This is important because, while a tire may appear to be in excellent condition on the exterior, you have no way of knowing the internal condition of the tire.[38]

Goodyear does not state a specified replacement criteria for its tires because of the number of variables involved. Goodyear indicates that the owner is ultimately responsible for determining the time for tire replacement, but does warn owners of ensuring proper load, inflation, and not allowing tires to sit for extended periods without moving. Goodyear's *RV Tire Booklet* specifically states that, "6 months loaded, with little or no rotation, is not good!"[39]

Continental states that "All tires (including spares) that were manufactured more than 10 years ago should be replaced with new tires, even if they appear to be useable from their external appearance and if the tread depth may have not reached the minimum wear-out depth."[40]

Bridgestone-Firestone states that tires should be regularly inspected after 5 years of service to determine if they can continue in service. Regardless of a tire's condition or tread depth, they recommended that tires more than 10 years old be taken out of service and replaced with new tires.[41]

Your tire sidewall should also indicate the load index, speed symbol, and any special tire application letters

or symbols. Keep in mind, our tire

Figure 93 Tire sidewall should contain load index and speed rating.

illustration example (Figure 91) is an LT tire. LT and ST tires have two load indexes (separated by a slash mark). This is because these tires may be used in applications where there are dual rear tires. The illustration in Figure 94 shows "119/116" on the sidewall, which indicates that, on a single rear-wheel application, it is appropriate for a 119 load index (or 2,998 lbs). For dual rear wheel applications, the 116 index (or 2,756 lbs) is appropriate.

If after reading this you're scratching your head thinking that the math here seems "bass ackwards," your math skills are impeccable. The reason that weight indexes are slightly less for dual rear wheel applications is an engineered reserve, in the event one of the duals fails.

75=852	90=1323	105=2039	120=3086	135=4806
76=882	91=1356	106=2094	121=3197	136=4938
77=908	92=1389	107=2149	122=3307	137=5071
78=937	93=1433	108=2205	123=3417	138=5203
79=963	94=1477	109=2271	124=3527	139=5357
80=992	95=1521	110=2337	125=3638	140=5512
81=1019	96=1565	111=2403	126=3748	141=5677

82=1047	97=1609	112=2469	127=3858	142=5842
83=1074	98=1653	113=2535	128=3968	143=6008
84=1102	99=1709	114=2601	129=4079	144=6173
85=1135	100=1764	115=2679	130=4189	145=6393
86=1168	101=1819	116=2756	131=4299	146=6614
87=1201	102=1874	117=2833	132=4409	147=6779
88=1235	103=1929	118=2910	133=4541	148=6944
89=1279	104=1984	119=2998	134=4674	149=7165

Figure 94 Load rating chart index - code = lbs.

The "P" on our tire example indicates the tire's speed rating. (I'm hesitant to discuss speed ratings in much detail here because we're talking about RV tires, and when you're driving a RV, speed is not your friend. Slow and steady is always safer. However, in the interest of full disclosure, in our example, the "P" refers to a speed index of 93 mph. There are tire speed ratings in excess of 200mph, but then again, that fact is useful only should you become a Jeopardy contestant one day.

G = 56	P = 94
J = 62	Q = 100
K = 68	R = 106
L = 75	S = 112
M = 81	T = 118
N = 87	U = 124

Figure 95 Chart referencing speed rating codes.

Remember, RVs are often heavy and require additional stopping distance. You simply cannot operate a RV like you would a regular passenger vehicle. Pay particular attention to your RV owner's manual and any associated documentation for the tires. Trailers with Goodyear trailer tires installed have a maximum manufacturer's speed rating of 65 mph. Goodyear motorhome tires have a 75-mph maximum speed rating.

Lastly, a tire may have a special tire application marking or symbol. In the tire illustration in Figure 94, the "M+S" indicates that the tire is rated to handle mud and snow well. Some tires may have a three-peak mountain symbol with a snowflake in the middle, which represents that the tire is effective in snow.

Tire sidewalls should also indicate the Uniform Tire Quality Grade (UTQG), which shows a relative grade for the tire based on actual manufacturer tests. For the tread wear grade, there is acceptance that the scoring is somewhat subjective; however, the higher the number, the better the tread ware performance.

The traction rating is a letter grade that is assigned to a tire based on performance testing of how the tire performs while skidding on a wet

surface. The higher the letter grade, the better the performance. Recently, AA grades have been allowed as tire performance, through innovation and improved design, continues to excel.

Figure 96 Additional information on the sidewall can include traction information and temperature ratings.

Lastly, the temperature grade is also a letter grade assigned to a tire based on its ability to withstand extreme heat and ability to dissipate extreme heat buildup.

Every tire sold in the United States must meet at least C grade requirements, which indicates that it can perform at sustained speeds of 85 mph. Again, the higher a tire's letter grade, the better the tire's performance rating.

Figure 97 A tire's sidewall indicates its maximum tire inflation pressure and maximum tire load.

Every tire sold in the United States is required to indicate its maximum load and maximum inflation pressure on its sidewall (see Figure 98). A tire's maximum load is determined using an industry standard inflation pressure, whose variables allow some flexibility for manufacturers in setting specific vehicle recommendations. Therefore, it is possible, for example, for a light truck (using a LT tire) to have a pressure setting for the vehicle that slightly exceeds what is indicated as the tire's maximum tire pressure on its sidewall.

Always default to the vehicle weight sticker as long as the tires are identical to the OEM tires that were provided by the original manufacturer.

Inflation

Tire inflation is critical to the safe operation of your RV. Most RVers have witnessed the ugly side of tire failures—fifth wheel trailer sides ripped off, significant damage to a motorhome's body, etc. There are far worse outcomes!

One of the worst results of tire failure is fire. Each year, many motorhome fires are caused by a rear dual tire failure that eventually catches fire and then, catastrophe. Between 2009 and 2013, more than 5,500 fires per year involved recreational vehicles,[42] many of which were attributed to tire failures.

As discussed earlier in the book, RVs bouncing up and down the road create some unique challenges when discussing the risk of fire. Construction materials, fuels, batteries, wiring, and a basement storage area full of who-knows-what all require your constant attention.

One major fire risk is improper tire inflation or tire failure. An improperly inflated tire can quickly heat up to the point of catching fire or exploding, of which either scenario presents extreme safety risks. Motorhomes with rear dual tires are particularly vulnerable. A flat on an inside dual is often difficult to detect. Once the tire has failed, the friction between the failed tire and the remaining tire quickly raises to a hazardous level. A tire that catches fire can quickly spread to other areas of a RV. A tire that explodes can send tire shrapnel in all directions, severing brake lines, fuel lines, LP gas lines, or a host of other problems.

You cannot prevent all tire failures. Road debris or a defective tire off the assembly line may be beyond your control, but an aggressive tire inspection routine could potentially save you thousands of dollars, or possible your life!

As far as inflation is concerned, continually monitor tire inflation with either a Tire Pressure Monitoring System (TPMS) or a tire gauge.

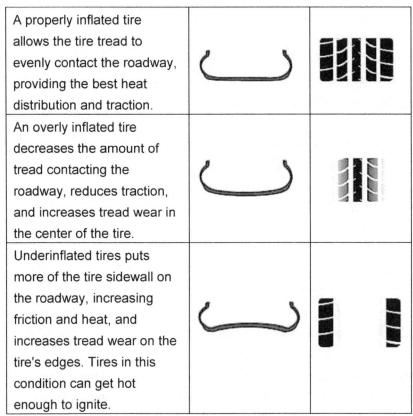

A properly inflated tire allows the tire tread to evenly contact the roadway, providing the best heat distribution and traction.		
An overly inflated tire decreases the amount of tread contacting the roadway, reduces traction, and increases tread wear in the center of the tire.		
Underinflated tires puts more of the tire sidewall on the roadway, increasing friction and heat, and increases tread wear on the tire's edges. Tires in this condition can get hot enough to ignite.		

Figure 98 Visual assessment of tire inflation scenarios.

A visual assessment of your tires is good, but is not a reliable method for determining a tire's under inflation until the tire is critically underinflated. If you think I'm wrong, test it. Let 10 lbs, then 20 lbs of air out of one RV tire and see if you can detect a difference in inflation in comparison to the remaining inflated tires. If you honestly can, then you're in the minority. The only way to be absolutely sure and safe while operating your RV is to use a reliable TPMS or tire gauge.

TPMS or air gauge

Because Tire Pressure Monitoring Systems (TPMSs) are becoming standard on most passenger vehicles, more and more folks are getting familiar with them. TPMS technology is also available for installation on your RV, but many folks are hesitant to install them.

TPMSs vary in design and installation; band systems have tire sensor mounts inside the tire, banded to the wheel; internal systems are part of the tire stem; and sensors simply replace the tire stem cap. Regardless the style, all TPMSs work essentially in the same way.

Tire sensors are registered in a central receiver by wheel position. Once installed, the sensors monitor a tire's air pressure and report that pressure to a central receiver (usually mounted somewhere in the driver's compartment). In the event of a low tire, a central receiver will produce a warning tone to alert the driver.

Most TPMSs allow you to set high and low pressures, and temperature alerts (all very handy information). A TPMS may be a little pricey but, in the scheme of things, is money well invested in my opinion.

For larger RVs, motorhomes, or trailers, antenna amplifiers can be installed to ensure that all of the tires on your rig are reporting properly. A RV TPMS can be installed with up to 18 sensors, thereby offering a TPMS that will protect you regardless of your RV configuration.

Some die-hard folks out there are convinced that the only foolproof method for checking your tires is to do so with a good-quality tire pressure gauge. These technology avoiders will remind you that batteries can fail, and that any device that contains electronics can malfunction at the most inopportune times. All are certainly true facts, but I would remind you that the only time you can check your tires with a pressure gauge is when you're sitting out on the pavement, stationary, and regardless of the weather conditions.

The reality is that, more often than not, tires fail or catch fire when you're driving down the road. Sometimes, issues like a dragging brake can start a tire fire while stationary because there is no moving air to cool the hanging brake, but this is less common. TPMS sensors can provide you with real-time tire pressure readings and, at a glance, you know the status of your tires. In the event of a TPMS sensor failure, you can begin more visual inspections of the tires while maintaining the peace-of-mind that the remaining tires are still monitored.

Where I will concede to the die-hards is the need to visually inspect your tires for damage or signs of unusual wear. A TPMS is not a replacement for checking your tires on your own; a TPMS is just an enhancement. Nothing is better than you rolling your eyeballs over each tire at a fuel stop or rest stop. A TMPS cannot detect uneven tire wear or other tire anomalies—you must detect those!

Tire problems

Keeping an eye on your tires offers you a much better chance of detecting a minor problem before it becomes a major problem. The beginning of this chapter provides you with information on what to look for as far as tire capacities, capabilities, and manufacture dates. What else do you need to look for?

Ultra violet (sun) and ozone damage

Tires produced today are the most reliable ever manufactured and have more technology in their designs than ever before. Tires manufactured today include ozone-resistant rubber compounds and waxes to fend off harmful ozone. When tires are used, the flexing and heat that are generated help bring these embedded waxes and protectants to the tires surface. Carbon-blended substances utilized during tire production are very effective at inhibiting harmful UV radiation. However, no tire (or anything else) is foolproof, or lasts forever.

Vigilantly inspect your tires for signs of abnormal wear and cracks. Any cracks (including small cracks in a sidewall) are an indication that a tire is beginning to suffer the effects of ozone and UV damage. At the first sign of these cracks, you should have the tires

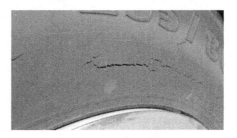

Figure 99 This tire's visible cracks indicate extensive damage. This tire is no longer road worthy.

professionally evaluated. Some limited cracking is OK, but there are very definite limits, specifically the depth of the cracks is critical.

Use of any tires with the amount of damage shown on Figures 100 and 101 should not be used by anyone. These tires are unsafe and should be replaced without hesitation. The color of a tire can provide some insight to its condition. If a tire looks faded, or has a gray tint, the tire is likely sun damaged beyond safe use.

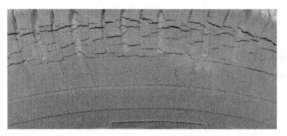

Figure 100 Badly cracked, this tire is absolutely unsafe.

A lot of tire products on the market claim UV and ozone protection, thus enhancing the functionality and life expectancy of your tire. Be cautious in this regard. While it seems counterintuitive that you should not use tire treatment and dressing, most tire manufacturers simply recommend cleaning your tires with mild soapy water and using no chemical treatments of any kind. Many tire products on the market include petroleum products that actually are harmful to your tire and should not be used. Not to imply are all bad, just be aware of the chemicals that tire dressings employ.

Tire wear bars

Federal Motor Vehicle Safety
Standards (FMVSS) now
require new tires to have tire
wear bars molded into the tire
tread. These tire wear bars
often appear as squares and
become visible only as your
tires wear. When the tire

Figure 101 Typical tire wear bar molded in the tire tread.

tread remaining measurement is at 2/32 inch, the tire wear bars will
be flush with the tire tread. At this point, the tires are worn out and
need to be replaced.

Other signs to look out for

Center wear is indicative of over inflation. In this example, the center tread shows clear signs of excessive wear as compared to outer edges of tire. In some cases, center wear is related to wheel misalignment.	
Edge or outside wear is indicative of underinflated tire; shoulders (outer edges) of tire will show extreme wear in comparison to tire's center tread. This condition can lead to tire fires.	
Camber wear is apparent with an exaggerated wear of either the outer- or innermost tread. Camber refers to the tire's angle. In RV applications, there should little to no camber. This type of tire wear indicates an alignment issue or suspension damage of some kind that should be evaluated promptly.	

Cup wear or patch wear can be difficult to distinguish. Cupped tires have smooth spots all over the tire surface and are caused by weak or damaged suspension components, thereby allowing tire to bounce and skid. Patch wear is usually more systematic (not random), suggested cause of which is due more to a tire out of round or balance. Regardless, both conditions should be evaluated promptly.	
Toe wear is similar to tire wear resulting from camber problem, but is less pronounced. A tire with toe wear will reveal an inner or outer shoulder that will not be nearly as worn or abused as tire wear from camber problem. Symptom usually points to alignment issue. As with all tire problems, evaluate promptly.	

Figure 102 Various indications of tire damage.

FUN FACTS
RV

The typical RV owner is 48 years old, married, with an annual household income of $62,000, higher than the median for all households.
(Source: RVIA.Org)

Conclusion

Congratulations! You've made it to the end of the book's primary text. The remaining pages contain pre-delivery inspection checklists, weight worksheets, and some state licensing and supplemental brake information, all of which are included as appendices.

This effort has been an incredible learning experience for me. I hope the text has been insightful and useful for you as well. RV ownership is on the rise, with record sales over these past few years. With more and more of us on the road, the need for more accurate information will only increase (as will the amount of disinformation and RV Park lore).

I've made every attempt to provide accurate information throughout this book's pages, and have gone to great lengths to research issues where conflicting information seemed the norm. From the beginning, I've challenged you to do your own research and become your own expert. For those areas where this book did not deliver for you, press on to find the information you need.

For as long as this book is available through demand publishing, a sister website (www.areyourvready.com) will be maintained and include the latest versions of weight worksheets and PDI checklists, which will be available for your download.

I ask that you please inform me (using the contact information at www.areyourvready.com) if you encounter any discrepancies in the book, or believe that additional information should be amended in a future edition.

Special Thanks

Special thanks to family and friends whom have suffered (and I mean **suffered**) for the past year as I've focused on completing this effort.

While it was fun and educational for me, for some it may have elicited more of an "Oh God, not the book again" response.

To all of you, a sincere thank you and a promise of no more writing, for a while...

Thank you again and SAFE TRAVELS.

Appendix One

Pre-Delivery Inspection Checklists

In chapter four, I discussed, in great detail, the need to perform a thorough pre-delivery inspection. Conducting an inspection provides you the best opportunity to detect issues before finalizing your purchase. Remember, a dealer (or private party selling their RV) will be more motivated to perform repairs in order to complete a sale. Once you own the unit, there is less of an incentive for them to hustle and get your repairs made. Of course dealers will perform warranty work and repairs as needed, the point being as long as the RV is on their tax roster, a dealer will be more enthusiastic to get things done.

These pre-delivery inspection checklists are a product of my research, reviews and lessons learned while purchasing our RVs. There are many sites out there touting their own home-grown checklists, but I found them to be hit-and-miss. I believe these checklists are the most thorough available.

For ease of use, the checklists are broken down into several categories. Motorhome specific, trailer specific and then major systems, exterior, interior, electric, plumbing, etc. The intent is for you to review the checklists, select the ones that fit your need and ignore the rest. Several checklist items are replicated across more than one topical area. This was necessary because of the menu approach to selecting the checklists you want to utilize.

The following checklists are included:

- MOTORHOME – Specific
- TRAILER – Specific
- WHEELS
- STORAGE COMPARTMENTS
- EXTERIOR – sidewalls and caps

- EXTERIOR – roof
- EXTERIOR – underbelly
- EXTERIOR – awnings
- EXTERIOR – slides
- WINDOWS
- INTERIOR
- KITCHEN
- BATHROOM
- AUDIO VISUAL
- GENERATOR
- UTILITIES
- PROPANE
- ELECTRICAL – AC and DC systems
- HVAC
- SAFETY

These checklists are available for download at
www.areyourvrady.com

MOTORHOME SPECIFIC	Notes
Drive shaft Inspect the driveline for apparent damage. The drive shaft should be solid with no play. U-Joints should be lubricated. Where the drive shaft connects to the transmission and rear differential should be relatively dry. Seeping is fairly common but there should be no obvious leaks. It should not be wet to the touch.	
Differential Inspect for damage and signs of leaks at the axels. Check the differential fluid. For used units, determine if fluid has ever been changed. Refer to owner's manual for the manufacturer's suggested maintenance interval.	
Engine appearance and overall condition Check engine and engine compartment. Is the engine clean? For used RVs is there a maintenance history? Are all covers and caps in place?	
Boots There are ball joint boots, tie rod cover boots, dust cover boots, steering dampening rod boots and other assorted boots depending on the chassis and manufacturer. Inspect each for damage or deterioration.	
Mileage For used units, is there a maintenance history that corresponds to the reported mileage?	

Bags For diesel pushers (or other chassis with air bags), carefully inspect the air bags for condition. They should be clean and uniform in color. Check for signs of cracking, indications of something rubbing against a bag or signs of fluid on the bag. Operate the air system and check the bags for leaks. This can be accomplished using leak detection fluid or a mixture of soap and water. Listen for the compressor running. If the compressor kicks on often with no application of brakes, it may be a sign of an air leak in the system.	
Engine oil – condition For used units, check engine oil. It should be clean and full. Ask for oil change records. For larger diesel engines, consider sending off an oil sample.	
Engine coolant – test strip For used units, check the cooling system using the appropriate test strips. Test strips are available at most automotive parts stores for most engine cooling system types. For larger diesel units, specific formula strips can be obtained at heavy truck fuel stops and maintenance shops.	
Power steering fluid Check the fluid level. For used units, does the fluid smell burned? Is it discolored? Wipe the fluid on a clean cloth. Is there any indication of debris in the fluid?	
Steering dampener If the RV is equipped with a steering dampener, visually and physically check it. It	

	should be securely mounted. It should be dry with no oil soiling the boot. Are there signs of leaks or damage?	
	Transmission fluid Most motorized units include the capability to check the transmission fluid. Refer to the chassis manufacturer manual for specific guidance. For used units, check the fluid level. Check records for transmission service. On some diesel pushers with Allison transmissions, there is a diagnostic check that can be initiated from the driver's seat and the status will read out on the transmission gear selector screen.	
	Hose condition Check all hoses condition. Hoses are subjected to extreme temperature swings, dirt, oils, atmospheric ozone and electrochemical degradation. Hoses should be pliable but not soft or spongy. Upper radiator hoses have the highest failure rate so check them carefully. Check around clamps and fasteners for splits, hairline cracks or dry rot.	
	Belt condition Belts are susceptible to the same problems hoses experience. Carefully check belts for cracks, signs of fraying or splits. Check the sides of the belt for glazing or signs of excessive heat.	
	Exhaust inspection Check the exhaust system for damage, leaks, and excessive rust. Are exhaust hangers all in place and in good condition?	

Smells Are there any unusual smells? Burning rubber, oil, wires? Is there a sulfur smell? If something unusual is detected, run it to ground. The smell of burning wires could be disastrous. Other smells may be emission related but take the time to investigate.	
Chassis battery, location, date, type Determine the location of the chassis battery. The chassis battery is the battery that supplies the needed 12-Volts DC to the OEM chassis. Inspect the chassis battery. Is it clean? What type battery is it? There are three types of batteries, Wet Cell (flooded), Gel Cell, and Absorbed Glass Mat (AGM). Gel and AGM are considered maintenance free style batteries. For used RV's, what is the in-service date for the installed battery? Is it near its end-of-service life?	
Leaks Inspect the chassis carefully. Are there signs of leaks? New or used, leaks can happen to all rigs.	
State inspection For used units, was there a state Inspection? Is it current? If the state requires an inspection and it's out of date, investigate why?	
Wiring Inspect the wiring and wiring bundles to make sure they are routed so that they will not get caught in moving parts or be exposed to extreme heated surfaces.	

Fuel filter

Check your fuel filter. They vary greatly in appearance and mounting location. For used units, determine when the filter was last changed. On diesel units, read the manufacturers manual. Some filters include water separators and have circuitry that will inform the driver water is present in the fuel.

Oil filter

Check the oil filter housing for signs of damage. On used units, check when the oil was changed last. If in question, change the oil.

Fuse box

Inspect the fuse box, new or used. Are all the fuses in place? Is there any sign of damage from a blown fuse and associated wiring? Is the box clean and weather proof?

Air filter

For all units, check the air filter. In larger diesel units, this can be tricky, but the filter is critical to proper and reliable operation. It should be clean. Replace on condition.

Engine starting and idle

Start the engine and let it idle for a few minutes. Is it smooth? Are there any unusual noises? Is there a high idle feature?

Exhaust, smoke

When the engine is running, is there any smoke from the exhaust? Is there smoke at idle? Some smoke from a diesel under load is common, but at idle, the exhaust should be relatively clear.

Mirrors

Inspect the mirrors for damage. Is the housing secure? Do the automatic adjustment controls function properly? Are they heated? Spend the time necessary to get your mirrors adjusted properly.

Lights

Check all the chassis lights and markers lamps. Check driving lights and high-beam function. Make sure the lights are aligned.

Gauges

Check all gauges for proper operation. Check lighting and for programmable operations, run through the menu operations and settings.

Heat and air conditioning controls

Check the chassis air conditioning in all settings, fresh and recirculating. Check the heater and various output settings for proper operation. Does the blower motor work in all speeds? Are there strange noises when changing air flow? If so, electric/vacuum doors could be blocked with debris. Is air circulating from the appropriately selected vents?

Chassis radio

Does the dash radio work in all modes? Does it have Navigation or Monitor capabilities? Bluetooth? Check for passwords on newer radios that may prevent changing settings.

Seat belts, driver, passenger and couch

Check all seatbelts in the coach for proper operation. Ensure latch is smooth to operate.

Turn signals

Check the operation of the turn signals. Ensure that the turn signal auto cancel function works appropriately when the steering wheel is returned to center.

Rear camera

Does the RV have a rear camera? Is it wired or wireless? If wireless, ensure the monitor is properly linked to the camera unit. Ensure there is no password installed in the system that would prevent changing settings.

Backup camera

Is the unit a rearview vision camera or just a backup camera? Rearview vision units are like electronic rearview mirrors, on all the time. Back up cameras are on only when the transmission is in reverse.

Side camera

Is the unit equipped with side mounted cameras for changing lanes? These cameras are linked to the turn signal switch and provide a side coach view, avoiding blind spots. Test each one for proper operation.

Driver passenger visors

If the coach is equipped with driver/passenger sun visors, check them carefully. Are they in good condition? Any cracks or blemishes that would make seeing through them difficult? Is the mounting arm easy to maneuver to the proper position for diving into the sun? When positioned out of the way, do they remain stationary? Are the visors motorized? If so, do they function properly?

Horn

Test the coach horn. Many larger coaches have two horns, selectable by a switch. These coaches include the regular car type horn and a large truck air horn.

Steering wheel

Check the operation of the tilt (possibly telescoping) wheel. Does it lock properly into position? Is it adequately adjustable? Is there play in the wheel? While driving, is the wheel centered? If not, that may be a sign of damaged steering components.

Windshield wipers

Test the windshield wipers and washer controls. Check the condition of the wiper blades and replace them if they seem dry or cracked. Ensure the windshield wiper reservoir is full and functions properly.

Air brake, air ride suspension controls and dump valve

For systems with air brakes, it is imperative to understand their operation. There are many great sources of instruction, including the chassis owner and operators manual. Spend the time necessary to understand proper air brake operation, air pressure requirements, parking brake operations, settings and brake adjustments. If your rig is equipped with an air dryer, its maintenance is critical to ensure safe and reliable air pressure is maintained.

	Navigation Many motorized RVs have navigation built into the dash radio or have an included, standalone navigation system. Is map current?	
	Leveling system controls In many motorized RVs, the automatic leveling controls are immediately available from the driver position. Operate the system, level the coach and then physically check the levelers. Retract the system when completed. Did the system operate smoothly? Strange noises? Was there an error?	
	Step well cover Many motorhomes have stepwell covers. Check the operation of the cover. Is it manual or motorized? If motorized, learn where the override mechanism is.	

TRAILER SPECIFIC	Notes
A frame tongue condition For travel trailers, thoroughly inspect the A frame tongue assembly and ball hitch coupling. Check for damage, unusual wear and excessive rust. Ensure the assembly is not bent or twisted in any way. Check that bolts are tight and intact. Check chain attachment points and any storage or LP storage boxes and platforms.	
Fifth wheel King Pin For fifth wheel trailers, carefully inspect the entire fifth wheel hitch assembly. Check the condition of the actual King-Pin and inspect for unusual or uneven wear. Is the king-pin damaged? Are there gouges on the pin? Are the attachment bolts properly torqued? Are there any signs of repair?	
Supplemental hitch equipment, sway bars, weight distributing hitch Many travel trailers use supplemental hitch equipment for a more stable and sure towing experience. If equipped, check these devices and attachment points for damage. Ensure connection points are properly mounted and torqued appropriately.	
Chains Chains are critical for safe operation. Inspect the chains for damage and replaced/repaired links. The chain should be clean, not rusty. The chain should be sufficient length to crisscross underneath the A frame to the rear of the tow vehicle and not bind when negotiating a tight turn.	

Breakaway box and connection cable

Virtually all towed RV units (with the exception of ultra-light units) are equipped with a breakaway device that will stop the RV in the event of a catastrophic separation from the tow vehicle. Inspect the breakaway box and cable. The cable, and key, should pull away from the breakaway box with some force but it should not pull out freely. Check the wiring to the breakaway box to ensure the unit is getting the necessary 12-Volts DC.

Umbilical connection and cable

Check the RV umbilical cable. Inspect for damage, cuts, kinks and apparent repairs. Check the cable end and ensure the connections are clean and all present. The umbilical should be firmly attached to the A frame or fifth wheel assembly.

Locks

If locks are included, check their operation and inspect them for damage. Ensure the keys fit and operate the locks BEFORE using. If a lock does not have a spare key, consider purchasing a new lock.

Tongue jack pad – operation

For travel trailers, operate the tongue jack sufficiently to raise the trailer beyond what would be required for connecting to your tow vehicle, then lower the trailer to the extreme. Does the tongue jack operate smoothly? Are there signs of damage from being dragged? If it articulates, does it lock into position to prevent damage from falling? Does it grind or slip? Does it operate smoothly?

Fifth wheel landing gear	
For fifth wheels, operate the front jacks (landing gear) sufficiently to raise the trailer beyond what would be required for connecting to your tow vehicle then lower the trailer to the extreme. Do the jacks extend smoothly? Are there signs of damage from being dragged? For manual systems with clips, are they present and in good operating condition?	

WHEELS	**Notes**
Tire date code	
What are the tire date codes? Are all tires the same or does it appear tires are mismatched? Please refer to tire section of the book for detailed tire information.	
Pressure	
Check the tire pressure of all tires. NOTE: Tire pressure on some units can be 120lbs (or more) cold so ensure you have the appropriate tire gauge.	
Tread	
Inspect the tires. How does the tread appear? Evenly worn across all tires? Are any of the tires damaged? Chunks of tread missing? Uneven wear?	
Side walls	
Carefully inspect the tire sidewalls. Are there bulges in the sidewalls? Is there any obvious damage to the sidewalls?	

Spare location, condition and access Does the unit include a spare? Condition of spare? How do you access the spare?	
Wheel torque Inspect the wheel torque settings. Were all the wheels in specification? If not, was one or more wheel off by more than 20%? If so, remove the wheel(s) and look for damage caused by the lugs being loose, oblong wear in the lug holes.	
Wheel condition, steel, aluminum Refer to your owner's manual for description of the wheels installed and care for the wheels in accordance with manual. Are the wheels damaged? Do they all match?	
Trailer brakes - condition For used units, consider removing the wheels and check each brake assembly. Are any brake assemblies damaged? Do all brakes appear to be wearing evenly?	

Condition (floor, side walls, ceiling)

Inspect each storage compartment carefully for signs of damage. Are the storage compartment floors sturdy enough for loading supplies? Are the side and rear walls sturdy enough to remain intact should items move in transit?

Signs of water infiltration

Carefully inspect each storage compartment for signs of water damage, either from infiltration or internal tank leaks. Is there evidence of a leak? Soiled floor or sidewall material? Is there evidence of repairs to any of the storage compartments? Do any of the compartments have worrisome odors?

Test lights in compartments

Test all compartment lights for proper operation.

Storage compartment doors

Ensure the doors operate properly. They should close tightly with minimal force. The weather seals should be flexible and intact completely surrounding the compartment door. The latch mechanism and striker should be free of any damage. Ensure you test the locking keys and mechanisms.

Test electrical connections

If a storage compartment has a 120-Volt AC or 12-Volt DC plug, test the plug for proper operation. Often, 120-Volt AC plugs are added in lower storage compartments for vacuums, outdoor entertainment systems, etc.

Test cable connections

If a coax connection is present, test the connection for signal by attaching a signal producing device. If possible, use a coax continuity tester.

Sliding trays, condition, operation, locks

Carefully inspect storage compartment trays. For sliding trays, be careful when extending the tray to its extended position in case the tray is not property attached or the limit catch fails. Does the tray slide with minimal effort? Do the locking mechanisms keep the tray stationary?

Access panels

Locate all access panels and investigate what is located behind them. Often, plumbing filters and bypass valve assemblies are located behind these access panels.

EXTERIOR - SIDE WALLS AND CAPS	Notes
Side wall condition Inspect for signs of damage, creases, dents, tears, cuts, bulges, discoloration, missing siding screws, or delamination.	
Front cap condition Inspect front cap for cracks, paint issues, sun damage, caulking issues, signs of water infiltration, and seals around all penetrations. Inspect seals and seams where siding and roof join.	
Graphics Condition of graphics, paint or decals.	
Rear cap condition Inspect rear cap for cracks, paint issues, caulking issues, signs of water infiltration, and seals around all penetrations and windows. Inspect seals and seams where siding and roof join.	
Window condition Inspect windows for cracks, chips, fog in double pane units, and hard water damage.	
Windows seals Carefully inspect caulk and seals around windows frames to ensure water tight fitment.	
Window screens Check for fitment, tears and locking clips.	

Trim	
Inspect the trim condition, seals and caulking.	
Entrance door	
Condition, check door for damage, day lock function, deadbolt, striker location and complete key sets. Does door shut properly? Does door close with minimal force? Is the latch to hold the entrance door functional? Door seal condition? Door screen condition?	
Sidewall vents	
Check condition, caulking, and if an internal flap is installed, does the flap function and move freely. Check for nests, bird and mud-dauber.	
Entrance hand rail	
Inspect condition of handrail. Ensure it functions properly and if it is a swing out model that it locks in position correctly. The handle should move freely when unlocked and be firm when locked into position.	
Entrance steps	
Ensure the steps operate smoothly. If electric, make sure the steps operate in conjunction with the door control. For motorized RVs, refer to the manual for step safety settings. Most steps have an override that retracts them when the RV ignition is turned on.	
LP storage door(s)	
Check function of doors, condition, weather seals, striker and latch. Doors should open and close with minimal effort and should be snug when shut.	

Electrical connection door Check condition of plug cover. Many are spring loaded. Ensure spring assembly closes the door tightly when not in use. Check seal to ensure effective water barrier.	
Water inlet door or cover For exterior water inlet covers, ensure cover is in working condition and fits snugly when the inlet is not in use to prevent dirt from getting into the water system. Replace if necessary.	
Sidewall light fixtures Ensure proper operation, check seal on fixture. The light should not have water or dirt inside the lens. Check the lens for cracks.	
Stepwell/steps lighting If equipped, ensure light fixtures operate correctly.	
Fold-out panel(s) If equipped, extend the soft-sides and exercise the fold-out panels to ensure smooth operation. Pay attention to how the material bunches and folds. It is important to get the material to lay properly when folding in to prevent damage. Check for tears, rips, holes, dirt, and especially mold. If mold is discovered, it is likely signs of an improperly sealing side.	

EXTERIOR - ROOF	Notes
Overall condition Using soft-sole shoes (like tennis shoes) get up on the RV roof. Most roofs are either Ethylene Propylene Diene Monomer (EPDM), commonly referred to as rubber. Other materials include fiberglass or metal, likely aluminum. You need to know what type roofing material is installed as each has specific care instructions and maintenance needs. Inspect for obvious signs of damage, tears, punctures, rips, soft spots, bubbles, or areas that appear discolored. There should be sealing material generously used across the roof of the RV wherever there is something mounted, like air conditioners, skylights, antennas, etc.	
Roofing material properly attached Each seam or seal should be generously protected by RV roofing sealant. Side walls, corners, edges and seams on the RV sides must be properly sealed to avoid costly water infiltration.	
Seals and caulking Carefully inspect every opening, screw head or attachment point to ensure adequate weathertight seal.	
Vents Carefully inspect the roof top vents and vent shrouds if installed. Check for cracks and signs of failure due to sun exposure. Generally these covers are inexpensive. If necessary, they should be replaced to avoid costly water damage.	

Skylights

Carefully inspect any installed skylights. Check for cracks and signs of failure due to sun exposure or stress. These covers, usually over showers, can be rather large and are more expensive than traditional vent covers but should be inspected and replaced with the same aggressiveness.

Air conditioner drains

There are several methods used for roof air conditioner units to drain. Check the manual for your unit and inspect the drains to ensure they are not plugged. Check the area around the air conditioner(s) to ensure the roof is not soft and that the air conditioner(s) have not created a depression in the roof.

OTA antenna

Check the antenna seal and that all the attachment screws are covered in sealant. Check any coax penetrations.

Satellite dish antenna

Check the antenna seal and that all the attachment screws are covered in sealant. Check and coax penetrations.

Solar panels

Solar panels can be large and heavy. Ensure the attachment points for the panels are properly secured and sealed well. Inspect the wiring penetration into the roof ensuring it is also properly sealed and weathertight. Ensure that no charging cables are loose or exposed as they may get caught by low hanging tree branches or other obstructions.

Penetrations All RV roof penetrations should be adequately sealed with RV roof sealant. Check the roof for penetrations where items may have been removed. If you find one, be inquisitive. It can be an indication of an issue that might require further investigation.	
Ladder attachment points RV roof ladders get a lot of use and can move and flex over time. Make sure the ladder attachment points are sealed. RV roof sealant can be removed to tighten ladder.	

EXTERIOR - UNDERBELLY	**Notes**
Fluid leaks Inspect the entire undercarriage for signs of leaks or areas that appear to be repaired, new panels or paint. If found, further inspect the area to determine the cause. Leaks are not uncommon in RV plumbing so signs of repairs should not necessarily be considered a red-flag or problematic.	
Frame condition Inspect the frame, end to end, for signs of damage, stress or repair. Check for excessive rust or evidence of repairs made to the frame. Be suspect of areas freshly painted with rubberized undercoating. Carefully inspect areas that appear to have repairs of any kind, especially if these repairs include welds. Improper welding can be dangerous. If new welds are discovered, consider having the welds inspected.	

Axles

Check axles carefully for damage or lack of routine maintenance. Check for large nicks and dents that would suggest substantial impact to the axel. Check attachment points for signs of stress or repair. Be cautious of new welds.

Suspension

Visually inspect the suspension and suspension attachment points. Check bolt and weld condition. Check for excessive rust or indications of replacement components.

Brake wiring

Where exposed, inspect the wiring to the brakes. It should not be hanging loose but should be neatly routed along the frame and axles. Make sure the cable is not broken, stretched, have splices or other signs of damage.

Plumbing

Carefully inspect the plumbing exposed on the bottom of the RV. Generally, the sections of pipe on the bottom of the RV underbelly are the last sections before terminating to a sewer hose connection. If there is a blade valve, inspect its operation. Make sure the exposed plumbing is properly mounted and secure. Pipes should not move freely. Make sure there is a functional sewer pipe end cap that properly seals.

Insulation

For areas where insulation can be inspected like basement walls, access panels or interior access doors, check for signs of damage, water infiltration and rodents.

Tanks

If it is possible, inspect the enclosed tanks. This will likely be a difficult task as the tanks are usually covered from the bottom by either the motorhome chassis or trailer belly pan. If an inspection is possible, look carefully for debris, signs of leaks, or odors. The UTILITES section includes exercising the tanks and checking their actual operation and condition.

Bottom skirt or belly pan

Motorized RV frames have material that is often attached to the actual chassis rails that forms a barrier to the subfloor of the RV. In motorized RVs, inspect the underbelly of the unit checking for holes, cracks or damage. Make sure the belly pan is tight against the bottom of the aft body. For RV trailers, many RV manufacturers use a material called "Coroplast". This material looks like plastic coated cardboard sheets and can run the length of the trailer forming a nice, reliable water resistant barrier. Regardless of the material, inspect that it is intact and in good condition. There should be no damage, cuts, holes or missing sections. The material should run from side to side and should be sealed where seams meet. Look for areas that seem to sag as this is potential evidence of a water leak. Remember, this is your protection while driving down the road in the rain. The better the material is positioned and attached, the better protected the bottom of the RV will be.

Leveling jacks – electric, hydraulic or manual Inspect the RV leveling jacks and pads. Using the manual, exercise the leveling jacks to ensure proper operations. When extended, inspect them for damage. Are they straight? Are the consistently mounted meaning all assemblies are fastened at the same angle? For hydraulic units, check the hoses and reservoir. For mechanical and electric, ensure the units are properly lubricated. For electric and hydraulic units, ensure you understand the back-up operating method in case of failure.	
Straps, rods, attachment points Underneath the RV, inspect straps connecting sewer pipes, exhaust pipes, wire bundles, hoses, etc. Make sure these straps and attachment points are solid and secure. Give them a tug. There should be little movement.	
Wire bundles Ensure wire bundles are properly covered and run neatly. They should be attached at regular intervals and should not have enough slack to allow debris to catch on or damage one. Where wire bundles articulate and move back and forth to support a RV slide room, make sure the bundle is secure and that there is sufficient room for the bundle to be protected from damage when the slide room retracts. Manufactures have a number of methods for accomplishing this. These attachments should be inspected regularly.	

EXTERIOR - AWNINGS	Notes
Mounting brackets, rollers, rods Carefully inspect the installed awning(s) attachment brackets and mounts. Are they secure? Caulked? Does the roller assembly appear in good condition? Are the end caps (if manufacturer installed) in place?	
Operation Extend each awning to its fully extended position and stop. Retract the awning. Pay particular attention to the process. Is it smooth? Does the awning catch on anything? Does it extend and retract evenly?	
Material condition With the awning(s) extended, inspect the material as carefully as possible for tears, rips, or punctures. Carefully inspect the stitching on the sides as this is often a failure point.	
Wind sensor Wind sensors will retract extended awnings when the winds pick up to a specific speed. These are wonderful awning accessories if installed. Ensure you understand the settings for this feature.	
Override, if automatic If the awning(s) is automatic, understand how to manually retract the awning in the event of a failure. Most automated awnings have a manual backup mode for emergencies.	

	Awning lights Some awnings have led light strips or other forms of illumination. Check that the lights function and are firmly attached the length of the awning.	
	Slide Toppers If equipped with awnings over the slides, check them using the same criteria as above. When deployed, ensure the fabric is taught and does not sag. Check the condition of the material.	

EXTERIOR - SLIDES		**Notes**
	Slide(s) seals Inspect weather seals and weather stripping. Check for dry rot, cuts or other apparent damage. Does the slide seal well when closed? Is it square, meaning both sides fit flush against the RV siding?	
	Slide(s) operation Do the slide(s) operate smoothly? Are there strange noises, like grinding or popping sounds? Does the slide lurch or shake? On the underside of the slide, does there appear to be any damage? Does the slide mechanism appear clean and lubricated? Any signs of repairs?	

Slide(s) locking mechanisms or locking bars RV slides come in several configurations. Some slides lock into place for travel by simply bringing them in. The slide rests on a raised bar that acts as a lock. Some slides utilize a locking bar that the operator installs inside the RV once the slides are brought in. Refer to the owner's manual for which type is utilized.	
Slide(s) emergency override Electric and hydraulic slides often include a mechanical override to operate the slide in case of failure. Sometimes these overrides require a special socket that can be operated with a ratchet drive or an electric drill. Some require a special wrench. Check the owner's manual and physically check for an override attachment point to ensure you understand proper operation.	
Slide toppers Check the attachment points and material for tears, rips and punctures. Check the stitching on the edges as this is often a failure point.	

Window screens

Check all window screens. Screens should fit snugly and have tabs for removal. Are there screens on all windows? Are any screens torn or damaged?

Window trim

Inspect the window trim around every window. The trim should be clean and neatly attached. Are there any signs of water damage?

Window seal

Inspect the caulk and material sealing the windows on the coach. Depending on the style of windows, this can be a difficult task. Carefully check for signs of water infiltration and damage. Are there any stains near the windows?

Window emergency exit latch and operation

Safety in an RV is critical. Locate the emergency exit which is often a window exit. Learn how to operate this emergency exit. Demonstrate its proper use to all occupants.

Drapes

Are the coach drapes clean and in good condition? Do the drape mounting rails or tabs all function properly? For sliding drapes, slide them open and closed. Do they move freely? Are all the tabs in place? Do any of the drapes have signs of water damage? If so, carefully examine why?

Window coverings, day night shades Many RV windows have dual stage blinds, also known as day-night shades. Check the operation of each of these shades. Are they in good condition? Do all shades function properly? Do any of the shades have signs of water damage? If so, examine why.	
Front window drop down shade Front coach shades, mechanical or electrical, are fairly common in motorhomes for privacy. If equipped, do the shades function properly? Any signs of damage? Any signs of water infiltration? Do the shades extend and retract smoothly?	

INTERIOR	Notes
Floor carpet Inspect the carpet throughout the RV. Is it clean? Any stains? Signs of repair? Check for water damage in slides and at slide thresholds. Give the carpet a tug with your hand. If the carpet has been damaged by water, some carpet may literally lift out in your hand. Press on the carpet pad. Does the pad spring back? If not, check thoroughly for water damage.	
Floor tile If your RV has floor tile, inspect it carefully for damage, cracks, missing grout and chips. Step on each tile. Do any move or feel loose? Do any rock back and forth?	

Subfloor condition – weak, soft spots

Inspect the floor carefully by walking on every portion of the floor you physically can. For sections you can't, perhaps under the master bed, press on the floor with your hands. Check for soft spots. If discovered, determine why. Is the flooring thin or is there some form of damage?

Water damage, stains

Where ever possible, inspect the floor, subfloor and underneath the floor from a basement access point. Water damage can often be repaired but only if discovered promptly. As important to discovering the damage is determining why the damage occurred. Has the issue been appropriately fixed to prevent future damage?

Transitions

Are flooring transitions intact? Are they secure? Are there signs of excess wear?

Carpet wraps

Carpet wraps in this context refers to carpet wrapped around and secured to baseboards on slides, to the bottom of cabinets, steps, bed frames, or other areas where the manufacturer has attached carpet other than directly to the floor. On slides, make sure the carpet is attached firmly and securely so that it will not roll up or separate when the slide is used. Is the carpet on stairs excessively worn?

Walls, condition, paper, material, coverings, holes

Inspect the walls of the RV for damage. Look for nail holes, exposed screw holes or areas where picture hangers have damaged the walls and may need repair. If used, is the wallpaper in good shape? Any peeling edges or corners?

Internal slide seals

Inspect the rubber seals on the interior of each slide. The material should be pliable with no tears or rips in the material. It should be securely attached.

Door trim

Inspect the trim surrounding any coach doors. Internal trim and weather seals should be securely attached and damage free.

Cabinets, condition, leaks, spills, hinges, latches

Inspect all cabinets one by one. Get a step stool if necessary for overhead cabinets. Inspect each one for cleanliness, damage and signs of leaks. Check under kitchen cabinets for signs of cleaners that may have spilled and caused damage. Check the hinges of the doors ensuring the doors swing freely, but securely. Check the latches to hold each door shut while traveling. It should take some effort to open cabinet doors.

Drawers, condition, slides, spills, latches

Inspect all drawers one by one, carefully. Inspect each one for cleanliness, damage and signs of leaks. Check the drawer glides ensuring the drawers slide open freely. Check

the drawer latches to hold each drawer shut while traveling.	
Ceiling, stains, sags, cuts, tears Don't forget to look up. Check the ceiling in each room and throughout the RV for signs of damage and leaks. Are there any signs of discoloration? Does the ceiling seem to sag in spots? If so, inspect the area carefully as this may be a sign of water infiltration.	
Ceiling vents, exhaust fans Inspect your ceiling vents. For air returns, check for filters that may need to be replaced or cleaned. For exhaust fans, check the fans controls and operation. If there is a mechanical interior cover, make sure the cover works appropriately and can fully close to ensure protection during the rain. If the controls are electric, check that they function properly.	
Ceiling fan If equipped, check that the ceiling fan operates properly. The fan should be securely mounted to the ceiling and should not excessively vibrate when running.	
Dinette booth Many RVs have built-in booth type dinettes. Often, this dinette can be reconfigured into a bed. Check the condition of the table and booth seating. Is everything clean and in good working condition? Does the table mechanism operate with minimal effort when converting to a bed? For dinette booths that allow storage under the bench seating, is this area in good condition? Any signs of spills or rodents?	

Dining table and chairs

For coaches with dining tables and chairs, check the condition of the table and leaf, if included. Does the table open properly? Is the table mounted to the floor? Are the chairs in good condition? Are there extra dining table chairs included? Some dining tables are not free standing but extend from a side wall mount. Check the mechanism that locks this style table in place.

Recliners

Carefully inspect your coach seating. Are the recliners in good working order? Are they attached to the floor? Do they have straps to keep them in place when traveling? Is the mechanical operation of the recliner mechanism smooth?

Couch

Is the couch clean? Any signs of damage, stains or rips? In motorhomes, is the couch configured as extra seating while the coach is in motion? If so, are the appropriate number of seatbelts included? Is the couch a jack knife style couch allowing for additional sleeping? If so, does it function smoothly? Is the couch a sleeper sofa with a traditional mattress or air mattress? Does the couch mattress open smoothly? Does the air mattress hold air? Are the controls easy to use? Is there an included remote control? What is the power source?

Loveseat

Is the loveseat clean and free of damage? In motorhomes, is the loveseat used for additional seating while traveling? Are there appropriate seatbelts?

Mattress

Check the condition of all mattresses in the coach. Are they clean? Free of stains, tears and rips? Are there any condition concerns? Are they traditional mattresses or specific RV length mattresses. If in doubt, measure the mattress dimensions so that bedding you purchase will properly fit.

Closet

Inspect the closet area(s) of your coach. Is there a clothes rod? Is it mounted securely? Are there closet doors? Do the doors include travel latches to keep the doors from opening/closing during travel?

Bed frame – storage under bed

Inspect the master bedroom bed platform. If the platform doubles as storage, check the storage area. If the mattress platform lifts, are there gas struts? Do the struts hold the bed in the elevated position? Is the storage area clean and useable?

Bunk bed condition

Many RV models offer bunk bed configurations for children. These bed and frames can sometimes articulate up and lock in a stow-a-way position. Are the bunks mounted securely? Are the mattresses clean and free of damage? Are there electronics in the bunk areas, like televisions or radios? If so, do they function properly? Do they have remotes? Are the bunks enclosed by a curtain? If so, is it clean and slide smoothly?

Pocket doors

In many RVs, doors to bedrooms and bathrooms may be in the form of a pocket door, a door that opens into a pocket in the wall. If you have pocket doors, do they slide smoothly? Is the hardware intact? Do the pocket doors have functional latches to keep them secured while traveling?

Accordion doors

In many RVs, doors to bedrooms and bathrooms may be in the form of an accordion door, a door that through a series of small folds, compresses to one side. If you have accordion doors, do they slide smoothly? Is the hardware intact? Do the accordion doors have functional latches to keep them secured while traveling?

Coffee table, end tables

Does the coach have coffee tables or end tables? Are they in good condition? Are there straps to hold the tables securely while traveling?

KITCHEN	Notes
Countertops Carefully examine your kitchen countertops and workspaces. Are the counters in good condition? Is there any damage to the counters? Knife cuts, splits or burns?	
Countertop extension panels and brackets Some RVs include a foldout countertop extension or slide out extension using a rail system. If included, is it in good condition? Does it function properly?	
Sink Inspect your sink and faucet assembly carefully. Using your hand, apply some downward pressure inside the sink observing for cracks. Is the sink sealed around the countertop? Is the drain or strainer basket appropriately sealed? Does the faucet function properly?	
Drains, leaks, water damage Inspect under kitchen cabinets with a flashlight and a careful gaze. Are there signs of leaks or water damage? Leaking plumbing is not uncommon and signs of previously leaks are not necessarily bad.	
Stovetop burners Inspect each burner on the stovetop and light each one ensuring they operate properly.	
Stovetop cover Many RVs have stove top covers which when in place, allow extra counter space for preparing meals. If included, check that these covers fit properly.	

Oven

Using the lighting method appropriate to your coach, warm the oven sufficiently to test proper operation.

Microwave or convection oven

Virtually all RVs include either a microwave or a convection oven unit. Using a bowl of water, test that the unit heats the water in a timely manner. Does the unit have an internal rack? Is the turntable in good condition and free of cracks?

Refrigerator, operation, AC, DC, LP

RV refrigerators come in all shapes, sizes and configurations. Based on the model included in the RV, run the refrigerator in all power configurations, LP Gas, Electric, and 12-Volt DC if appropriate. Allow the refrigerator to run sufficiently in each mode to ensure cooling.

Ice maker

On a PDI, it will be difficult to check the icemaker unless the unit has been powered for some period prior to your arrival. Check the icemaker for obvious signs of damage.

Water line

If the refrigerator is equipped with in the door water, check the location of the water line feeding the unit. These water lines are a notorious source of leaks and headaches for owners. Periodically inspect the water line for signs of leaks. For winterization, pay particular attention to this line.

	Filter	
	On new units, ensure a new water filter is installed into the refrigerator prior to use. On used units, consider simply removing the filter and replacing it.	
	Cabinets	
	Carefully inspect all cabinets one by one. Get a step stool if necessary for overhead cabinets. Inspect each one for cleanliness, damage and signs of leaks. Check under kitchen cabinets for signs of cleaners that may have spilled and caused damage. Check the hinges of the doors. Ensure the doors swing freely but securely. Check the latches that hold each door shut while traveling. It should take some effort to open cabinet doors.	
	Pantry	
	Inspect the pantry, if equipped, for cleanliness and signs of spilled food, liquids or rodents.	
	Dish washer	
	If equipped, test the dishwasher. Run a short cycle to ensure water flow and proper drainage.	

BATHROOM	**Notes**
Toilet	
Inspect the toilet(s) carefully. Does the bowl seal properly? Does the bowl trap open appropriately when depressing the foot control or activating the electronic flush control?	

Signs of leaks Pay particular attention in the RV bathroom for signs of leaks or damage. Does the floor feel mushy near the toilet? Any signs of discoloration? Check carefully around the shower fixture and vanity for leaks. Look inside the vanity for signs of leaks.	
Sink and vanity, caulk Is the bathroom sink and vanity appropriately caulked and sealed?	
Sink faucet Test the vanity faucet. Does the faucet work properly? Is there appropriate water pressure?	
Shower Inspect the RV shower (tub if equipped) for any signs of damage. Apply pressure to the floor of the shower to see if there are any cracks in the enclosure. For showers with glass (or glass-like) sliding doors, do the doors have a locking mechanism for traveling?	
Shower faucet Test the shower faucet. Does the faucet work properly? Is there appropriate water pressure?	
Drains Monitor the drains while using each faucet. Do the drains run smoothly? Do any drains run slowly? Any smells from the drains?	
Skylight Many RV showers have a skylight which aside from offering some natural light, allows additional headroom. These skylights are often	

a source of water infiltration. Carefully check the seal of the skylight for indication of leaks. Are there any signs of damage or cracks?	
Washer/Dryer If equipped, check these connections. Inspect the water connections. Inspect the dryer vent for proper seal and operation. Remember, if equipped, this represents an additional winterization step. If included, check the washer/dryer for proper operation. Does the washer fill when operated? Does the dryer get warm after one minute of operation? Are the manuals included?	

A/V ENTERTAINMENT SYSTEM	Notes
Televisions Check the televisions in the RV. Are there remote controls? Do the televisions work from the OTA antenna? Do the televisions work from the cable input? Are the television manuals in the RV?	
TV safety straps Depending on how and where your RVs televisions are mounted, there may be safety straps to hold the unit in place to avoid vibration. Carefully check how your televisions are mounted. Are there clips beside or behind the television that would indicate straps should be used? Does the television move freely?	

TV slides and articulating arms Some RVs mount interior and exterior televisions on slides or articulating arms. If your coach has any of these television systems, understand how they lock into position.		
Audio equipment, remotes, manuals If the coach has stereo equipment installed, check the unit for proper operation. Does the unit have a remote? Is the unit Bluetooth? If so, try pairing a music device. Check to see if the unit has a password installed that might preclude reprogramming. Are the manuals available?		
Speakers For audio visual entertainment systems equipped with additional speakers, test the speakers to ensure they function properly and that sound is well distributed through the coach.		
DVD / Blueray player Does the RV have a DVD or Blueray player? If so, test the unit to ensure proper operation with your RVs television and signal distribution system. Is the remote available? Is the manual available?		
Audio switching equipment Some RVs have elaborate audio switching centers to provide input from various audio devices. Some of these systems can be very intimidating. If equipped, locate the manual for this switching center. Test the switch to make sure it works by connecting an audio device, like an IPod or similar audio player.		

Video switching equipment Some RVs have elaborate video switching centers to provide input from various video sources. Some of these systems can be very intimidating. If equipped, locate the manual for this switching center. Test the switch to make sure it works by switching between whatever on-board video devices are attached.	
Antenna signal splitter and switch A very common accessory in the RV world is the Winegard amplified antenna switch. This wall plate sized switch provides the means to select between over the air antenna signal and cable television signal. The wall plate has a push button on-off switch that controls the onboard amplifier that provides power to the OTA antenna mounted on the roof of the coach. It is important to note, when this amplifier is ON, the cable television signal is switched OFF.	
OTA antenna crank Many coaches include an OTA antenna that is mounted on articulating arms that raise and lower the antenna using a hand crank inside the coach. Locate this crank and ensure the antenna crank functions properly.	
Satellite dish equipment Provided there is service, connect and test the coach satellite antenna and receiver for proper operation.	

GENERATOR	Notes
Condition Inspect the condition of the generator. Are there any signs of damage or overheating? Any apparent leaks? Are all panels in place?	
Hours If used, how many hours does the generator have? Based on the manual, is there evidence of the proper maintenance being performed? If multiple hour meters are present, i.e. on the unit and one inside the RV, are the hours in sync?	
Remote panel configuration and operation For generator installations with remote panels inside the RV, test the panel operation to ensure it functions properly.	
Automatic Generator Start (AGS) For coaches with AGS, set up a scenario that will force the AGS to initiate. Does it function properly? Manual will include start scenarios.	
Fluid levels Check all fluid levels on the generator.	
Access to compartment and locking mechanism Does the generator have adequate access to perform maintenance and routine fluid inspections? If tray mounted, does the extension tray function smoothly? Are there signs of rust or damage? When retracted, does the generator lock into position properly?	

Fuel source

Most on-board generators are plumbed to use the chassis fuel system. Ensure your generator is set up this way. For units that rely on alternate fuel methods, ensure the impacts of dual fuel are acceptable to you while traveling.

Exhaust inspection, auxiliary pipe to vent above RV

While running the generator, inspect the exhaust system. Are there any apparent issues with the exhaust? Are there any signs of exhaust leaks like suit stains or burn marks along the exhaust path? For units with exhaust extensions, are all the parts necessary to attach the extension included?

Starting

Test the generator by starting. The unit should start easily. For diesel units, after priming and glow-plug, the unit should start promptly. Run the generator for several minutes. Does it run smoothly? Are there any unusual noises or vibrations?

Switch over from shore power to generator power

Test the switch over from shore power to generator power. Refer to your RV owner's manual for the exact sequence and process. Generally, a unit will switch from shore power to generator power shortly after the transfer switch detects steady power.

Transfer switch operation	
Test the transfer switch operation by switching from shore power to generator power and back again. Does the transfer occur without disrupting 120-Volt devices in the coach?	

UTILITIES	Notes
Shore power connection point On units where the shore power cable is not hard-wired, carefully inspect the shore power connection assembly. If it is accessible from the exterior side wall, does the weatherproof cover function properly? Are the connections clean? Is the assembly caulked are securely mounted? Does the umbilical cord "lock" into place?	
Shore power cable condition Carefully inspect your shore power cable. Check for cuts or damage to the cable. Inspect the plug end of the cable. Is the cable in serviceable condition? Is the plug clean and complete?	
Shore power cable length How long is your shore power cable? For lengths shorter than 30 feet, consider purchasing an extension for a total of at least 50 foot.	
Date of batteries For new RVs, check the battery in-service date. The batteries should not be "new-old-stock". For used RVs, what is the in-service date for the installed batteries? Are they approaching end-of-life service life?	

Batteries

Locate your coach batteries. What type are they? 6-Volt or 12-Volt? The coach batteries supply the needed 12-Volts DC to the coach for lights, auxiliary power accessories, electric slide motors, appliance controllers, and more. Inspect the coach batteries. Are they clean and free of damage?

Battery disconnect switch location and operation

Locate the RV battery disconnect switch. Check the functionality of the switch. When switched, is 12-Volt DC power terminated? Are there multiple switches? Is so, understand the path for each.

Dry cell, wet cell, sealed

What type batteries are installed? There are three types of batteries, Wet Cell (flooded), Gel Cell, and Absorbed Glass Mat (AGM). Gel and AGM are considered maintenance free style batteries.

Coax inlet

Test the coach coax inlet by attaching a signal producing device. If possible, use a coax continuity tester to validate the integrity of the coax runs. For external coax inlets, does the cover provide proper weather protection?

Satellite inlet

It is unlikely that you'll be able to test satellite coax without an actual satellite antenna and receiver being installed. For new units, where these accessories are installed, the dealer can show test screens with one of the satellite service source pages. For used units, testing the coax with a coax continuity tester may be the best option available to you.

Telephone inlet

Telephone service at RV parks is becoming a thing of the past just as telephone jacks are more and more uncommon in RVs. If the coach has a telephone jack inlet, check the weather cover for effectiveness. If you wish to test the telephone jack, find service or use a tone generator.

Solar power panel inlet

Some coaches have solar power wiring installed at the factory. If the RV does, check the power inlet cover to ensure it is weather tight. Some units have the inlet on the roof, some on the forward wall while others are located in basement storage areas. Check the owner's manual for specific information.

Fresh water inlet

Check your fresh water inlet connection. Is the connection clean? Is there a washer and debris filter installed? Does the hose connection ring turn freely?

Water manifold systems

Many RVs are configured with very elaborate water manifold systems, allowing each hot/cold water feed to be independently controlled. This is an outstanding feature to have should you ever need to isolate a water feed source. If the RV includes this manifold design, locate it and review the proper operation of the individual valves. If the system includes a specific valve for the water bypass, understand the configuration it must be in for winterizing purposes.

Anderson valve (if equipped)

Many water distribution systems in RVs are controlled by an Anderson Valve. This multi-position valve allows the RV owner to select fresh water tank fill, fresh tank use with pump, city water source, and winterization. Check the operation of the valve. Is the selector knob providing the source indicated? Is the knob selector firm and sure when switching between positions? Does the valve selector leak at all? If it does leak, the valve is likely failing and should be replaced.

Outside shower

Locate the outside shower (if equipped) and test. Are there leaks? Adequate water pressure from the pump? Any damage to the hand-held wand or hose?

Black tank flush

These systems are available from various manufacturers but their purpose is much the same. These systems are connected to a water source using a garden hose (NEVER your drinking hose) and this water inlet sprays clean water into the black tank to help keep the tank as clean as possible. If your system is equipped, test it and ensure the jets in the black tank operate properly.

Waste water sewer connection

While not the most glamorous part of RVing, understanding the proper method of emptying the black and gray tanks is critical. Check the connection on the RV to attach the sewer hose to. Is the pipe and connection point sturdy? Does the sewer pipe have a functional cap? On the bayonet mount, are the tabs on the pipe intact?

Gray dump valve location and operation Locate the gray tank waste water valve(s). The tank waste water valves are operated by pulling the handle out which opens a blade valve, allowing waste water to discharge from the tank. Test the operation by connecting a sewer hose to the RV waste water sewer connection. Add some water to the gray water tank. Open the gray tank dump valve. Does waste water flow? Was the valve smooth to operate? When closed, does waste water stop flowing?	
Black dump valve location and operation Locate the black tank waste water valve(s). The tank waste water valves are operated by pulling the handle out which opens a blade valve, allowing waste water to discharge from the tank. Test the operation by connecting a sewer hose to the RV waste water sewer connection. Add some water to the black water tank. Open the black tank dump valve. Does waste water flow? Was the valve smooth to operate? When closed, does waste water stop flowing?	
Outside faucet and/or shower For units with exterior faucets, check the water fixture by running some water. Does the faucet operate properly?	
Outside kitchen Some units offer outside kitchen accessories including gas stoves and refrigerators while others offer only a LP Gas line connection. Depending on your unit, check the accessories carefully for proper operation. If equipped, does the refrigerator operate properly using the appropriate power source for the unit? Does it	

operate in multiple power modes? Does the gas grill light properly?	
Fresh water tank drain The fresh water tank should have a means to drain the tank. Draining is necessary for tank cleansing and for winterization. Locate the low water drain for the fresh tank and ensure it operates properly.	
Winterizing bypass valve and operation Winterizing plumbing systems vary greatly but some general rules remain. Most often, systems have a bypass. This bypass can be very elaborate or simply bypass the water heater. It may be in the water bay, water heater cabinet, behind the water heater, attached to the water manifold or as part of the Anderson valve. Regardless, identify where the bypass valve is located and understand how it is used.	
Water heater drain There are two main water heater manufacturers, Suburban and Atwood. While the water heaters are similar, there are subtle differences. Please refer to the manual that supports the unit installed in your RV for specific maintenance instructions. Generally, the Suburban unit drain plug is the anode rod. In the Atwood unit, the drain plug is just that, a simple plug. Locate the water heater and determine which plug type is installed. Consider buying a special drain plug socket to make removal and installation easier. Often the plugs are difficult to get to and cross-threading the plug could lead to an expensive repair bill.	

Water heater anode rod (if equipped)

Suburban water heaters use an anode rod to protect the internal tank lining. The anode rod is a sacrificial device that allows contaminants in the water to attack the anode rather than the tank walls. That's why keeping an eye on the anode rod is so important. It should be inspected periodically and replaced when less than one-third of original size.

Water heater tank blow off valve

Water heaters are protected by a blow off valve, just like a traditional home water heater. Periodically, check the valve. Is it clean? Evidence of leaks? Does it operate properly?

Water heater, electric and propane

Test your water heater using the available heating sources. Many RV units are electric and LP gas. Ensure both heating sources are functioning properly.

Water pump operation

Test your on-board water pump. With water in the fresh water tank and ALL faucets in the off position, turn the pump on. The pump should run momentarily building water pressure in the system then turn off. If the pump continues to run, see if a faucet was accidentally left on. If not, being searching for a potential leak.

Convenience panel switches and control

Many RVs have a convenience panel which is a common location where many of the RV functions are controlled. This may be a panel near the main door, switches and controls inside a cabinet, or maybe a tablet like device that controls the RV system functions wirelessly. Regardless, locate where the controls are and exercise each one of them. Are all the switches marked? Do all the controls properly function? Don't leave the PDI process believing some switches are just spares. Each switch or control should have a definite function.

Tank controls and status gauges

Locate the controls and status gauges (if equipped) for your batteries and each of the storage tanks. The fresh, gray and black tanks should include a level indicator. The batteries should have charge status indicator. Locate these and ensure you understand how to check each.

PROPANE	Notes

Compartment location

Locate the propane storage compartment. On many motorhomes, the LP tank is located in a storage bay near the driver's compartment. On travel trailers, the LP tanks are often mounted on the A frame hitch assembly and many fifth wheels have the propane in forward storage bays. Is the storage area free of damage? Are the tanks protected from road debris? Are the tanks in a protective housing with adequate tank tie downs and locking mechanisms?

Compartment condition

Is the storage compartment or protective housing in good shape? Do the storage doors (if equipped) shut securely? Does the protective cover (if equipped) latch down securely to prevent coming off while driving down the road?

Propane bottle condition, number How many propane bottles does your RV have? Are they in good, serviceable condition? Are they clean with minimal rust? Are warning labels clearly visible?	
OPD valves The National Fire Protection Association, P58, LP Gas Code 1998, requires new LP tanks, 4 to 40 pounds, include an overfill prevention device, OPD. This device can be easily recognized by the triangular shaped handle on the LP tank. This device prevents accidental over-charging of the tank thus avoiding potential catastrophic failure. Check your tank(s) for this valve.	
Gauges Many motorhomes and some trailers have LP status gauges inside the coach in the convenience panel area. Some units have gauges on the actual LP tanks. Is the RV equipped with LP tank level gauges? Do the tanks have valve level gauges? Are they in good working order?	
Condition of hoses Check the condition of all the LP hoses and lines. Metal lines should be securely mounted to the RV chassis. Rubber hoses should be clean, pliable and not cracked or show signs of excessive wear. If rubber hoses pass through the RV structure, there should be protective material in the pass-thru to ensure the hose does not chafe and fail from vibration.	

Emergency shut of valve – hooked to detector Some RV units may have an emergency gas flow shut off valve that is wired to a LP gas detector in the coach. In the event LP gas was detected, the valve should close.	
Regulators Visually inspect the regulator attached to the LP gas tank(s). Is the regulator clean and damage free? Are the connections to the regulator secure?	
Tank selection – switch location, operation For RVs with more than a single tank, the unit should be equipped with a tank selector. If applicable to your unit, locate the tank selector. Most often, it is physically located next to one of the tanks. These selectors can be manual, requiring the user to physically select the tank for LP to be drawn from, or automatic, switching to a second tank when the primary is empty. Refer to your RV owner's manual for instructions on your units LP tank selector. Determine which type you have and learn its appropriate settings and operation.	

Lights

Most RV light fixtures, aside from lamps, are 12-Volt DC, powered through the coach converter or directly from the coach batteries. Do all the coach lights work?

AC power outlets

Test all 120-Volt AC outlets when the coach is connected to shore power using an outlet tester. Do all the outlets work? Do any outlets show a wiring fault?

GFCI outlets

Test all 120-Volt AC GFCI outlets using the same procedures as the standard 120-Volt outlets. Do all the outlets work? Do any outlets show a wiring fault? Test the GFCI circuit by pressing the test switch. Did the GFCI circuit trip?

12 volt DC ports

Many RVs come with some 12-Volt DC accessory ports. These ports look like the traditional cigarette lighter plug ports found in passenger cars. Test the accessory plugs using a phone charger or any other 12-Volt DC accessory device you have access to. Do they all work properly?

USB ports

Many RVs come with some USB charging ports. These ports look like the USB ports on your personal computer. Test the USB charging ports using a phone charger or any other USB accessory device you have access to. Do they all work properly?

AC power when generator is running

With the generator running, check all the RVs outlets for power. Are all outlets working?

AC power to appropriate plugs via inverter

With no shore or generator power, check the outlets powered by the coach inverter. Often, a limited number of outlets are wired to the RV inverter. Do the outlets have power?

DC operable while on shore power or generator

Do the 12-Volt DC lights, fans and other 12-Volt DC accessories work while on shore and generator power?

Battery charging from shore power

Check that the coach batteries are charging once connected to shore power. Some RVs will have a meter showing charging status while some units have a power information center. Depending on the unit, verify that the batteries are charging.

Transfer switch

Check for proper operation of the coach transfer switch. The transfer switch is responsible for managing electrical input to the coach. When connected to shore power, you should hear a thud from the transfer switch and then the coach should have 120-Volt AC available from shore power. If you change to generator power, the transfer switch should swap from shore power to generator power. Again, you should hear a slight thud when the transfer switch changes configuration. Check the status of the system for proper operation.

Battery charging when generator is running Check that the coach batteries are charging once the generator is running. Some RVs will have a meter showing charging status, some units have a power information center. Depending on your unit, verify that the batteries are charging.	
Solar There are a number of ways solar panels can be installed on coaches. If you have solar panels installed, check the product manuals for information on verifying that the panels are providing a charge to the batteries. Depending on the output of the panels, the system may have a very elaborate charging and status panel. Some panels that just provide a minimal amount of charge back to the battery will likely be wired directly back to the battery using a simple charging module.	
120-Volt circuit breaker location Your coach should have an electrical panel located either in the basement, an interior cabinet or access panel. Locate the 120-Volt AC circuit breaker panel. Not to be confused with the 12-Volt DC fuse box, the 120-Volt AC circuit breakers operate just as they do in a traditional house. The panel should include individual circuits for all major appliances, air conditioners, residential refrigerators, washer-dryers, and outlets. Check to make sure all the circuit breakers are in operational condition.	

12-Volt DC fuses	
Locate the 12-Volt DC fuse box. These fuses are linked to the 12-Volt DC devices, lights, appliances, appliance controllers, and accessories in your coach. Check to make sure the fuses are marked and that they are all in working order.	

HVAC	**Notes**
Thermostat Locate the thermostat control(s) and check for proper operation. Thermostats vary greatly between brands. Ensure you understand specifically what is wired to the thermostat. In some units, there are multiple thermostats. Check the owner's manual for the unit to understand system operation and test that each system operates appropriately.	
Furnace control if separate from thermostat In some RVs, furnace systems are wired to a dedicated thermostat. If a separate control is installed, check the thermostat for proper operation.	
Furnace Carefully inspect the furnace. Does the furnace ignite based on control from the thermostat? Does it provide heat quickly? Are the filters clean? Check for debris and clean the intake area with a vacuum.	

Air conditioner

Test each air conditioner unit for proper operation. If more than one unit is installed, they may be controlled from independent thermostats. Check this operation. Do the units cool quickly when operated? Is the air temperature from the units in range based on the owner's manual? Test using a laser-thermometer if possible. Are the filters in place and clean?

Electric heat

If equipped with an electric heat source, test the unit for proper operation. Does the unit heat quickly? Does the unit have a thermostat? Is it equipped with a timer? Is it equipped with a remote? Is the owner's manual available? If the unit has exposed heat elements, are they protected by a safety cover? If the unit is portable, does it have a safety shut-off if knocked over?

Heat strips

Some HVAC units include heat strips operated through the thermostat. Test for warm air from the HVAC when operated.

Heat Pump

Heat pumps are effective in some circumstances to warm the RV and operate by bringing in warmer outside air, back through the RV air conditioning system. This may be difficult to test, depending on temperatures at the time of your PDI.

Ceiling fan If equipped, test the ceiling fan. Does the fan operate properly? Does the unit vibrate excessively? Are all the blades in good condition?	
Vent fans Operate all ceiling vent fans and carefully inspect each fan cover for damage. Do the fans operate by switch or thermostat? Do they make any unusual noises while running?	

SAFETY	**Notes**
Fire extinguishers Check the coach for fire extinguishers. Ideally, there should be a fire extinguisher immediately available in the kitchen area, the main entrance door and one immediately available in the bedroom area. Are the extinguishers within their indicated service dates? Does the mounting hardware work properly by allowing the extinguisher to be removed with minimal effort?	
Smoke detectors Test each smoke detector. If the units are battery only, consider installing new batteries and annotating the date on a maintenance schedule to remind you to change the batteries annually.	

LP gas detector Some RV units may have an emergency, gas flow shut off valve that is wired to a LP gas detector in the coach. In the event LP gas was detected, the valve should close.	
CO detector Check the CO detector. Units should have a test function. If combined with a smoke detector unit, follow the test instructions in the owner's manual. If the unit is battery only, consider installing new batteries.	

Appendix Two

Weight Calculation Worksheets

The following pages contain a series of worksheets that will help you calculate your RVs weight. Depending on which type RV you have and your proximity to a scale will determine which worksheet will work best for you. There are worksheets for most RVs and for the three most common type scales. Before taking your RV to weigh, please review the worksheet closely to ensure you understand the task at hand. It would be frustrating to go to the trouble of getting your RV weighed only to miss a significant step.

In an effort to keep these worksheets concise, they are filled with acronyms and abbreviations. I've provided them below for review. Getting your RV weighed is one of the most important things you can do as a safe RV operator. In the event you discover you're overweight, be diligent in correcting the issue.

If you prefer a printed copy of these worksheets, they are available at www.areyourvready.com.

Acronyms and abbreviations:

CCC (cargo carrying capacity): This value is provided so that you are aware of how much cargo can be added to your RV. It is established by the manufacturer and is determined before adding any options and after-market items.

Curbside: Passenger side of the RV that is adjacent to the curb when parked.

GAW (gross axle weight): Actual weight placed on axles from vehicle chassis and any added equipment and attached trailer. Actual weight on the axle; not the total amount axle rating (see GAWR).

GAWR (gross axle weight rating): Rating that applies to any axle on any platform; maximum allowable weight for specified axle.

GCWR (gross combined weight rating): Absolute maximum weight that combined tow vehicle and towed vehicle can weigh. GCWR could be a motorhome and dinghy, a motorhome and enclosed trailer, a pickup and fifth-wheel trailer, or any combination of vehicles. In this case, the GCWR includes everything from the RV itself, to the fuel, water, luggage, propane, Cheetos and soda— everything. The GCWR weight rating is often overlooked, which can lead to dangerous vehicle conditions.

GTW (gross trailer weight): Actual weight of fully loaded trailer when weighed; not to be confused with GTWR, which represents the maximum allowable weight for a trailer.

GVW (gross vehicle weight): Actual weight of a loaded vehicle when weighted; not to be confused with GVWR.

GVWR (gross vehicle weight rating): Maximum allowable weight for an RV based on manufacturer design specifications; rating includes everything you've loaded into an RV as well (e.g., propane, food, water, cargo, etc.).

MWL (manufacturer's weight label): Placard, plate or label applied to the vehicle by the manufacturer that details the specific weight capacities for the vehicle, including gross axel and vehicle weight ratings.

Pin weight: Weight of the fifth-wheel applied to the tow vehicle through the fifth wheel hitch. Fifth-wheel pin weight is approximately 20% of trailer gross weight.

Street side: Side of a RV that, when parked, is adjacent to active traffic, or the driver's side.

Tongue weight (synonymous with hitch weight): Weight a trailer imposes on a tow vehicle through a hitch. Tongue weights vary based on trailer and hitch style.

UVW (unloaded vehicle weight rating): Weight of a RV without any options or accessories of any kind.

WDH: Weight Distributing Hitch.

Available Worksheets

WORKSHEETS FOR WEIGHING RV BY INDIVIDUAL WHEEL POSITION	
For Class A, Class B, Class C, Unattached Tow Vehicles and Pickup Campers	Use Worksheet #1
For Fifth Wheel Trailers and Tow Vehicles	Use Worksheet #2
For Travel Trailers and Tow Vehicles	Use Worksheet #3

WORKSHEETS FOR WEIGHING RV ON SEGMENTED SCALES (LIKE CAT)

For Class A, Class B, Class C, Unattached Tow Vehicles and Pickup Campers	Use Worksheet #4
For Fifth Wheel Trailers and Tow Vehicles	Use Worksheet #5
For Travel Trailers and Tow Vehicles	Use Worksheet #6

WORKSHEETS FOR WEIGHING RV ON SEGMENTED SCALES (LIKE CAT) WHERE SCALE CAN ACCOMMODATE WEIGHING HALF THE RV

For Class A, Class B, Class C, Unattached Tow Vehicles and Pickup Campers	Use Worksheet #7
For Fifth Wheel Trailers and Tow Vehicles	Use Worksheet #8
For Travel Trailers and Tow Vehicles	Use Worksheet #9

WORKSHEETS FOR WEIGHING RV ON SINGLE AXLE SCALES

For Class A, Class B, Class C, Unattached Tow Vehicles and Pickup Campers	Use Worksheet #10
For Fifth Wheel Trailers and Tow Vehicles	Use Worksheet #11
For Travel Trailers and Tow Vehicles	Use Worksheet #12

WORKSHEETS FOR WEIGHING RV ON SINGLE AXLE SCALES WHERE SCALE CAN ACCOMMODATE WEIGHING HALF THE RV

For Class A, Class B, Class C, Unattached Tow Vehicles and Pickup Campers	Use Worksheet #13
For Fifth Wheel Trailers and Tow Vehicles	Use Worksheet #14
For Travel Trailers and Tow Vehicles	Use Worksheet #15

WORKSHEET #1 - INDIVIDUAL WHEEL POSITION WEIGHT
For Class A, Class B, Class C, Unattached
Tow Vehicles and Pickup Campers

INSTRUCTIONS		
CURB SIDE WEIGHTS (in lbs)	Position the Vehicle as directed by the Weighing Official. The number of scales available will determine the need to reposition the Vehicle.	STREET SIDE WEIGHTS (in lbs)
VEHICLE WEIGHTS BY WHEEL POSITION		
1.	Enter Steer Axle GAW.	2.
Calculate Steer Axle GAW: (1+2=3).		3.
4.	Enter Drive Axle GAW.	5.
Calculate Drive Axle GAW: (4+5=6).		6.
7.	Enter Tag Axle GAW (if equipped).	8.
Calculate Tag Axle GAW (if equipped): (7+8=9).		9.
CALCULATIONS		
Enter Vehicle GAWR for the Steer Axle as indicated on the Vehicle MWL.		10.
Steer Axle GAW (line 3) MUST be less than GAWR (line 10).		**STOP** Verify
Enter Vehicle GAWR for the Drive Axle as indicated on the Vehicle MWL.		11.
Drive Axle GAW (line 6) MUST be less than GAWR (line 11).		**STOP** Verify

Enter Vehicle GAWR for the Tag Axle (if equipped) as indicated on the Vehicle MWL.	12.
Tag Axle GAW (line 9) MUST be less than GAWR (line 12).	🛑 Verify
Calculate the GVW for the Vehicle. Add Steer Axle GAW (line 3), Drive Axle GAW (line 6) and Tag Axle GAW (line 9): (3+6+9=13).	13.
Enter the Vehicle GVWR from the Vehicle MWL.	14.
The GVW (line 13) MUST be less than the GVWR of the Vehicle (line 14). If not, the Vehicle exceeds its GVWR and this MUST be resolved.	🛑 Verify

WORKSHEET #2 - INDIVIDUAL WHEEL POSITION WEIGHT
Fifth Wheel Trailers and Tow Vehicles

CURB SIDE WEIGHTS (in lbs)	INSTRUCTIONS	STREET SIDE WEIGHTS (in lbs)
	Position the Tow Vehicle and Trailer as directed by the Weighing Official. The number of scales available will determine the need to reposition the Vehicles.	
TOW VEHICLE ONLY WEIGHT		
1.	Enter Steer Axle GAW.	2.
Calculate Steer Axle GAW: (1+2=3).		3.
4.	Enter Drive Axle GAW.	5.
Calculate Drive Axle GAW: (4+5=6).		6.
Calculate Uncoupled Tow Vehicle GVW: (3+6=7).		7.
TOW VEHICLE AND FIFTH WHEEL TRAILER		
8.	Enter Steer Axle GAW.	9.
Calculate Steer Axle GAW: (8+9=10).		10.
11.	Enter Drive Axle GAW.	12.
Calculate Drive Axle GAW: (11+12=13).		13.
Calculate Coupled Tow Vehicle GVW: (10+13=14).		14.

15.	Trailer Axle 1 GAW.	16.
Calculate Trailer Axle 1 GAW: (15+16=17).		17.
18.	Trailer Axle 2 GAW.	19.
Calculate Trailer Axle 2 GAW: (18+19=20).		20.
21.	Trailer Axle 3 GAW.	22.
Calculate Trailer Axle 3 GAW: (21+22=23).		23.
Calculate Total Trailer GAW: (17+20+23=24).		24.

WHEEL POSITION WEIGHING IS NOW COMPLETE

CALCULATIONS

Enter Tow Vehicle GAWR for the Steer Axle as indicated on the Tow Vehicle MWL.	25.
Steer Axle GAW (line 3) and Steer Axle GAW (line 10) MUST each be less than the Steer Axle GAWR (line 25).	**STOP** Verify
Enter Tow Vehicle GAWR for the Drive Axle as indicated on the Tow Vehicle MWL.	26.
Drive Axle GAW (line 6) and Drive Axle GAW (line 13) MUST each be less than the Drive Axle GAWR (line 26).	**STOP** Verify
Enter Trailer GAWR for the Trailer Axles as indicated on the Trailer MWL.	27.
Trailer GAW (lines 17, 20 and 23) MUST each be less than the Trailer GAWR (line 27).	**STOP** Verify
Calculate the GCW for the Tow Vehicle and Trailer. Add Total Trailer GAW (line 24) and Tow Vehicle GVW (line 14): (14+24=28).	28.

382

Enter the Tow Vehicle GCWR from the Tow Vehicle manufacturer weight label.	29.
The GCW (line 28) MUST be less than the GCWR of the Tow Vehicle (line 29). If not, the Tow Vehicle and Fifth Wheel exceed their gross combined weight rating and this MUST be resolved.	**STOP** Verify

TRALER WEIGHT CALCULATIONS	
ENTER the Coupled Tow Vehicle GVW (line 14).	30.
ENTER the Uncoupled Tow Vehicle GVW (line 7).	31.
Calculate the Fifth Wheel Pin Weight. Subtract the Tow Vehicle uncoupled GVW (line 31) from the Tow Vehicle Coupled GVW (line 30): (30–31=32)	32.
ENTER the Total Trailer GAW (line 24).	33.
Calculate the GTW by adding the Pin Weight (line 32) to the Total Trailer GAW (line 33): (32+33=34).	34.
Enter the Trailer GVWR from the Trailer MWL.	35.
The Trailer GTW (line 34) MUST be less than the GVWR of the Fifth Wheel (line 35). If not, the Fifth Wheel has exceed its maximum designed weight and this MUST be corrected.	**STOP** Verify

WORKSHEET #3 - INDIVIDUAL WHEEL POSITION WEIGHT
Travel Trailers and Tow Vehicles

INSTRUCTIONS		
CURB SIDE WEIGHTS (in lbs)	Position the Tow Vehicle and Trailer as directed by the Weighing Official. The number of scales available will determine the need to reposition the Vehicles. Weight data will be collected with WDH disconnected and connected.	STREET SIDE WEIGHTS (in lbs)
TOW VEHICLE ONLY WEIGHT		
1.	Enter Steer Axle GAW.	2.
Calculate Steer Axle GAW: (1+2=3).		3.
4.	Enter Drive Axle GAW.	5.
Calculate Drive Axle GAW: (4+5=6).		6.
Calculate Uncoupled Tow Vehicle GVW: (3+6=7).		7.
TOW VEHICLE AND TRAVEL TRAILER WEIGHT DISTRIBUTING HITCH NOT CONNECTED		
8.	Enter Steer Axle GAW.	9.
Calculate Steer Axle GAW: (8+9=10).		10.
11.	Enter Drive Axle GAW.	12.
Calculate Drive Axle GAW: (11+12=13).		13.
14.	Trailer Axle 1 GAW.	15.

Calculate Trailer Axle 1 GAW: (14+15=16).		16.
17.	Trailer Axle 2 GAW.	18.
Calculate Trailer Axle 2 GAW: (17+18=19).		19.
20.	Trailer Axle 3 GAW.	21.
Calculate Trailer Axle 3 GAW: (20+21=22).		22.
Calculate Coupled Tow Vehicle GVW: (10+13= 23).		23.
Calculate Total Trailer GAW: (16+19+22=24).		24.

**TOW VEHICLE AND TRAVEL TRAILER
WEIGHT DISTRIBUTING HITCH CONNECTED**

25.	Enter Steer Axle GAW.	26.
Calculate Steer Axle GAW: (25+26=27).		27.
28.	Enter Drive Axle GAW.	29.
Calculate Drive Axle GAW: (28+29=30).		30.
31.	Trailer Axle 1 GAW.	32.
Calculate Trailer Axle 1 GAW: (31+32=33).		33.
34.	Trailer Axle 2 GAW.	35.
Calculate Trailer Axle 2 GAW: (34+35=36).		36.

37.	Trailer Axle 3 GAW.	38.
Calculate Trailer Axle 3 GAW: (37+38=39).		39.
Calculate Coupled Tow Vehicle GVW: (27+30=40).		40.
Calculate Total Trailer GAW: (33+36+39=41).		41.

CALCULATIONS	
Enter Tow Vehicle GAWR for the Steer Axle as indicated on the Tow Vehicle MWL.	42.
Steer Axle GAW (lines 3, 10 and 27) MUST each be less than Steer Axle GAWR (line 42).	STOP Verify
Enter Tow Vehicle GAWR for the Drive Axle as indicated on the Tow Vehicle MWL.	43.
Drive Axle GAW (lines 6, 13 and 30) MUST each be less than Drive Axle GAWR (line 43).	STOP Verify
Enter Trailer GAWR for the Trailer Axles as indicated on the Trailer manufacturer weight label.	44.
Trailer Axle GAW, (line 16, 19, 22, 33, 36 and 39) MUST each be less than Trailer GAWR (line 44).	STOP Verify
Calculate GCW – METHOD ONE, WITHOUT WDH: Add Tow Vehicle GVW (line 23) and Total Trailer GAW (line 24). This is the total weight of the Tow Vehicle and Trailer: (23+24=45).	45.
Calculate GCW – METHOD TWO, WITH WDH: Add Tow Vehicle GVW (line 40) and Total Trailer GAW (line 41). This is the total weight of the Tow Vehicle and Trailer: (40+41=46).	46.

 Line 45 and Line 46 should be essentially the same. If not, either a calculation is in err or something was changed between weighing.

Enter Tow Vehicle GCWR from the Tow Vehicle MWL.	47.
The GCW (lines 45 and 46) MUST each be less than the Tow Vehicle GCWR (line 47). If not, the Tow Vehicle and Travel Trailer exceed their designed combined maximum weight rating and this MUST be resolved.	**STOP** Verify

TRALER WEIGHT CALCULATIONS

ENTER the Coupled Tow Vehicle GVW (line 23).	48.
ENTER the Uncoupled Tow Vehicle GVW (line 7).	49.
Calculate TONGUE WEIGHT: Subtract the Uncoupled Tow Vehicle GVW (line 49) from the Coupled Tow Vehicle GVW (line 48): (48–49=50).	50.
ENTER Total Trailer GAW (line 24).	51.
Calculate the GTW by adding the Tongue Weight (line 50) to the Total Trailer GAW (line 51): (50+51=52).	52.
Enter Trailer GVWR from the Trailer MWL.	53.
The Trailer GTW (line 52) MUST be less than the Trailer GVWR (line 53). If not, the Travel Trailer has exceed its maximum designed weight and this MUST be corrected.	**STOP** Verify

WORKSHEET #4 - SEGMENTED SCALES
For Class A, Class B, Class C, Unattached Tow Vehicles and Pickup Campers

INSTRUCTIONS	WEIGHT DATA (in lbs)
Position Vehicle so that axles are centered on separate scale segments.	
Enter Steer Axle GAW.	1.
Enter Steer Axle GAWR from Vehicle MWL.	2.
Steer Axle GAW (line 1) MUST be less than the Steer Axle GAWR (line 2).	**STOP** Verify
Enter Drive Axle GAW.	3.
Enter Drive Axle GAWR from Vehicle MWL.	4
Drive Axle GAW (line 3) MUST be less than the Drive Axle GAWR (line 4).	**STOP** Verify
Enter Tag Axle GAW (if equipped).	5.
Enter Tag Axle GAWR from Vehicle MWL.	6.
Tag Axle GAW (line 5) MUST be less than the Tag Axle GAWR (line 6).	**STOP** Verify
Calculate Vehicle GVW: (1+3+6=7)	7.
Enter Vehicle GVWR from Vehicle MWL.	8.
The Vehicle GVW (line 7) MUST be less than the Vehicle GVWR (line 8).	**STOP** Verify

WORKSHEET #5 - SEGMENTED SCALES
Fifth Wheel Trailers and Tow Vehicles

INSTRUCTIONS	
Position Tow Vehicle and Fifth Wheel Trailer so that axles are centered on separate scale segments. All weights recorded in pounds (lbs).	
TOW VEHICLE ONLY WEIGHT	
Enter Steer Axle GAW.	1.
Enter Drive Axle GAW.	2.
Calculate Uncoupled Tow Vehicle GVW: (1+2=3).	3.
TOW VEHICLE AND FIFTH WHEEL TRAILER COUPLED	
Enter Steer Axle GAW.	4.
Enter Drive Axle GAW.	5.
Enter Fifth Wheel Trailer GAW.	6.
Calculate Coupled Tow Vehicle GVW: (4+5=7).	7.
CALCULATIONS	
Calculate the Fifth Wheel Pin Weight. Subtract the Tow Vehicle Uncoupled GVW (line 3) from the Tow Vehicle Coupled GVW (line 7): (7 – 3 = 8)	8.
Enter Tow Vehicle Steer Axle GAWR as indicated on the Tow Vehicle MWL.	9.

Tow Vehicle Steer Axle Uncoupled GAW (line 1) and Steer Axle Coupled GAW (line 4) MUST each be less than Steer Axle GAWR (line 9).	**STOP** Verify
Enter Tow Vehicle Drive Axle GAWR as indicated on the Tow Vehicle MWL.	10.
Tow Vehicle Drive Axle Uncoupled GAW (line 2) and Drive Axle Coupled GAW (line 5) MUST each be less than Drive Axle GAWR (line 10).	**STOP** Verify
Enter Trailer GVWR as indicated on the Trailer MWL.	11.
Calculate Fifth Wheel GTW by adding the Pin Weight (line 8) and the Fifth Wheel GAW (line 6): (8+6=12)	12.
Fifth Wheel GTW (line 12) MUST be less than the Fifth Wheel GVWR (line 11).	**STOP** Verify
Enter Tow Vehicle GCWR from the Tow Vehicle MWL.	13.
Calculate the GCW for the Tow Vehicle and Trailer. Add Total Trailer GAW (line 6) and Tow Vehicle GVW (line 7): (6+7=14).	14.
GCW (line 14) MUST be less than the Tow Vehicle GCWR (line 13). If not, the Tow Vehicle and Fifth Wheel exceed their designed combined maximum weight rating and this MUST be resolved.	**STOP** Verify

WORKSHEET #6 - SEGMENTED SCALES
Travel Trailers and Tow Vehicles

INSTRUCTIONS	
Position Tow Vehicle and Travel Trailer so that axles are centered on separate scale segments. Weight data will be collected with WDH disconnected and connected. All weights recorded in pounds (lbs).	
TOW VEHICLE ONLY WEIGHT	
Enter Steer Axle GAW.	1.
Enter Drive Axle GAW.	2.
Calculate Uncoupled Tow Vehicle GVW: (1+2=3).	3.
TOW VEHICLE AND TRAVEL TRAILER WEIGHT DISTRIBUTING HITCH NOT CONNECTED	
Enter Steer Axle GAW.	4.
Enter Drive Axle GAW.	5.
Enter Travel Trailer GAW.	6.
Calculate Coupled Tow Vehicle GVW: (4+5=7).	7.
TOW VEHICLE AND TRAVEL TRAILER WEIGHT DISTRIBUTING HITCH CONNECTED	
Enter Steer Axle GAW.	8.
Enter Drive Axle GAW.	9.
Enter Travel Trailer GAW:	10.

Calculate Coupled Tow Vehicle GVW: (8+9=11).	11.

CALCULATIONS	
Enter Tow Vehicle Steer Axle GAWR as indicated on the Tow Vehicle MWL.	12.
Tow Vehicle Steer Axle GAW (lines 1, 4 and 8) MUST each be less than Steer Axle GAWR (line 12).	**STOP** Verify
Enter Tow Vehicle Drive Axle GAWR as indicated on the Tow Vehicle MWL.	13.
Tow Vehicle Drive Axle GAW (lines 2, 5 and 9) MUST each be less than Drive Axle GAWR line 13.	**STOP** Verify
Enter Travel Trailer GAWR as indicated on the manufacturer weight label.	14.
Trailer GAW (lines 6 and 10) MUST each be less than Trailer GAWR (line 14).	**STOP** Verify
Enter Trailer GVWR as indicated on the Trailer MWL.	15.
Calculate the Travel Trailer Tongue Weight. Subtract the Tow Vehicle Uncoupled GVW (line 3) from the Tow Vehicle Coupled GVW (line 7): (7–3=16)	16.
Calculate the Travel Trailer GTW by adding the Tongue Weight (line 16) and the Travel Trailer GAW (line 6): (16+6=17).	17.
Travel Trailer GTW (line 17), MUST be less that the Travel Trailer GVWR (line 15).	**STOP** Verify
Calculate the GCW- METHOD ONE, WITHOUT WDH: Add Total Trailer GAW (line 6) and Tow Vehicle GVW (line 7): (6+7=18).	18.
Calculate the GCW- METHOD TWO, WITH WDH: Add Total Trailer GAW (line 10) and Tow Vehicle GVW (line 11): (10+11=19).	19.

⚠	Line 18 and Line 19 should be essentially the same. If not, either a calculation is in err or something was changed between weighing.
Enter the Tow Vehicle GCWR from the Tow Vehicle MWL.	20.
GCW (line 18 and 19) MUST each be less than the GCWR of the Tow Vehicle (line 20). If not, the Tow Vehicle and Travel Trailer exceed their designed combined maximum weight rating and this MUST be resolved.	**STOP** Verify

WORKSHEET #7 - WIDE SEGMENTED SCALE WEIGHT

For Class A, Class B, Class C, Unattached Tow Vehicles and Pickup Campers

INSTRUCTIONS
Position Vehicle so that axles are centered on separate scale segments. This worksheet is used for scales that have sufficient room to allow you to reposition the vehicle so that only half the Vehicle is on the scale. This will allow calculation of Vehicle weight by corner. All weights are recorded in pounds (lbs).

VEHICLE ONLY WEIGHT – COMPLETELY ON SCALE	
Enter Steer Axle GAW.	1.
Enter Drive Axle GAW.	2.
Enter Tag Axle GAW (if equipped).	3.
Calculate Tow Vehicle GVW: (1+2+3=4).	4.

VEHICLE ONLY – HALF VEHICLE ON SCALE		
LEFT	Enter appropriate side of Steer Axle on the scale. Subtract that value from line 1 and enter the opposite side axle weight.	RIGHT
LEFT	Enter appropriate side of Drive Axle on the scale. Subtract that value from line 2 and enter the opposite side axle weight.	RIGHT
LEFT	Enter appropriate side of Tag Axle on the scale. Subtract that value from line 3 and enter the opposite side axle weight.	RIGHT

CALCULATIONS	
Enter the Vehicle Steer Axle GAWR as listed on the Vehicle MWL.	5.
Steer Axle GAW (line 1) MUST be less than GAWR (line 5).	**STOP** Verify

Enter the Vehicle Drive Axle GAWR as listed on the Vehicle MWL.	6.
Drive Axle GAW (line 2) MUST be less than GAWR (line 6).	**STOP** Verify
Enter the Vehicle Tag Axle GAWR as listed on the Vehicle MWL.	7.
Tag Axle GAW (line 3) MUST be less than GAWR (line 7).	**STOP** Verify
Enter Vehicle GVW (line 4).	8.
Enter the Vehicle GVWR from the Vehicle MWL.	9.
The GVW (line 8) MUST be less than the GVWR (line 9). If not, the Vehicle exceeds its GVWR and this MUST be resolved.	**STOP** Verify

WORKSHEET #8 - WIDE SEGMENTED SCALE WEIGHT
Fifth Wheel Vehicles and Tow Vehicles

INSTRUCTIONS	
Position Tow Vehicle and Fifth Wheel Trailer so that axles are centered on separate scale segments. This worksheet is used for scales that have sufficient room to allow you to reposition the Tow Vehicle and Trailer so that only half of each Vehicle is on the scale. This will allow calculation of Vehicle weight by corner. All weights are recorded in pounds (lbs).	

TOW VEHICLE ONLY WEIGHT – COMPLETELY ON SCALE	
Enter Steer Axle GAW.	1.
Enter Drive Axle GAW.	2.
Calculate Tow Vehicle GVW: (1+2=3).	3.

TOW VEHICLE ONLY – HALF VEHICLE ON SCALE		
LEFT	Enter appropriate side of Steer Axle on the scale. Subtract that value from line 1 and enter the opposite side axle weight.	RIGHT
LEFT	Enter appropriate side of Steer Axle on the scale. Subtract that value from line 2 and enter the opposite side axle weight.	RIGHT

COUPLED TOW VEHICLE - FIFTH WHEEL TRAILER ATTACHED COMPLETELY ON SCALE	
Enter Steer Axle GAW.	4.
Enter Drive Axle GAW.	5.
Enter Fifth Wheel Trailer GAW:	6.
Calculate Coupled Tow Vehicle GVW: (4+5=7).	7.

Calculate Fifth Wheel Pin Weight. Subtract Tow Vehicle GVW (line 3) from Coupled Tow Vehicle GVW (line 7): (7–3=8)	8.	

COUPLED TOW VEHICLE - FIFTH WHEEL TRAILER ATTACHED HALF ON SCALE		
LEFT	Enter appropriate side of Steer Axle on the scale. Subtract that value from line 4 and enter the opposite side axle weight.	RIGHT
LEFT	Enter appropriate side of Drive Axle on the scale. Subtract that value from line 5 and enter the opposite side axle weight.	RIGHT
LEFT	Enter appropriate side of Trailer Axle on the scale. Subtract that value from line 6 and enter the opposite side axle weight.	RIGHT
CALCULATIONS		
Enter Tow Vehicle Steer Axle GAWR as indicated on the Tow Vehicle MWL.	9.	
Tow Vehicle Steer Axle GAW (line 1) and Coupled Tow Vehicle GAW (line 4) MUST each be less than Tow Vehicle Steer Axle GAWR (line 9).	**STOP** Verify	
Enter Tow Vehicle Drive Axle GAWR as indicated on the Tow Vehicle MWL.	10.	
Tow Vehicle Drive Axle GAW (line 2) and Coupled Tow Vehicle GAW (line 5) MUST each be less than Tow Vehicle Drive Axle GAWR (line 10).	**STOP** Verify	
Enter Fifth Wheel GAWR as indicated on the Trailer MWL.	11.	
Fifth Wheel GAW (line 6) MUST be less than Trailer Axles GAWR (line 11).	**STOP** Verify	
Enter Fifth Wheel Trailer GVWR as indicated on the Trailer MWL.	12.	

Calculate Fifth Wheel GTW by adding the Fifth Wheel Pin Weight (line 8) and the Fifth Wheel Trailer GAW (line 6): (6+8=13).	13.
Fifth Wheel Trailer GTW (line 13) MUST be less that the Fifth Wheel Trailer GVWR (line 12).	**STOP** Verify
Enter Tow Vehicle GCWR from the MWL.	13.
Calculate GCW by adding Tow Vehicle GVW (line 3) to the Trailer GTW (line 13): (3+13=14).	14.
GCW (line 14) MUST be less than the Tow Vehicle GCWR (line 13). If not, the Tow Vehicle and Fifth Wheel exceed their designed combined maximum weight rating and this MUST be resolved.	**STOP** Verify

WORKSHEET #9 - WIDE SEGMENTED SCALES
Travel Trailers and Tow Vehicles

INSTRUCTIONS
Position Tow Vehicle and Travel Trailer so that axles are centered on separate scale segments. This worksheet is used for scales that have sufficient room to allow you to reposition the Tow Vehicle and Trailer so that only half of each Vehicle is on the scale. This will allow calculation of Vehicle weight by corner. Weight data will be collected with WDH disconnected and connected. All weights recorded in pounds (lbs).

TOW VEHICLE ONLY WEIGHT – COMPLETELY ON SCALE	
Enter Steer Axle GAW.	1.
Enter Drive Axle GAW.	2.
Calculate Uncoupled Tow Vehicle GVW: (1+2=3).	3.

TOW VEHICLE ONLY WEIGHT – HALF VEHICLE ON SCALE		
LEFT	Enter appropriate side of Steer Axle on the scale. Subtract that value from line 1 and enter the opposite side axle weight.	RIGHT
LEFT	Enter appropriate side of Drive Axle on the scale. Subtract that value from line 2 and enter the opposite side axle weight.	RIGHT

COUPLED TOW VEHICLE - TRAVEL TRAILER ATTACHED WEIGHT DISTRIBUTING HITCH NOT CONNECTED COMPLETELY ON SCALE	
Enter Steer Axle GAW.	4.
Enter Drive Axle GAW.	5.
Enter Travel Trailer GAW:	6.
Calculate Coupled Tow Vehicle GVW: (4+5=7)	7.

	COUPLED TOW VEHICLE - TRAVEL TRAILER ATTACHED WEIGHT DISTRIBUTING HITCH NOT CONNECTED HALF ON SCALE	
LEFT	Enter appropriate side of Steer Axle on the scale. Subtract that value from line 4 and enter the opposite side axle weight.	RIGHT
LEFT	Enter appropriate side of Drive Axle on the scale. Subtract that value from line 5 and enter the opposite side axle weight.	RIGHT
LEFT	Enter appropriate side of Trailer Axle on the scale. Subtract that value from line 6 and enter the opposite side axle weight.	RIGHT

COUPLED TOW VEHICLE - TRAVEL TRAILER ATTACHED WEIGHT DISTRIBUTING HITCH CONNECTED COMPLETELY ON SCALE	
Enter Steer Axle GAW.	8.
Enter Drive Axle GAW.	9.
Enter Travel Trailer GAW:	10.
Calculate Coupled Tow Vehicle GVW: (8+9=11)	11.

	COUPLED TOW VEHICLE - TRAVEL TRAILER ATTACHED WEIGHT DISTRIBUTING HITCH CONNECTED HALF ON SCALE	
LEFT	Enter appropriate side of Steer Axle on the scale. Subtract that value from line 8 and enter the opposite side axle weight.	RIGHT
LEFT	Enter appropriate side of Drive Axle on the scale. Subtract that value from line 9 and enter the opposite side axle weight.	RIGHT
LEFT	Enter appropriate side of Trailer Axle on the scale. Subtract that value from line 10 and enter the opposite side axle weight.	RIGHT

CALCULATIONS	
Enter Tow Vehicle Steer Axle GAWR as indicated on the Tow Vehicle MWL.	12.
Tow Vehicle Steer Axle GAW (line 1), (line 4) and (line 8) MUST each be less than Steer Axle GAWR (line 12).	**STOP** Verify
Enter Tow Vehicle Drive Axle GAWR as indicated on the Tow Vehicle MWL.	13.
Tow Vehicle Drive Axle GAW (line 2), (line 5) and (line 9) MUST each be less than Drive Axle GAWR (line 13).	**STOP** Verify
Enter Trailer GVWR as indicated on the Trailer MWL.	14.
Calculate Trailer Tongue Weight. Subtract the GVW of Uncoupled Tow Vehicle (line 3) from the Coupled Tow Vehicle GVW (line 7): (7−3=15).	15.
Calculate Trailer GTW. Add Trailer Tongue Weight (line 15) and the Travel Trailer GAW (line 6). (15+6=16)	16.
Travel Trailer GTW (line 16) MUST be less that the Travel Trailer GVWR (line 14).	**STOP** Verify
Enter the Tow Vehicle GCWR from the Tow Vehicle MWL.	17.
Calculate GCW. Add Tow Vehicle GVW (line 7) and the Travel Trailer GAW (line 6). (6+7=18).	18.
The GCW (line 18) MUST be less than the GCWR of the Tow Vehicle (line 17). If not, the Tow Vehicle and Travel Trailer exceed their designed combined maximum weight rating and this MUST be resolved.	**STOP** Verify

WORKSHEET #10 - SINGLE AXLE SCALE
For Class A, Class B, Class C, Unattached Tow Vehicles and Pickup Campers

INSTRUCTIONS	WEIGHT DATA (in lbs)
Position the Vehicle on the scale platform, one axle set at a time, so that each axle is centered on the platform as best possible. Once a weight is established, move to the next axle. All recorded weights are in pounds (lbs).	
Enter Steer Axle GAW.	1.
Enter Vehicle Front Axle GAWR as listed on the Vehicle MWL.	2.
The Steer Axle GAW (line 1) MUST be less than the Front Axle GAWR (line 2).	**STOP** Verify
Enter Drive Axle GAW.	3.
Enter Vehicle Drive Axle GAWR as listed on the vehicle MWL.	4
The Drive Axle GAW (line 3) MUST be less than the Drive Axle GAWR (line 4).	**STOP** Verify
Enter Vehicle Tag Axle GAW (if equipped).	5.
Enter Vehicle Tag Axle GAWR as listed on the Vehicle MWL.	6.
The Tag Axle GAW (line 5) MUST be less than the Tag Axle GAWR (line 6).	**STOP** Verify
Calculate Vehicle GVW: Add Steer Axle GAW (line 1), Drive Axle GAW (line 3) and Tag Axle GAW (line 6): (1+3+5=7).	7.
Enter Vehicle GVWR as listed on the Vehicle MWL.	8.
The GVW (line 7) MUST be less than the GVWR (line 8).	**STOP** Verify

WORKSHEET #11 - SINGLE AXLE SCALE
Fifth Wheel Trailers and Tow Vehicles

INSTRUCTIONS	
Position the Tow Vehicle and Fifth Wheel on the scale platform, one axle set at a time, so that each axle is centered on the platform as best possible. Once a weight is established, move to the next axle. All recorded weights are in pounds (lbs).	
TOW VEHICLE ONLY WEIGHT	
Enter Steer Axle GAW.	1.
Enter Drive Axle GAW.	2.
Calculate Tow Vehicle GVW: (1+2=3).	3.
COUPLED TOW VEHICLE - FIFTH WHEEL TRAILER ATTACHED	
Enter Steer Axle GAW.	4.
Enter Drive Axle GAW.	5.
Calculate Coupled Tow Vehicle GVW: (4+5=6).	6.
Calculate Fifth Wheel Pin Weight by subtracting Tow Vehicle GVW (line 3) from Coupled Tow Vehicle GVW (line 6): (6–3=7).	7.
Enter Fifth Wheel Axle One GAW.	8.
Enter Fifth Wheel Axle Two GAW.	9.
Enter Fifth Wheel Axle Three GAW.	10.
Calculate Trailer Total GAW: Add Trailer Axle One (line 8), Trailer Axle Two (line 9) and Trailer Axle Three (line 10): (8+9+10 = 11).	11.

403

CALCULATIONS	
Enter Tow Vehicle Steer Axle GAWR as indicated on the Tow Vehicle MWL.	12.
Tow Vehicle Steer Axle GAW (line 1) and Coupled Tow Vehicle Steer Axle GAW (line 4) MUST each be less than Steer Axle GAWR (line 12).	**STOP** Verify
Enter Tow Vehicle Drive Axle GAWR as indicated on the Tow Vehicle MWL.	13.
Tow Vehicle Drive Axle GAWR (line 2) and Coupled Tow Vehicle Drive Axle GAW (line 5) MUST each be less than Drive Axle GAWR (line 13).	**STOP** Verify
Enter Trailer GAWR as indicated on the Trailer MWL.	14.
Each Fifth Wheel Axle GAW (lines 8, 9 and 10) MUST each be less than the Trailer GAWR (line 14).	**STOP** Verify
Enter Trailer GVWR as indicated on the Trailer MWL.	15.
Calculate Trailer GTW. Add the Fifth Wheel Pin Weight (line 7) and the Fifth Wheel Trailer Total GAW (line 11): (7+11=16).	16.
Trailer GTW (line 16) MUST be less than the Trailer GVWR (line 15).	**STOP** Verify
Enter Tow Vehicle GCWR from the Tow Vehicle MWL.	17.
Calculate GCW. Add Coupled Tow Vehicle GVW (line 6) and Total Trailer GAW (line 11): (6+11=18)	18.
GCW (line 18) MUST be less than the Tow Vehicle GCWR (line 17) If not, the Tow Vehicle and Fifth Wheel exceed their designed combined maximum weight rating and this MUST be resolved.	**STOP** Verify

WORKSHEET #12 - SINGLE AXLE SCALE
Travel Trailers and Tow Vehicles

INSTRUCTIONS	
Position the Tow Vehicle and Fifth Wheel on the scale platform, one axle set at a time, so that each axle is centered on the platform as best possible. Once a weight is established, move to the next axle. Weight data will be collected with WDH disconnected and connected. All weights recorded in pounds (lbs).	
TOW VEHICLE ONLY WEIGHT	
Enter Steer Axle GAW.	1.
Enter Drive Axle GAW.	2.
Calculate Tow Vehicle GVW: (1+2=3).	3.
COUPLED TOW VEHICLE - TRAVEL TRAILER ATTACHED WEIGHT DISTRIBUTING HITCH NOT CONNECTED	
Enter Steer Axle GAW.	4.
Enter Drive Axle GAW.	5.
Calculate Coupled Tow Vehicle GVW: (4+5=6)	6.
Enter Travel Trailer Axle One GAW.	7.
Enter Travel Trailer Axle Two GAW.	8.
Enter Travel Trailer Axle Three GAW.	9.
Calculate Total Trailer GAW: Add Axle One GAW (line 7), Axle Two GAW (line 8) and Axle Three GAW (line 9): (7+8+9=10)	10.

COUPLED TOW VEHICLE - TRAVEL TRAILER ATTACHED WEIGHT DISTRIBUTING HITCH CONNECTED	
Enter Steer Axle GAW.	11.
Enter Drive Axle GAW.	12.
Calculate Coupled Tow Vehicle GVW: (11+12=13).	13.
Enter Travel Trailer Axle One GAW.	14.
Enter Travel Trailer Axle Two GAW.	15.
Enter Travel Trailer Axle Three GAW.	16.
CALCULATIONS	
Enter Tow Vehicle Steer Axle GAWR as indicated on the Tow Vehicle MWL.	17.
Tow Vehicle Steer Axle GAW (line 1, line 4 and line 11) MUST each be less than Steer Axle GAWR (line 17).	**STOP** Verify
Enter Tow Vehicle Drive Axle GAWR as indicated on the Tow Vehicle MWL.	18.
Tow Vehicle Drive Axle GAW (line 2, Line 5 and line 12) MUST each be less than Drive Axle GAWR (line 12).	**STOP** Verify
Enter Trailer GAWR as indicated on the Trailer MWL.	19.
Each Trailer GAW (line 7, line 8, line 9, line 14, line 15 and line 16) MUST each be less than the Trailer GAWR (line 19).	**STOP** Verify
Enter Trailer GVWR as indicated on the Trailer MWL.	20.
Calculate Trailer Tongue Weight. Subtract the Tow Vehicle GVW (line 3) from Coupled Tow Vehicle GVW (line 6): (6–3=21).	21.

Calculate GTW. Add Tongue Weight (line 21) and the Travel Trailer Total GAW (line 10): (21+10=22).	22.
Total GTW (line 22) MUST be less that the Trailer GVWR (line 20).	🛑 Verify
Enter Tow Vehicle GCWR from the Tow Vehicle MWL.	23.
Calculate GCW. Add Coupled GVW (line 6) and Total Trailer GAW (line 10): (6+10=24).	24.
The GCW (line 24) MUST be less than the Tow Vehicle GCWR (line 23). If not, the Tow Vehicle and Travel Trailer exceed their designed combined maximum weight rating and this MUST be resolved.	🛑 Verify

WORKSHEET #13 – WIDE SINGLE AXLE SCALE WEIGHT
For Class A, Class B, Class C, Unattached Tow Vehicles and Pickup Campers

INSTRUCTIONS	
Position Vehicle so that axles are centered on the scale platform. This worksheet is used for scales that have sufficient room to allow you to reposition the Vehicle so that only half the Vehicle is on the scale. This will allow calculation of Vehicle weight by corner. Once a weight is established, move to the next axle. All weights recorded in pounds (lbs).	

VEHICLE ONLY WEIGHT – COMPLETELY ON SCALE		
Enter Steer Axle GAW.	1.	
Enter Drive Axle GAW.	2.	
Enter Tag Axle GAW (if equipped).	3.	
Calculate Tow Vehicle GVW: Add Steer Axle GAW (line 1), Drive Axle (line 2) and Tag Axle (line 3) and Drive Axle (line 2): (1+2+3=4).	4.	

VEHICLE ONLY – HALF VEHICLE ON SCALE		
LEFT	Enter appropriate side of Steer Axle on the scale. Subtract that value from line 1 and enter the opposite side axle weight.	RIGHT
LEFT	Enter appropriate side of Drive Axle on the scale. Subtract that value from line 2 and enter the opposite side axle weight.	RIGHT
LEFT	Enter appropriate side of Tag Axle on the scale. Subtract that value from line 3 and enter the opposite side axle weight.	RIGHT

CALCULATIONS	
Enter Vehicle Steer Axle GAWR as listed on the Vehicle MWL.	5.
Steer Axle GAW (line 1) MUST be less than GAWR (line 5).	**STOP** Verify

Enter Vehicle Drive Axle GAWR as listed on the Vehicle MWL.	6.
Drive Axle GAW (line 2) MUST be less than GAWR (line 6).	**STOP** Verify
Enter Vehicle Tag Axle GAWR as listed on the Vehicle MWL.	7.
Tag Axle GAW (line 3) MUST be less than GAWR (line 7).	**STOP** Verify
Enter Vehicle GVWR from the Vehicle MWL.	8.
The GVW (line 4) MUST be less than the GVWR (line 8). If not, the Vehicle exceeds its GVWR and this MUST be resolved.	**STOP** Verify

WORKSHEET #14 - WIDE SINGLE AXLE SCALE WEIGHT
Fifth Wheel Vehicles and Tow Vehicles

INSTRUCTIONS
Position Tow Vehicle and Fifth Wheel Trailer so that axles are centered on the scale platform. This worksheet is used for scales that have sufficient room to allow you to reposition the Tow Vehicle and Trailer so that only half the Tow Vehicle and Trailer axles are on the scale platform at once. This will allow calculation of Vehicle weight by corner. Once a weight is established, move to the next axle. All weights recorded in pounds (lbs).

TOW VEHICLE ONLY WEIGHT – CENTERED ON SCALE PLATFORM	
Enter Steer Axle GAW.	1.
Enter Drive Axle GAW.	2.
Calculate Tow Vehicle GVW: (1+2=3).	3.

TOW VEHICLE ONLY – HALF VEHICLE ON SCALE PLATFORM		
LEFT	Enter appropriate side of Steer Axle on the scale. Subtract that value from line 1 and enter the opposite side axle weight.	RIGHT
LEFT	Enter appropriate side of Steer Axle on the scale. Subtract that value from line 2 and enter the opposite side axle weight.	RIGHT

COUPLED TOW VEHICLE - FIFTH WHEEL TRAILER ATTACHED CENTERED ON SCALE PLATFORM	
Enter Steer Axle GAW.	4.
Enter Drive Axle GAW.	5.
Enter Fifth Wheel Trailer Axle One GAW:	6.
Enter Fifth Wheel Trailer Axle Two GAW:	7.

410

Enter Fifth Wheel Trailer Axle Three GAW:	8.
Calculate Coupled Tow Vehicle GVW. Add Steer Axle GAW (line 4) and Drive Axle GAW (line 5): (4+5=9).	9.
Calculate Fifth Wheel Pin Weight. Subtract Tow Vehicle GVW (line 3) from Coupled Tow Vehicle GVW (line 9): (9–3=10)	10.

COUPLED TOW VEHICLE - FIFTH WHEEL TRAILER ATTACHED HALF ON SCALE PLATFORM		
LEFT	Enter appropriate side of Steer Axle on the scale. Subtract that value from line 4 and enter the opposite side axle weight.	RIGHT
LEFT	Enter appropriate side of Drive Axle on the scale. Subtract that value from line 5 and enter the opposite side axle weight.	RIGHT
LEFT	Enter appropriate side of Trailer Axle One on the scale. Subtract that value from line 6 and enter the opposite side axle weight.	RIGHT
LEFT	Enter appropriate side of Trailer Axle Two on the scale. Subtract that value from line 7 and enter the opposite side axle weight.	RIGHT
LEFT	Enter appropriate side of Trailer Axle Three on the scale. Subtract that value from line 8 and enter the opposite side axle weight.	RIGHT

CALCULATIONS	
Enter Tow Vehicle Steer Axle GAWR as indicated on the Tow Vehicle MWL.	11.
Tow Vehicle Steer Axle GAW (line 1) and Coupled Tow Vehicle GAW (line 4) MUST each be less than Tow Vehicle Steer Axle GAWR (line 11).	STOP Verify
Enter Tow Vehicle Drive Axle GAWR as indicated on the Tow Vehicle MWL.	12.
Tow Vehicle Drive Axle GAW (line 2) and Coupled Tow Vehicle GAW (line 5) MUST each be less than Tow Vehicle Drive Axle GAWR (line 12).	STOP Verify

Enter Fifth Wheel GAWR as indicated on the Trailer MWL.	13.
Fifth Wheel GAW (line 6. line 7 and line 8) MUST each be less than Trailer Axles GAWR (line 13).	**STOP** Verify
Enter Fifth Wheel Trailer GVWR as indicated on the Trailer MWL.	14.
Calculate Fifth Wheel GTW: Add Fifth Wheel Pin Weight (line 10) and the Fifth Wheel Trailer GAW (line 6, line 7 and line 8): (6+7+8+10=15).	15.
Fifth Wheel Trailer GTW (line 15) MUST be less that the Fifth Wheel Trailer GVWR (line 14).	**STOP** Verify
Enter Tow Vehicle GCWR from the MWL.	16.
Calculate GCW by adding Tow Vehicle GVW (line 3) to the Trailer GTW (line 15): (3+15=17).	17.
GCW (line 17) MUST be less than the Tow Vehicle GCWR (line 16). If not, the Tow Vehicle and Fifth Wheel exceed their designed combined maximum weight rating and this MUST be resolved.	**STOP** Verify

WORKSHEET #15 – WIDE SINGLE AXLE SCALE WEIGHT
Travel Trailer and Tow Vehicle

INSTRUCTIONS
Position Tow Vehicle and Travel Trailer so that axles are centered on the scale platform. This worksheet is used for scales that have sufficient room to allow you to reposition the Tow Vehicle and Trailer so that only half the Tow Vehicle and Trailer axles are on the scale platform at once. This will allow calculation of Vehicle weight by corner. Weight data will be collected with WDH disconnected and connected. Once a weight is established, move to the next axle. All weights recorded in pounds (lbs).

TOW VEHICLE ONLY WEIGHT – CENTERED ON SCALE PLATFORM

Enter Steer Axle GAW.	1.
Enter Drive Axle GAW.	2.
Calculate Tow Vehicle GVW: (1+2=3).	3.

TOW VEHICLE ONLY WEIGHT
HALF OF VEHICLE ON SCALE PLATFORM

LEFT	Enter appropriate side of Steer Axle on the scale. Subtract that value from line 1 and enter the opposite side axle weight.	RIGHT
LEFT	Enter appropriate side of Drive Axle on the scale. Subtract that value from line 2 and enter the opposite side axle weight.	RIGHT

COUPLED TOW VEHICLE - TRAVEL TRAILER
WEIGHT DISTRIBUTING HITCH NOT CONNECTED
CENTERED ON SCALE PLATFORM

Enter Steer Axle GAW.	4.
Enter Drive Axle GAW.	5.
Calculate Coupled Tow Vehicle GVW: (4+5=6)	6.

Enter Travel Trailer Axle One GAW.	7.
Enter Travel Trailer Axle Two GAW.	8.
Enter Travel Trailer Axle Three GAW.	9.
Calculate Trailer Total GAW: (7+8+9=10)	10.

COUPLED TOW VEHICLE - TRAVEL TRAILER ATTACHED WEIGHT DISTRIBUTING HITCH NOT CONNECTED HALF ON SCALE		
LEFT	Enter appropriate side of Steer Axle on the scale. Subtract that value from line 4 and enter the opposite side axle weight.	RIGHT
LEFT	Enter appropriate side of Drive Axle on the scale. Subtract that value from line 5 and enter the opposite side axle weight.	RIGHT
LEFT	Enter appropriate side of Trailer Axle One on the scale. Subtract that value from line 7 and enter the opposite side axle weight.	RIGHT
LEFT	Enter appropriate side of Trailer Axle Two on the scale. Subtract that value from line 8 and enter the opposite side axle weight.	RIGHT
LEFT	Enter appropriate side of Trailer Axle Three on the scale. Subtract that value from line 9 and enter the opposite side axle weight.	RIGHT

COUPLE TOW VEHICLE - TRAVEL TRAILER WEIGHT DISTRIBUTING HITCH CONNECTED CENTERED ON SCALE PLATFORM	
Enter Steer Axle GAW.	11.
Enter Drive Axle GAW.	12.

Calculate Coupled Tow Vehicle GVW: (11+12=13)	13.
Enter Travel Trailer Axle One GAW.	14.
Enter Travel Trailer Axle Two GAW.	15.
Enter Travel Trailer Axle Three GAW.	16.

TOW VEHICLE - TRAVEL TRAILER ATTACHED **WEIGHT DISTRIBUTING HITCH CONNECTED** **HALF ON SCALE**		
LEFT	Enter appropriate side of Steer Axle on the scale. Subtract that value from line 11 and enter the opposite side axle weight.	RIGHT
LEFT	Enter appropriate side of Drive Axle on the scale. Subtract that value from line 12 and enter the opposite side axle weight.	RIGHT
LEFT	Enter appropriate side of Trailer Axle One on the scale. Subtract that value from line 14 and enter the opposite side axle weight.	RIGHT
LEFT	Enter appropriate side of Trailer Axle Two on the scale. Subtract that value from line 15 and enter the opposite side axle weight.	RIGHT
LEFT	Enter appropriate side of Trailer Axel Three on the scale. Subtract that value from line 16 and enter the opposite side axle weight.	RIGHT

CALCULATIONS	
Enter Tow Vehicle GAWR for the Steer Axle as indicated on the Tow Vehicle MWL.	17.
Tow Vehicle Steer Axle GAW (line 1, Line 4 and line 11) MUST each be less than Steer Axle GAWR (line 17).	**STOP** Verify

415

Enter Tow Vehicle GAWR for the Drive Axle as indicated on the Tow Vehicle MWL.	18.
Tow Vehicle Drive Axle GAW (line 2, Line 5 and Line 12) MUST each be less than Drive Axle GAWR (line 18).	**STOP** Verify
Enter Trailer GAWR as indicated on the Trailer MWL.	19.
Travel Trailer GAW (line 7, line 8, line 9, line 14, line 15, and line 16) MUST each be less than the Trailer GAWR (line 19).	**STOP** Verify
Enter Trailer GVWR as indicated on the Trailer MWL.	20.
Calculate Trailer Tongue Weight. Subtract the Tow Vehicle GVW (line 3) from the Coupled Tow Vehicle GVW (line 6): (6–3=21)	21.
Calculate GTW. Add Trailer Total GAW (line 10) and Trailer Tongue Weight (line 21): (21+10=22)	22.
GTW (line 22) MUST be less that the Trailer GVWR (line 20).	**STOP** Verify
Enter Tow Vehicle GCWR from the Tow Vehicle MWL.	23.
Calculate GCW. Add Coupled Tow Vehicle GVW (line 6) and Trailer Total GAW (line 10): (6+10=24)	24.
The CGW (line 24) MUST be less than the GCWR (line 23). If not, the Tow Vehicle and Travel Trailer exceed their designed combined maximum weight rating and this MUST be resolved.	**STOP** Verify

Appendix Three

Driver's License Requirements

Do you need to get a special driver's license to operate that shiny new RV you just bought? Great question. Many folks, including life-long, die-hard RVers may quickly tell you no. Your salesman might hedge the question. For the majority of RV owners, the quick answer is most RVs sold do not require a special license to operate. The better answer is to check with your local Department of Motor Vehicles because the rules surrounding special licensing for RVs is constantly evolving.

I invested a substantial amount of time compiling a snapshot in time of licensing requirements, state by state. It was a tedious and frustrating undertaking. It should not have been. In this day and age of immediate access to data, one would assume locating this information would be simple. It wasn't. In fact, it was far from it. While there are a number of sites that have reference data posted, it is often out dated, contradictory or simply incorrect. I contacted one site administrator to inform them the information they had posted for my state of residence was incorrect. For my efforts, I was berated by the site owner who decried how impossible it was to manage and continually update the information. I completely understand the frustration but if that's the purpose of your site, then manage to that expectation. When I encountered conflicting information, I relied on official state publications for resolution. In a handful of instances, state guidance was contradictory which prompted me to contact the individual Department of Motor Vehicle office to seek clarification. Incredibly, the end result was that they were often unclear as to what the specific rules were and that is documented in the section below.

417

So why are there differences between state licensing requirements? While the Federal Motor Carrier Safety Improvement Act of 1999, definitions section, exempts "recreational vehicles operating under their own power"[43] from the requirement that their operators obtain Commercial Drivers Licenses (CDL), each state retains the power to require more stringent rules, up to and including requiring CDLs or what are often referred to as "Non-Commercial CDLs". Confusing? Yes it is... The bottom line is each state controls specifically how they wish to manage their driver's license programs.

As of this writing, I tried to carefully document and represent requirements for each of the 50 states using the latest published driver's license manual, official electronically posted licensing requirements, and/or electronic definitions from the states information portals. There is a lot of *"legalese"* to wade through. I purposefully kept the specific language used by the state where possible. Of the 50 states, 43 specifically exempt CDL requirements for RVs. 19 states require some form of specific license while 31 have no apparent requirements for additional licensing of any kind. For states where some form of additional license is necessary, notice the requirement often stems from exceeding the 26,000 pound weight threshold.

Driver's license requirements for RVs by state

Alabama: Per the 2016 Code of Alabama, Title 32, Motor Vehicles and Traffic, Chapter 6, Licenses and Registration, Article 1A, Uniform Commercial Driver License Act: Commercial driver license required; "Exceptions: Commercial driver license requirements do not apply to drivers of vehicles used for personal use such as recreational vehicles which would otherwise meet the definition of a commercial motor vehicle". No state references to any RV specific driver's license requirements found.

Alaska: Alaska driver's license manual, July 2014 states: "Those exempted from the commercial driver licensing requirements include drivers of recreational, military and emergency vehicles." No state references to any RV specific driver's license requirements found.

Arizona: Arizona 28-3102, Exceptions to driver license classes; Definitions, Section A: "a person who operates an authorized emergency vehicle, a farm vehicle or a recreational vehicle may operate the vehicle with a class A, B, C, D or G license". Section 5. "Recreational vehicle" means a motor vehicle or vehicle combination that is more than twenty-six thousand pounds gross vehicle weight rating and that is designed and exclusively used for private pleasure, including vehicles commonly called motor homes, pickup trucks with campers, travel trailers, boat trailers and horse trailers used exclusively to transport personal possessions or persons for noncommercial purposes. References indicate special licensing required for RVs over 26,000 pounds while they are defined as noncommercial vehicles.

Arkansas: The Arkansas CDL manual does not specifically exempt RVs from the CDL requirement. Arkansas, Title 27, Transportation, A.C.A. 27-23-111, Content of Commercial Driver's License, Classifications, Expiration and Renewal, provides definition of Class A, B, C and D licenses based on vehicle weight. No state references to any RV specific driver's license requirements.

California: Does have specific license requirements based on the type and weight of the RV. Class A license required for any combination of vehicles, if any vehicle being towed has a gross vehicle weight rating of more than 10,000 pounds; any vehicle towing more than 1 vehicle; any trailer bus; any vehicle under Class B or Class C. Class B license required for any single vehicle with a gross vehicle weight rating of more than 26,000 pounds; any single vehicle with 3 or more axles, except any single 3-axle vehicle weighing less than 6,000 pounds; any 3 or more axle vehicle or vehicle with a gross vehicle weight rating of more 26,000 pounds towing another vehicle with a gross vehicle weight rating of 10,000 pounds or less; any motor home over 40 feet in length; any vehicle covered under Class C. Class C license required for any 2-axle vehicle with a gross vehicle weight rating of 26,000 pounds or less, including when such vehicle is towing a trailer with a gross vehicle weight rating of 10,000 pounds or less; any 3-axle vehicle weighing 6,000 pounds or less; any 2-axle vehicle weighing 4,000 pounds or more unladen when towing a trailer not exceeding 10,000 pounds gross vehicle weight rating; any motor home of 40 feet in length or less; any 5th wheel trailer under 10,000 pounds if not for hire or under 15,000 pounds with endorsement; or vehicle towing another vehicle with a gross vehicle weight rating of 10,000 pounds or less.

Colorado: Department of Revenue, Division of Motor Vehicles, Rules and Regulations for Classification of Driver's Licenses, Title 42, Section 42-2-402 exempts RVs from CDL. No other appropriate references for special licensing were evident. Colorado is one of the states I contacted and received conflicting information from Department of Motor Vehicle employees.

Connecticut: Connecticut Department of Motor Vehicles, Connecticut Statute 95-2602: "Any motor vehicle... or combination of motor vehicle and trailer where the gross weight of the trailer is more than 10,000 pounds requires a Class 2 license". The Connecticut CDL manual does exclude RVs from commercial vehicle category but has special licensing requirements for certain RVs based on weight.

Delaware: State of Delaware, Division of Motor Vehicles, Driver's License Services: "No special licenses are required when operating personal recreation vehicles, commercial motor vehicles for military purpose and emergency vehicles used in the preservation of life or property". The following defines these waived vehicles: Section C: "Recreational vehicles or trailers which provide temporary living quarters and are used solely for recreational purposes". No state references to any RV specific driver's license requirements.

Florida: Florida statute 322.53 (2) (d) exempts all RV's from CDL requirement, regardless of weight and has no apparent requirement for special licensing.

Georgia: Georgia Code, Title 40, Motor Vehicles and Traffic, Chapter 5, Article 7 specifies that recreational vehicles are not commercial vehicles, however Class E or Class F license required for vehicles in excess of 26,000 pounds.

Hawaii: The Hawaii CDL manual excludes recreational vehicles. However, Hawaii license categories implies that special licenses are required for recreational vehicles based on their weights.

Idaho: Idaho Statutes, Title 49, Motor Vehicles, Chapter 3, exempts recreational vehicles from CDL requirements with no special apparent licensing requirements.

Illinois: Illinois Compiled Statutes, 625 ILCS 5, Illinois Vehicle Code, Section 6-500, excludes recreational vehicles from CDL requirements when operated for personal use. Illinois does require special licensing for vehicles above 16,000 pounds or towing above 10,000 pounds.

Indiana: Indiana Department of Revenue, IC 9-24-6, Commercial Driver's License, Exempted Vehicles: IC9-24-6-1: "this chapter does not apply to a motor vehicle that meets any of the following conditions: (1) Is registered as a recreational vehicle." No state references to any RV specific driver's license requirements.

Iowa: State driver's license fact guide states the following are exempt from CDL requirements: "Recreational Vehicle. A person operating a recreational vehicle for personal or family use OR a person operating a vehicle with less than 26,001 gross vehicle weight rating towing a travel trailer or fifth wheel trailer for personal or family use". **Note:** For RVs over 26,000 pounds, special licensing is implied.

Kansas: Kansas Department of Revenue, Driver's License Facts: Recreational vehicles that fit into one of the below categories requires either a Class A or B CDL. Class A CDL: Allows you to drive any combination of vehicles with a combined gross vehicle weight rating 26,001 pounds or more, if the gross vehicle weight rating of the vehicle or vehicles being towed is in excess of 10,000 pounds. Class B CDL: Allows you to drive a single vehicle with a gross vehicle weight rating of 26,001 pounds or more, or any such vehicle with a trailer with a gross vehicle weight rating of no more than 10,000 pounds.

Kentucky: Kentucky State Law 281A.050, Drivers excluded from CDL requirement: The provisions of this chapter shall not apply to, (4) Drivers of vehicles that: (a) Are designed as temporary living quarters for recreational, camping, or travel use; and (b) Operate on their own motor power or are mounted on or drawn by another vehicle. No state references to any RV specific driver's license requirements.

Louisiana: Louisiana Laws, Revised Statutes, Title 32, Motor vehicles and traffic regulation, RS 32:408, Examination of applicants required; classes of licenses: Class "E" Driver's License: "Personal Vehicle" Permits the operation of and any personal use of recreational vehicle or combination of vehicles... No reference to RV's being defined as noncommercial vehicles. No state references to any RV specific driver's license requirements.

Maine: Maine Revised Statutes, Title 29-1 Motor Vehicles Heading, license types does not specifically address recreational vehicles, nor does the Maine CDL manual exempt recreational vehicles. The standard noncommercial Class C license authorizes a person to operate recreational vehicles for personal use.

Maryland: Maryland Department of Transportation requires a special noncommercial Class A or Class B license for specific RV types and weights. For units over 26,000 pounds, a Class A or B license is required. For units with a combined weight of 26,000 pounds or more, towing 10,001 pounds or more, requires a Class A noncommercial license. Maryland 11-109.1, exempts recreational vehicles from the commercial vehicle category.

Massachusetts: No specific exemption in CDL language for recreational vehicles. The standard Class D license is good for all vehicles up to 26,000 pounds. **_Note:_** I called the motor vehicle division and was informed that a Class D license is appropriate for all recreational vehicles, regardless of size however, personnel were unable to provide a specific reference.

Michigan: The Michigan Commercial Driver's License Program provides the following exemption: "The following people do NOT need a Commercial Driver License: Individuals operating motor homes or other vehicles used exclusively to transport personal possessions or family members, for non-business purposes." No state references to any RV specific driver's license requirements.

Minnesota: Minnesota Statutes 169.011 Definitions, (b) For purposes of chapter 169A: (1) "a commercial motor vehicle does not include a farm truck, an authorized emergency vehicle, or a recreational vehicle"... No state references to any RV specific driver's license requirements.

Mississippi: Mississippi Code, MS 63.1.78, provides a broad exemption, stating: "(1) Except as otherwise specifically provided in this article, the provisions of this article shall be inapplicable to the following persons and vehicles: (e) Any vehicle which is used strictly and exclusively to transport personal possessions or family members for nonbusiness purposes." The standard Class R license is all that is required, no specific RV license needed.

Missouri: Missouri Revised Statutes, Chapter 302, Drivers' and Commercial Drivers' Licenses Section 302.775, states CDL requirements do not apply to: "(5) Any person driving or pulling a recreational vehicle, as defined in sections 301.010 and 700.010, for personal use;" ... No state references to any RV specific driver's license requirements.

Montana: Montana Code Amended, 61-1-101 states that vehicles will not be considered commercial vehicles if they are not used to transport goods for compensation or for hire. There are no specific requirements for RV driver's license.

Nebraska: Nebraska 60-465, Commercial Motor Vehicle Defined, states commercial motor vehicles do not include (b) any recreational vehicle as defined in section 60-347 or motor vehicle towing a cabin trailer as defined in 60-314 and 60-339. The Nebraska standard Class O operator's license is all that's required to operate a RV.

Nevada: Nevada 483.850 provides that the following are exempt from Nevada CDL requirements. Recreational vehicle drivers using a RV for non-commercial purposes may be required to obtain special noncommercial licenses depending on size and weight. Nevada requires a special license endorsement for towing trailers over 10,000 pounds. Noncommercial Class A or Class B are defined as follows: Class A: any combination of vehicles with a gross combined weight rating of 26,001 pounds, if the gross vehicle weight rating of the trailing vehicle is over 10,000 pounds. The holder may also drive a Class B or Class C vehicle. Class B: any single vehicle with a gross vehicle weight rating of 26,001 pounds or more, or any vehicle which is towing another vehicle that does not have a gross vehicle weight rating of more than 10,000 pounds.

New Hampshire: New Hampshire, SAF-C 1801.02, Exemption from the Commercial Driver's License Requirements: (a)(2) Persons who drive recreational vehicles... The driver's license manual states that the Class D license is specifically good for

425

vehicles up to 26,000 pounds. _NOTE:_ This implies that a special license is required for vehicles above 26,001 pounds.

New Jersey: New Jersey 39:3-10.11: Definitions relative to commercial driver's license specifically excludes recreational vehicles. No specific licensing requirements for RVs.

New Mexico: New Mexico, Title 18 Transportation and Highways, Chapter 19 Motor Vehicle Procedures, License and Permits, Part 5 Driver's License Section 18.19.5.30, E.: Recreational vehicles: a vehicle licensed as a recreational vehicle under the provisions of Section 66-1-4 NMSA 1978 and used as a recreational vehicle, drivers are excluded from requiring a CDL. A Class E license is required for individuals who are exempt from CDL requirements for recreational vehicles larger than 26,000 pounds.

New York: New York Statue 5-19-501 exempts "personal use vehicles" from CDL requirements. Caution: The New York CDL manual specifically address recreational vehicles and states that a special license for heavy vehicles is required for vehicles above 26,000 pounds. Aside from the CDL license exemption, I was unable to find specific "consistent" information on these special licenses.

North Carolina: North Carolina 20-37.16, Content of License; Classifications and Endorsements states: (e) The requirements for a commercial driver's license do not apply to vehicles used for personal use such as recreational vehicles." However, recreational vehicles larger than 26,000 pounds do require a non-commercial Class A or B license according to North Carolina Motor Vehicle Code, Chapter 20, Article 2.

North Dakota: North Dakota 39-06, 2-01, Uniform Commercial Driver's License Act, Section 39-06.2-06 exempts "when the vehicle being driven is a house car or a vehicle towing a travel trailer being solely use for personal rather than commercial purposes." No specific state requirements for any special license.

Ohio: Ohio, 4506.01 Commercial Driver's Licensing definitions, excludes recreational vehicles. No special state RV licensing required.

Oklahoma: Under Title 47 of the Oklahoma Statutes, the exemption for CDL exists for a vehicle that is self-propelled or towed ... "equipped to serve as temporary living quarters for recreational, camping or travel purposes and is used solely as a family or personal conveyance." Oklahoma Class D license is valid for vehicles designed and used solely as recreational vehicles, regardless of weight.

Oregon: Oregon, Title 59, Oregon Vehicle Code, Section 801.208 excludes recreational vehicles operated for personal use from commercial vehicle regulations. No specific driver's license requirements found.

Pennsylvania: Pennsylvania Title 18, Section 1603, Definitions, excludes any motorhome or recreational trailer operated solely for personal use from commercial vehicle regulations. Based on weight however, a non-commercial Class A or B license is required for configurations over 26,000 pounds.

Rhode Island: Rhode Island, Title 31, Motor and Other Vehicles, Chapter 31-10.3-16 excludes from CDL requirements: (5) "Any person operating a vehicle for personal or family use such as a motorized camper or travel trailer equipped with permanent living and sleeping facilities used for camping activities". No state references to any RV specific driver's license requirements.

South Carolina: South Carolina Code of Laws, Title 56 Motor Vehicles, (C) (4) excludes operators of recreational vehicles from requiring CDL. However, noncommercial Class E or Class F license may be necessary. Class E vehicles are non-commercial single unit vehicles that do not exceed 26,000 pounds gross vehicle weight. Class F vehicles are non-commercial combination vehicles that exceed 26,000 pounds gross vehicle weight.

South Dakota: South Dakota Codified Laws, 32-12A-1, part 29 states: "Recreational vehicle, a vehicle which is self-propelled or permanently towable by a light duty truck and designed primarily not for use as a permanent dwelling but as temporary living quarters for recreational, camping, travel, or seasonal use; does not require the operator to obtain a CDL." No state references to any RV specific driver's license requirements.

Tennessee: Tennessee Code Annotated, Title 55 Motor and Other Vehicles, Chapter 50, Uniform Classified and Commercial Driver's License, (12) (A) defines commercial vehicles as used in commerce. (B) (IV) specifically exempts recreational vehicles. No state references to any RV specific driver's license requirements.

Texas: Texas Transportation Code, Title 7, Vehicles and Traffic, Subtitle B, Section 522.004, specifically exempts recreational vehicles driven for personal use. Subsection (b) states "In this section, "recreational vehicle" means a motor vehicle primarily designed as temporary living quarters for recreational camping or travel use. The term includes a travel trailer, camping trailer, truck camper, and motor home." Texas Transportation Code, Title 7, Vehicles and Traffic, Subtitle B, Section 521.001, may require non-commercial Class A or B license depending on the weight of the recreational vehicle.

Utah: Utah State Legislature, Utah Code, Title 53, Chapter 3, Uniform Driver License Act, 53-3-102, (4)(b)(iv) exempts the following vehicles from CDL requirements: "recreational vehicles that are not used in commerce and are driven solely as family or personal conveyances for recreational purposes". No state references to any RV specific driver's license requirements.

Vermont: Vermont Statutes, Title 23: Motor Vehicles, Chapter 39: Commercial Driver's License Act, Section 4103, (4) states commercial vehicles are motor vehicles designed or used to transport passengers or property. Section (B)(ii) specifically excludes recreational vehicles as long as they are used exclusively for noncommercial purposes. No state references to any RV specific driver's license requirements.

Virginia: Virginia, Code of Virginia, 46.2-341.4, definitions sections states: The following shall be excluded from the definition of commercial motor vehicle: "any vehicle when used by an individual solely for his own personal purposes, such as personal recreational activities". No state references to any RV specific driver's license requirements.

Washington: Washington State Legislature, RCW 46.25.050, Commercial driver's license required, Exceptions, Restrictions, Reciprocity. Exemptions include: (1) (c) Operating a recreational vehicle for noncommercial purposes. No state references to any RV specific driver's license requirements.

West Virginia: West Virginia Code, Uniform Commercial Driver's License Act, Article One, Section 17E-1-8, exempts recreational vehicles from CDL requirements. No state references to any RV specific driver's license requirements.

Wisconsin: Wisconsin Legislature, 343.055 Commercial driver license waivers, Section (1) Operators Waived (d) states: Recreational vehicle operators. "The operator of the commercial motor vehicle is a person operating a motor home, or a vehicle towing a 5th-wheel recreational vehicle or single-unit recreational vehicle and the vehicle or combination, including both units of a combination towing vehicle and the 5th-wheel recreational vehicle or recreational vehicle, is both operated and controlled by the person and is transporting only members of the person's family, guests or their personal property". No state references to any RV specific driver's license requirements.

Wyoming: Wyoming State Code 31-7-109 defines classes of licenses, Class A, B or C. These licenses are based on weight and configuration. The Wyoming State CDL requirements exempt recreational vehicles up to 26,000 pounds. Above 26,000 pounds requires a Class A, B or C license.

Appendix Four

Auxiliary Braking

Like the topic of weight, the issue of supplemental braking can get you in the middle of some finger pointing and heated discussions. Supplemental braking includes all types of trailers, to include vehicles towed behind motorhomes – which I would argue by definition, are trailers. These rules seem very straight forward to most, but to some, the ambiguities of the various laws creates enough gray area for them to simply ignore the issue. A few years ago, I had a fellow RVer at a campground argue that the car he was "towing" behind his motorhome could not possibly be considered a trailer. I asked him if it was not a trailer, then what possibly could it be? "A car", he replied.

For the sake of clarity, I believe that a vehicle you "tow" behind a tow vehicle that is hooked up with a tow bar and safety-tow-chains, squarely fits the definition of a trailer. The following chart details what the specific requirements are for supplemental brakes in all 50 states.

Supplemental brake requirements by state

STATE	SUPPLEMENTAL BRAKEN REQUIRED WHEN:
Alabama	Trailer weighs 3,000 pounds or more and if trailer exceeds 40% of tow vehicle weight.
Alaska	Trailer weighs 5,000 pounds or more. Breakaway system required.

Arizona	Trailer weighs 3,000 pounds or more.
Arkansas	Trailer weighs 3,000 pounds or more. Breakaway system required.
California	Trailers manufactured after 1940 weighing 6,000 pounds or more that travel 20 mph or higher. Trailers manufactured after 1966 weighing more than 3,000 pounds must have brakes on at least two wheels. RVs weighing more than 1500 pounds.
Colorado	Trailer weighs 3,000 pounds or more. Breakaway system required.
Connecticut	Trailer weighs 3,000 pounds or more. Breakaway system required.
Delaware	Trailer weighs 4,000 pounds or more.
District of Columbia	Trailer weighs 3,000 pounds or more. Breakaway system required
Florida	Trailer weighs 3,000 pounds or more.
Georgia	Trailer weighs 3,000 pounds or more.
Hawaii	Trailer weighs 3,000 pounds or more.
Idaho	Trailer weighs 1,500 pounds or more. Breakaway system required.

Illinois	Trailer weighs 3,000 pounds or more. Breakaway system required if towed vehicle weighs 5,000 pounds or more.
Indiana	Trailer weighs 3,000 pounds or more.
Iowa	Trailer weighs 3,000 pounds or more.
Kansas	Vehicle combination at 20mph must be able to stop within 40 feet on dry, hard surface.
Kentucky	Refer to Kentucky vehicle code. Kentucky requires various combinations of vehicles and trailers to be able to stop within defined limits.
Louisiana	Trailer weighs 3,000 pounds or more.
Maine	Trailer weighs 3,000 pounds or more.
Maryland	Trailer weighs 3,000 pounds or more. Breakaway system required.
Massachusetts	Trailer weighs 10,000 pounds or more.
Michigan	Trailer weighs 15,000 pounds or more.
Minnesota	Trailer weighs 3,000 pounds or more. Breakaway system required if towed vehicle is 6,000 pounds or more
Mississippi	Trailer carrying 2,000 pounds or more. Breakaway system required.

Missouri	Trailers coupled by fifth wheel and kingpin.
Montana	Trailer weighs 3,000 pounds or more. Breakaway system required.
Nebraska	Trailer weighs 3,000 pounds or more. Breakaway system required if towed vehicle is 6,500 pounds or more.
Nevada	Trailer weighs 3,000 pounds or more. Breakaway system required.
New Hampshire	Trailer weighs 3,000 pounds or more. Vehicle combination at 20mph must be able to stop within 30 feet on dry, hard surface.
New Jersey	Trailer weighs 3,000 pounds or more. Breakaway system required.
New Mexico	Trailer weighs 3,000 pounds or more.
New York	Trailer weighs 3,000 pounds or more.
North Carolina	Trailer weighs 4,000 pounds or more. Every "house trailer" weighing 1,000 pounds or more.
North Dakota	Breakaway system required.
Ohio	Trailer weighs 3,000 pounds or more.

Oklahoma	Trailer weighs 3,000 pounds or more.
Oregon	Vehicle combination weighing less than 8,000 pounds must stop within 25 feet from 20 miles per hour. Combinations over 8,000 pounds must stop within 35 feet from 20 miles per hour.
Pennsylvania	Breakaway system required.
Rhode Island	Trailer weighs 4,000 pounds or more. Breakaway system required.
South Carolina	Trailer weighs 3,000 pounds or more.
South Dakota	Every trailer must be equipped with a braking system.
Tennessee	Trailer weighs 3,000 pounds or more. Breakaway system required.
Texas	Trailer weighs 4,500 pounds or more.
Utah	Vehicle combination at 20mph must be able to stop within 40 feet on dry, hard surface.
Vermont	Trailer weighs 3,000 pounds or more. Breakaway system required.
Virginia	Trailer weighs 3,000 pounds or more.
Washington	Trailer weighs 3,000 pounds or more.

West Virginia	Trailer weighs 3,000 pounds or more. Breakaway system required.
Wisconsin	Trailer weighs 3,000 pounds or more.
Wyoming	Vehicle combination at 20mph must be able to stop within 40 feet on dry, hard surface.

Endnotes

---

[1]"What is a Recreational Vehicle (RV)?" *RVIA.ORG*, Recreational Vehicle Industry Association, 28 August 2013.

[2] "Ideal RV length for fitting into National Park Campsites," Camperreport.com, Improve Photography, LLC, 10 September 2016.

[3] Broom, Kevin. "Travelers save when they go RVing study reveals," RVIA.org, Recreational Vehicle Industry Association, 11 December, 2016.

[4] "Publication 936, Main Content, Part One, Home Mortgage Interest,"irs.gov, Internal Revenue Service, 2017 Tax Publications.

[5]"Market Reports," December 2016 Year End Data, *RVIA.org.* Recreational Vehicle Industry Association, 27 February 2017.

[6]"Ford Boosting Motorhome Chassis Production," *RV Business.Com.* RV Business, Delivering RV Industry News, February 2013.

[7]"XC Series," fcccrv.com/chassis/xc/.com. Freightliner Custom Chassis, February 2017.

[8]"Market Reports," December 2016 Year End Data, RVIA.org. Recreational Vehicle Industry Association, 27 February 2017.

[9]"Market Reports," March 2016 Year End Data, RVIA.org. Recreational Vehicle Industry Association, 27 February 2017.

[10]"Market Reports," December 2016 Year End Data, RVIA.org. Recreational Vehicle Industry Association, 27 February 2017.

[11]"CAT Scale Mission," *About*, Catscale.com, CAT Scale Company, 27 March 2017.

[12]"RV Safety and Education Foundation," Wheel Position Weighing, *RVsafety.com,* RV Safety and Education Foundation, 20 October 2016.

[13]"Overweight RVs and Underinflated Tires are a Serious Problem," RV Weight Mobile Weigh Station, rvweigh.com, RV Weigh, March 2017.

[14]"Are you Overweight?" SmartWeigh Escapees RV Club, escapees.com, Escapees RV Club, Escapee Inc., December 2016.

[15]"On-Site Weighing of RVs and Toads,"weighttogollc.com, Weigh To Go LLC, December 2016.

[16]"Common Weight Distribution and Sway Control," Etrailer.com, E-Trailer Inc., December 2016.

[17]Bjornstad, Erik, "Symptoms of Stale Gas," bellperformance.com, Bell Performance, Inc., 2017.

[18]"Carbon Monoxide Poisoning," frequently asked questions, cdc.gov, Center for Disease Control and Prevention, US Department of Health, 2017.

[19]"Standard for Smoke Alarms,", UL217, standardscatalog.ul.com, Underwriters Laboratory, October 2015.

[20]"Standard for Single and Multiple Station Carbon Monoxide Alarms," UL2034, standardscatalog.ul.com, Underwriters Laboratory, March 2017.

[21]"Standard for Residential Gas Detectors," UL1484, standardscatalog.ul.com, Underwriters Laboratory, April 2016.

[22]"Standards and Codes, NFPA 1192: Standards on Recreational Vehicles," National Fire Protection Association, nfpa.org, National Fire Protection Association, 2015.

[23]"Propane cylinder overfilling prevention devices (OPS)," Public Education, National Fire Protection Association, nfpa.org, 2002.

[24]"49 CFR §180.205 – General requirements for recertification of specification cylinders," U.S. Government Publishing Office, Electronic Code of Federal Regulations, ecfr.gov, 2017.

[25]"18 USC 926A – Interstate Transportation of Firearms: US Government Publishing Office, gpo.gov, January 3, 2012.

[26]Woodbury, Chuck, "Carry a gun in your RV or Plan to?" rvtravel.com, referenced March 2017.

[27]"DC to AC amperage conversion, Knowledgebase and Tools, The Inverter Store, batterystuff.com, Battery Stuff LLC.

[28]"Starting Batteries and Deep-Cycle Batteries," Lead Batteries, aboutbatteries.batterycouncil.org, Battery Council International, 2017.

[29]"British Thermal Unit Conversion Factors," Sources and Laws of Energy, US Energy Information Administration, eia.gov, referenced October 2016.

[30]Cummins-Onan RV Generators, Cummins Power Generation, Minneapolis MN 55432, "The RV Generator Handbook," Cummins, Inc., 2012.

[31]"Motorized Equipment in National Parks," 36 *Code of Federal Regulations* §2.12, "Audio Disturbance," nps.gov, Department of the Interior, referenced March 2017.

[32]"Buying a Portable Generator," Power Load Requirements, starting and running watts, steadypower.com, Coffman Electrical Equipment Company, 2016.

[33]"RAM Trucks – Owner's Manual," RAM Truck Line, m.ramtrucks.com, Fiat Chrysler America FCA, 2017.

[34]"My Chevrolet – Owner's Manuals on Demand," Chevrolet Owner's Center, my.chevrolet.com, General Motors Corporation, 2017.

[35]"Ford 2016 RV and Trailer Towing Guide," Ford Motor Corporation, fleet.ford.com, Ford Motor Corp, 2017.

[36]"Toyota Tundra Owner's Manual," Toyota documents on-line, Toyota.com, Toyota Motor Corporation, 2017.

[37]"Tire Plant Codes," Resources, Tire Safety Group, tiresafetygroup.com, Safety Group, LLC, 2012.

[38]"Do I need new tires?" Michelin, Help and Support, Michelin.com, Michelin North America, 2017.

[39]"Tire Replacement Guidelines and Sidewall Weathering," Goodyear RV Tires, goodyearrvtires.com, Goodyear Tire and Rubber Company, 2017.

[40]"Tire Knowledge," Continental Tire Knowledge Center, continental-tires.com, Continental Tires Inc., 2017.

[41]"Firestone Tire Warranties," Firestone Support and Knowledge Center, firestonetire.com, Bridgestone Americas Tire Operations, LLC, 2015.

[42]Quasius, Mark, "RV Fire Protection," Family Motor Coaching, fmcmagazine.com, Family Motor Coach Association, 2016.
[43] https://www.gpo.gov/fdsys/pkg/FR-2007-02-20/html/E7-2823.htm

Made in the USA
Coppell, TX
28 May 2020

26605902R00246